Pilots of the
Battle of Britain

John G. Bentley with Mark T. Jones

RAVETTE PUBLISHING

First published in 2010

by Ravette Publishing Limited
PO Box 876
Horsham
West Sussex RH12 9GH

ISBN: 978-1-84161-342-0

Dedicated To
'The Few'

"It can hardly be said that the RAF Spitfire squadrons
have superior fighting material to the enemy.
It is my considered opinion that the only reason
why we are managing to maintain the balance of fighter power
is due entirely to the outstanding flying and leadership of the pilots."

Squadron Leader H J Wilson
(Later Group Captain) October 1940

Pilots of No. 32 Squadron take a break in the sunshine between patrols at Hawkinge 31st July 1940 (also front cover). Picture courtesy of the Francois Prins Collection

Pilots of the Battle of Britain

Contents

A Brief Background to the Conflict

Following a series of 'territorial acquisitions' by Nazi Germany between 1936 and 1938, Britain declared war on 3rd September 1939. This was an act finally instigated by the German invasion of Poland on September 1st.

The speed and might of the German campaign was to become known as 'Blitzkrieg'. Within hours, the Polish Air Force had been overwhelmed and the ground defences crumbled.

Both the French and British governments had given an ultimatum to Germany to withdraw from Poland, but the ultimatum was ignored, resulting in the automatic declaration of war on Germany at 11 am on September 3rd.

A British Expeditionary Force representing the British Army was immediately despatched to mainland Europe where it could unite with Britain's Allies - the French, Belgian and Dutch armies.

The seas and oceans were a war zone immediately, and within 48 hours of Britain's declaration of war on Germany, allied shipping losses to U-Boats were 41, and a total of 53 merchant ships had been lost. RAF bombers responded by attacking German warships in the Heligoland Bight region, but quickly lost six of the twenty-four attacking aircraft.

Despite the initial surge of aggression, the winter of 1939-40 saw little action for the British Expeditionary Force. However, on May 10th 1940, Germany invaded the Lowlands of Europe, penetrating Holland, Belgium, Luxembourg and Northern France on the same day. The Dutch and Belgian armies quickly fell to the superior might of the Third Reich while the French and British armies were forced to retreat.

Despite determined resistance by the British and French armies, by 19th May, it was known that the war in mainland Europe could not be won and plans were laid to try to evacuate the British Army from Dunkirk: "Operation Dynamo". Dynamo was an unprecedented success and over 338,000 troops were safely brought back to English shores in just nine days.

Churchill's Inspirational Leadership

Against the backdrop of these dire circumstances on May 19th, newly elected Prime Minister Winston Churchill made his first broadcast to the British people by radio;

Extracts of Winston Churchill's Broadcast from London, May 19th 1940
'Be ye men of Valour'

I speak to you for the first time as Prime Minister in a solemn hour for the life of our country, of our empire, of our allies, and above all, of the cause of freedom. A tremendous battle is raging in France and Flanders; the Germans, by a remarkable combination of air bombing and heavily armoured tanks, have broken through the French defences, north of the Maginot Line and strong columns of their armoured vehicles are ravaging the open country, which for the first day or two was without defenders. They have penetrated deeply and spread alarm and confusion in their tracks.

Behind them there are now appearing infantry in lorries and behind them again the large masses are moving forward. The re-groupment of the French armies to make head against and also to strike at this intruding wedge has been proceeding for several days, largely assisted by the magnificent efforts of the Royal Air Force. We must not allow ourselves to be intimidated by the presence of these armoured vehicles in unexpected places behind our lines. If they are behind our Front, the French are also at many points fighting actively behind theirs. Both sides are therefore in an extremely dangerous position. And if the French army and our own army are well handled, as I believe they will be, if the French retain that genius for recovery and counter attack for which they have so long been famous and if the British army shows the dogged endurance and solid fighting power of which there have been so many examples in the past, then a sudden transformation of the scene might spring into being.

It would be foolish, however, to disguise the gravity of the hour. It would be still more foolish to lose heart and courage or to suppose that well trained, well-equipped armies, numbering three or four millions of men can be overcome in the space of a few weeks or even months by a scoop or raid or mechanised vehicles, however formidable. We may look with confidence to the stabilisation of the Front in France and to the general engagement of the masses, which will enable the qualities of the French and British soldiers to be matched squarely against those of their adversaries . . .

In the air, often at serious odds, often at odds hitherto thought overwhelming, we have been clawing down three or four to one of our enemies; and the relative balance of the British and German Air Forces is now considerably more favourable to us than at the beginning of the battle. In cutting down the German bombers, we are fighting our own battle as well as that of France. My confidence in our ability to fight it out to the finish with the German Air Force has been strengthened by the fierce encounters which have taken place and are taking place. At the same time, our heavy bombers are striking nightly at the tap-root of German mechanised power, and have already inflicted serious damage upon the oil refineries on which the Nazi effort to dominate the world directly depends.

We must expect that as soon as stability is reached on the Western Front, the bulk of that hideous apparatus of aggression which gashed Holland into ruin and slavery in a few days will be turned upon us.

Our task is not only to win the battle, but to win the war. After this battle in France abates its force, there will come the battle for our Island, for all that Britain is, and all that Britain means. That will be the struggle. In that supreme emergency we shall not hesitate to take every step, even the most drastic, to call forth from our people the last ounce and the last inch of effort of which they are capable. The interests of property, the hours of labour, are nothing compared to the struggle of life and honour, for right and freedom, to which we have vowed ourselves . . .

Today is Trinity Sunday. Centuries ago words were written to be a call and a spur to the faithful servants of Truth and Justice:

"Arm yourselves, and be ye men of valour, and be in readiness for the conflict; for it is better for us to perish in battle than to look upon the outrage of our nation and our altar. As the Will of God is in Heaven, even so let it be."

Operation Dynamo –
A Monumental Success

The official expectancy of the success of the operation was low. Heavy casualties and the loss of perhaps seventy-five percent of Britain's professional army were expected. However, thanks to the valiant effort of the Royal Air Force and the combined efforts of the Royal Navy and an Armada of civilian small ships, over 338,000 troops were evacuated from the beaches of Dunkirk.

National rejoicing verged on euphoria. In an effort to refocus the nation on the task that lay ahead, Churchill made a speech to the House of Commons on June 4th, 1940.

'Wars are not won by evacuations'

When, a week ago today, Mr. Speaker, I asked the House to fix this afternoon as the occasion for a statement, I feared it would be my hard lot to announce the greatest military disaster in our long history. I thought, and some good judges agreed with me, that perhaps 20,000 or 30,000 men might be re-embarked. But it certainly seemed that the whole of the French First Army and the whole of the British Expeditionary Force north of the Amiens-Abbeville gap would be broken up in the open field or else would have to capitulate for lack of food and ammunition. These were the hard and heavy tidings for which I called upon the House and the nation to prepare themselves a week ago . . .

The enemy attacked on all sides with great strength and fierceness, and their main power, the power of their far more numerous Air Force, was thrown into the battle or else concentrated upon Dunkirk and the beaches. Pressing in upon the narrow exit, both from the east and from the west, the enemy began to fire with cannon upon the beaches by which alone the shipping could approach or depart. They sowed magnetic mines in the channels and seas; they sent repeated waves of hostile aircraft, sometimes more than a hundred strong in one formation, to cast their bombs upon the single pier that remained, and upon the sand dunes, on which the troops had their eyes for shelter. Their U-boats, one of which was sunk, and their motor launches took their toll of the vast traffic which now began. For four or five days an intense struggle reigned. All their armoured divisions, or what was left of them, together with great masses of infantry and artillery, hurled themselves in vain upon the ever-narrowing, ever-contracting appendix within which the British and French Armies fought.

He continued: The Royal Air Force, which had already been intervening in the battle, so far as its range would allow, from our home bases, now used part of its main metropolitan fighter strength, and struck at the German bombers and at the fighters, which in large numbers protected them. This struggle was protracted and fierce. Suddenly the scene has cleared, the crash and thunder has for the moment, but only for the moment, died away. A miracle of deliverance, achieved by valour, by perseverance, by perfect discipline, by faultless service, by resource, by skill, by unconquerable fidelity, is manifest to us all. The enemy was hurled back by the retreating British and French troops. He was so roughly handled that he did not hurry their departure seriously.

Sir, we must be very careful not to assign to this deliverance the attributes of a victory. Wars are not won by evacuations. But there was a victory inside this deliverance, which should be noted. . .

We are told that Herr Hitler has a plan for invading the British Isles. This has often been thought of before.

So I have, myself, full confidence that if all do their duty, if nothing is neglected, and if the best arrangements are made, as they are being made, we shall prove ourselves once again able to defend our Island home, to ride out the storm of war, and to outlive the menace of tyranny, if necessary for years, if necessary alone. At any rate, that is what we are going to try to do. That is the resolve of His Majesty's Government, every man of them. That is the will of Parliament and the nation. The British Empire and the French Republic, linked together in their cause and in their need, will defend to the death their native soil, aiding each other like good comrades to the utmost of their strength. We shall go on to the end, we shall fight in France, we shall fight on the seas and oceans, we shall fight with growing confidence and growing strength in the air, we shall defend our Island, whatever the cost may be.

"We shall fight on the beaches, we shall fight on the landing grounds, we shall fight in the fields and in the streets, we shall fight in the hills; we shall never surrender!"

11

This was to be their Finest Hour . . .

By June 1940, Holland, Belgium and France had surrendered. Determined to squash any suggestion that Britain might succumb to the German onslaught despite there being an imminent threat of invasion, Churchill delivered a powerful speech to a full House of Commons on the 18th of June 1940.

There are a good many people who say, "Never mind. Win or lose, sink or swim, better die than submit to tyranny - and such a tyranny." And I do not dissociate myself from them . . . We must not forget that from the moment when we declared war on September the 3rd it was always possible for Germany to turn all her Air Force upon this country . . .

In the meanwhile, however, we have enormously improved our methods of defence, and we have learned, what we had no right to assume at the beginning, namely, that the individual aircraft and the individual British pilot have a sure and definite superiority . . .

What General Weygand called the Battle of France is over.

The Battle of Britain is about to begin. Upon this battle depends the survival of Christian civilization. Upon it depends our own British life, and the long continuity of our institutions and our Empire. The whole fury and might of the enemy must very soon be turned on us. Hitler knows that he will have to break us in this Island or lose the war.

If we can stand up to him, all Europe may be free and the life of the world may move forward into broad, sunlit uplands. But if we fail, then the whole world, including the United States, including all that we have known and cared for, will sink into the abyss of a new Dark Age made more sinister, and perhaps more protracted, by the lights of perverted science.

Let us therefore brace ourselves to our duties, and so bear ourselves that, if the British Empire and its Commonwealth last for a thousand years, men will say, "This was their finest hour."

The RAF in France

When the BEF had been despatched to France, so too were support aircraft from the RAF.

However, Air Vice Marshal Hugh Dowding was extremely anxious that his precious resources should not be ploughed into a lost cause. Although Lord Beaverbrook (who had been appointed head of aircraft production) had significantly increased the number of fighter aircraft being manufactured each month, the real issue for Dowding was the supply of pilots, who took eighteen months to fully train.

When the evacuation of the British Expeditionary Force was first discussed on May 19th, Dowding urged that no more aircraft be sent to uphold the battle for mainland Europe. Initially he was overruled, and a further ten squadrons were despatched. However, a week later when Operation Dynamo commenced, the RAF were withdrawn from European hostilities, save providing protection for the evacuating troops and dropping them essential supplies.

Huge progress in aircraft design had been made by every manufacturing nation during the mid to late 1930's.

Of the 400 aircraft the RAF had taken to France, fifty of these were Lysander 'army co-operation' aircraft, which were primarily used for reconnaissance. A further 220 were light, twin-engined bombers, the Fairey Battle and Bristol Blenheim. Of the 130 British fighters, the Gladiator biplane and twin-engine Blenheim fighter-bombers were no match for the Messerschmitt Bf 109. The onus therefore fell on the pilots of the Hawker Hurricane to both shoot down the Luftwaffe bombers as they attacked the troops below and to hold off the single-seat Messerschmitt Bf 109 fighters.

The RAF did not use any heavy bombers in the battle for France, whereas the Luftwaffe had Heinkel He 111s. Dornier Do 17s and Junkers Ju 88s. The Junkers Ju 88 was an aircraft capable of both medium-level bombing and dive-bombing. However, it was the Junkers Ju 87 'Stuka' dive-bomber, which proved to be the key attack aircraft for the Germans during the European Blitzkrieg offensives.

Luftwaffe pilots had battle experience gained over Spain during the Spanish civil war, and modern aircraft, encompassing many of the latest technologies including fuel injected carburettors. These counteracted the effects of negative 'G's on the engines when the pilots went into a steep dive.

During the battle for Dunkirk, the Luftwaffe flew 1,882 bombing missions and 1,997 fighter sorties. However, Goering's Air Force failed to cut off to destroy the evacuating forces although it did inflict serious damage on the Allied Naval effort, sinking nine destroyers, damaging 22 others and sinking or seriously damaging 89 merchant vessels.

The RAF and French Air Force had shown their teeth in the battle for France, and again at Dunkirk. The Luftwaffe had suffered significant losses amounting to 28% of its total strength. 1,428 of its aircraft were destroyed, (1,129 to enemy action and 229 in accidents). A further 488 were seriously damaged, reducing the effectiveness of the Luftwaffe by 36%.

The RAF flew 660 sorties over the beaches of Dunkirk, but amid intense opposition sustained some significant losses. 37 Bristol Blenheims were shot down on June 2nd alone.

During the evacuation of Dunkirk, the RAF shot down 240 enemy planes for the loss of 170.

Despite this, the troops on the ground complained that more cover could have been provided by 'the Brylcreem Boys' (a nickname given by tommies for pilots in the RAF).

By June 6th, the RAF's strength of 1,078 front-line fighter aircraft had been reduced to 475 and the lives of 60 precious pilots had been lost.

Above: Hurricanes re-arming in France

Operation 'Sea Lion'

Hitler's plan for the invasion of Britain had been in development for many months. However, he had regularly tried to encourage Britain to co-exist in peace alongside Nazi Germany, knowing the value of Britain's Navy and Commonwealth of countries was to be embraced, rather than challenged. Hitler also knew that if there was no war against Britain, the likelihood of America's might being unleashed against Germany was unlikely.

Hitler generally spoke of the British Commonwealth in a complimentary way, once emphasising his position . . . *"with great admiration of the British Empire, of the necessity for its existence and of the civilisation that Britain has brought to the world".*

His controversial decision to halt the German Armour 30 miles short of the beaches of Dunkirk was a further demonstration of his desire not to embark on all-out warfare with the British Empire. He referred to this decision at a later date as being a 'sporting gesture'.

When Winston Churchill was elected to replace Neville Chamberlain as Prime Minister on May 10th, he made it very plain that peace with Nazi Germany was not a possibility.

After the successful evacuation of the BEF from Dunkirk, the German army prepared to invade British shores. The following weeks were vital to Britain and while Hitler continued to offer diplomatic solutions, British resources and the civil defence structure grew rapidly.

When General Jodl presented his final revision of plans for the invasion of Britain to Hitler on June 30th, Hitler was still hopeful of peace. On July 2nd, after considering Jodl's invasion plans, he issued a directive that *"a landing in England is possible, provided that air superiority can be attained and certain other conditions fulfilled . . .*

. . . all preparations must be undertaken on the basis that the invasion is still only a plan and has not yet been decided upon".

Left:
Adolf Hitler speaks to the Reichstag in the Kroll Opera after the end of the Balken campaign May 4, 1940

During the next weeks, Goering's Luftwaffe started to make 'probing' attacks, measuring the size and effectiveness of the RAF's radar-aided defence mechanism. Hitler continued to discuss his options with his advisors. Speaking for the German Navy, Admiral Raeder outlined the difficulties he faced in the sweeping and laying of mines and the preparation of the invasion fleet. Raeder urged that the invasion should only be attempted as 'a last resort'. Hitler agreed. Jodl however suggested that the task could be approached rather like a 'river crossing', with a broad front over which the Luftwaffe acted as artillery. He insisted that the first wave of landings must be strong and a sea-lane secured that could be kept free from attack by the Royal Navy.

As Goering's attacks intensified, Jodl presented a much more detailed plan on July 13th, supported by most of Hitler's key personnel. It involved 13 divisions landing over three days: Six divisions from Army Group A, which were to land between Ramsgate and Bexhill and four divisions landing between Brighton and the Isle of Wight. Meanwhile, three divisions from Army Group B would land further to the West, in Lyme Bay.

28 further divisions would follow including airborne and armoured divisions. As a result of this plan and the support it received from all three services, Hitler issued a new directive entitled: **"Preparations for the Landing Operation against England".**

It read:

"As England, in spite of her hopeless military situation still shows no sign of willingness to come to terms, I have decided to prepare, and if necessary, to carry out, a landing operation against her. The aim of this operation is to eliminate the English mother country as a base from which the war against Germany can be continued, and, if it should be necessary, to occupy it completely".

This operation, called 'Lion' by Jodl in his memorandum of July 12th, was now renamed by Hitler, 'Sea Lion'. Hitler made one further offer of peace on July 19th which the Foreign Secretary, Halifax, rejected three more precious days later. Each day enabled Britain to be slightly further prepared for the Battle that was to come. . .

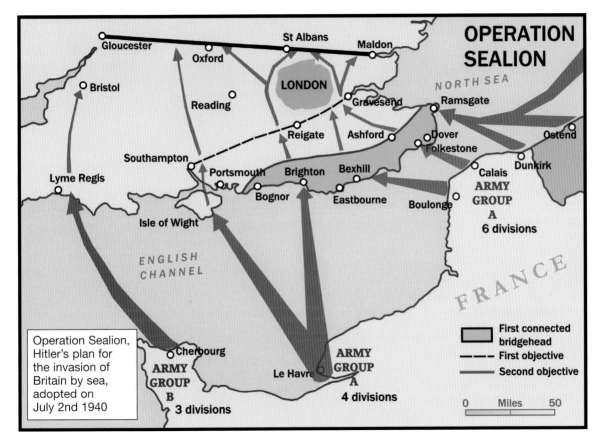

OPERATION SEALION

NORTH SEA

ENGLISH CHANNEL

FRANCE

Gloucester
Oxford
St Albans
Maldon
Bristol
Reading
LONDON
Gravesend
Ramsgate
Ostend
Southampton
Reigate
Ashford
Dover
Folkestone
Dunkirk
Lyme Regis
Portsmouth
Brighton
Bexhill
Calais
ARMY GROUP A
6 divisions
Isle of Wight
Bognor
Eastbourne
Boulonge
Cherbourg
ARMY GROUP B
3 divisions
Le Havre
ARMY GROUP A
4 divisions

Operation Sealion, Hitler's plan for the invasion of Britain by sea, adopted on July 2nd 1940

First connected bridgehead
First objective
Second objective

0   Miles   50

The Structure of RAF Fighter Command

As Britain slowly prepared for war it was fortunate to have Air Chief Marshal Sir Hugh Dowding overseeing the events. Dowding recognised the importance of defensive measures and he was one of the first people to see and realise the potential of radar working alongside a modern air force.

In his role as Chief of Fighter Command, he ensured that radar was put to good use and that radar stations were placed in strategic locations, especially along the south and east coasts of England. Fighter Command was to be at the forefront of operations as the Battle of Britain approached. He organised it into a series of groups, each being responsible for a geographical area of Britain.

These groups were then subdivided into sectors and each sector appointed a main airfield with satellite airfields under its control. Each sector base had its own operations room and maintenance and repair facilities for the aircraft.

Increasingly the production of fighter aircraft had been given priority and the number of fighter squadrons had risen from thirteen in 1936 (about 208 aircraft) to thirty-nine (about 624 aircraft) by September 1939. This growth continued throughout 1940.

By now, Dowding had ensured that many grass runways were replaced with concrete.

The RAF, aided by Radar and working with the integrated support of the Observer Corps and both Anti-aircraft Batteries and Barrage Balloon deployments, now had to be ready for its greatest test. Both Radar and the Observer Corp were necessary because Radar could only 'generally' establish the size of enemy formations, their height and speed up to 60 miles away.

The experienced teams who manned Royal Observer Corp points complimented this technology by bringing more accurate information through actual sightings and were also able to view intruders approaching under Radar's visibility 'ceiling' .

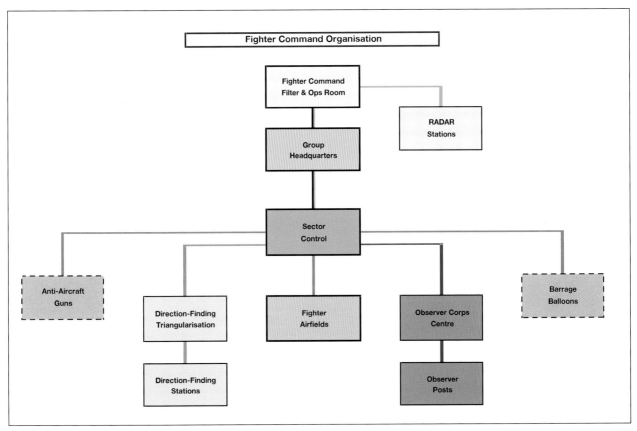

Fighter Command Organisation

Fighter Command
Filter & Ops Room

RADAR
Stations

Group
Headquarters

Sector
Control

Anti-Aircraft
Guns

Direction-Finding
Triangularisation

Fighter
Airfields

Observer Corps
Centre

Barrage
Balloons

Direction-Finding
Stations

Observer
Posts

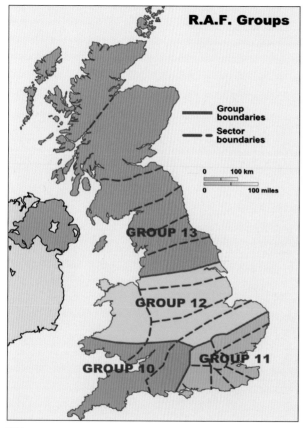

R.A.F. Groups

Group boundaries
Sector boundaries

0   100 km

0   100 miles

GROUP 13

GROUP 12

GROUP 10

GROUP 11

Four Fighter Command Groups were initially established. Stanmore in Middlesex (the Headquarters of Fighter Command) was central to them all.

13 Group covered the parts of northern England which were not covered by 12 Group, together with southern Scotland and Northern Ireland. **Air Vice Marshal Richard Saul** was placed in command.

12 Group was commanded by **Air Vice Marshal Trafford Leigh-Mallory.** It controlled the Midlands, East Anglia and industrial north of England up to Lancashire and Yorkshire.

11 Group covered London and the south-east of England. **Air Vice Marshal Keith Park** was appointed to lead this Group, likely to be the most active in the event of German aggression being unleashed.

10 Group covered Wales and the south-west of England under the leadership of **Air Vice Marshal Sir Quintin Brand.**

The Leadership of Fighter Command

The leadership of RAF Fighter Command was a significant factor in the outcome of the Battle of Britain.

Air Chief Marshal Sir Hugh Dowding

Left:
Air Chief Marshal
Sir Hugh
Dowding

Fighter Command, under the leadership of Air Chief Marshal Sir Hugh Dowding had rapidly become a modern branch of the RAF with modern fighters being developed and new technology being used to its optimum.

Dowding was a 'moderniser'. He was keen for the RAF to become 'a sharp instrument in the hands of skilled surgeons (tacticians)'.

He had learnt to fly as a young man at the Brooklands Aero Club. Within months of being accepted into the Royal Flying Corps (RFC) he had his 'wings' and a short while later was fighting for the RFC in the First World War.

After only one year with the Corps, Dowding was to be given the command of No 16 squadron. During the First World War, Dowding was to meet three people who were to play an important part in his life and in the coming war; Major Keith Park (a New Zealander), Major Trafford Leigh-Mallory and Major Sholto-Douglas.

By the end of the First World War Dowding held the rank of Brigadier-General.

Dowding's wife died at a young age after the first

war and from that time he was totally focussed on his work. The RFC evolved into the RAF and Dowding was soon championing the cause of metal monoplanes instead of the traditional wooden structured biplanes. He was one of the team of senior officials that gave their approval to the Hurricane and the Spitfire - aircraft that were going to prove invaluable in the future.

Dowding was appointed Chief of Fighter Command in 1936. In this role he ensured that radar was put to good use and oversaw the creation of the world's first integrated defence system, utilising the Observer Corps, Radar, Barrage Balloons, Anti-aircraft guns and Fighter aircraft.

Air Vice Marshal Keith Park

Air Chief Marshal Keith Rodney Park was the son of a Scottish geologist born in Thames, New Zealand. He joined the New Zealand Territorial Army and when the first world war broke out, joined an artillery battery. As a non-commissioned officer he participated in the infamous Gallipoli landings at Anzac Cove. In the trench warfare that followed, he

distinguished himself and was commissioned to become a second lieutenant. Unusually, he transferred from the New Zealand Army to the British Army.

Left: Air Vice Marshal Sir Keith Park

After Gallipoli his unit was transferred to the Somme, where he developed an interest in the value of aerial reconnaissance. After being blown off his horse by a shell, he was hospitalised in England, but 'unfit for service' in the unit he had been serving with, joined the

Royal Flying Corps in December 1916.

He soon became an accomplished flyer and instructor, serving with No. 48 Squadron at la Bellevue (near Arras). He flew Bristol twin seat reconnaissance aircraft. Within a week his squadron was moved near to Dunkirk and with increased success against German fighters, was awarded the Military Cross on August 17th 1917 and soon promoted to Captain.

Before the end of the First World War, he had become a respected leader of men, had received a Bar to his Military Cross and had been accreditted with 5 aircraft destroyed and 14 'probables'.

After the war he received a permanent commission as a Captain within the newly formed Royal Air Force. He served as Flight Commander of No. 25 Squadron from 1919 to 1920, before taking up a position as commander at the School of Technical Training. He had further interim appointments before becoming Staff Officer to Air Chief Marshal Dowding in 1938.

With the onset of war, he was promoted to Air Vice Marshal and placed in charge of No. 11 Group, responsible for the fighter defence of London and south east England in April 1940. He organized fighter patrols over France during the evacuation of the BEF from Dunkirk. He flew a personalised Hawker Hurricane between his airfields throughout the Battle of Britian and earned a reputation as a clear-minded tactician with a good grasp of strategic issues.

Park died as Sir Keith Park in 1975 having earned a GCB, KBE, MC & Bar, and DFC.

Air Vice-Marshal Sir Trafford Leigh-Mallory

Leigh-Mallory was born in 1892, in Cheshire. He joined the Territorial Battalion of the King's (Liverpool) Regiment on the outbreak of World War I, and received a commission to serve with the Lancashire Fusiliers.

He was seconded to the Royal Flying Corps in July 1916 and promoted to Major in the Royal Air Force following its formation in 1918. He was mentioned in dispatches and awarded the Distinguished Service Order.

In 1921 he was given a commission in the RAF with the rank of Squadron Leader, and joined the School of Army Co-operation, (which he later commanded for three years).

Above: Air Vice Marshal Leigh-Mallory

Air Vice-Marshal Sir Quintin Brand

Quintin Brand was born in Beaconsfield, South Africa in 1893. He had a distinguished career during the First World War as part of the Royal Flying Corps and Royal Air Force, being awarded the Distinguished Service Order, Military Cross and Distinguished Flying Cross.

His last success ('kill') as a fighter pilot was to shoot down a German bomber during the very last air raid on England of the First World War.

During peacetime, he made the first flight from England to the Cape in 1920, in a Vickers Vimy Bomber, taking some six weeks (although the actual flying time was only 109 hours). Together with his co-pilot, after two crashes, they finally reached their destination in a third aircraft supplied by the South African government. They were both knighted. Quintin went on to become Director General of Aviation in Egypt between 1932 and 1936 and the Director of Repair and Maintenance at the Air Ministry between 1937 and 1939. He assumed the role of Air Officer Commanding No. 10 Group, Fighter Command between 1939 and 1941.

He was given command of No. 12 Group in 1937. Five years later, he moved across to No. 11 Group and was promoted to Air Marshal and appointed Air Officer Commanding-in-Chief Fighter Command.

Leigh-Mallory was killed in November 1944 in a flying accident.

He finally retired from the RAF in 1943 and died in Rhodesia in March 1968 aged 74.

Air Vice-Marshal Richard Saul

During the Battle of Britain, Saul was responsible for the aircraft and four sector stations defending the North of England, Scotland and strategically important targets which included the Naval base at Scapa Flow.

His career started as an observer on aircraft which included the RE8 and BE2 during the First World War.

Saul was an all round sportsman representing the Royal Air Force in both rugby and hockey, and won the RAF tennis championship outright.

His appointment as commander of 13 Group followed his position as the Senior Air Staff Officer at Fighter Command Headquarters, the post previously held by Keith Park. It was Saul's organisational ability that assisted Dowding to shape Fighter Command structure into an effective fighting force during the late 1930s.

The Opposing Air Forces

The commercial success of German aviation in the ten years prior to World War Two provided the opportunity for the restructuring and equipping of an organisation that would soon take on a military guise.

The Luftwaffe was not officially born until March 1935, when it was realised that Germany had secretly built what appeared to be the world's most powerful and modern Air Force. All this had been done under the disguise of aero-sports clubs, glider clubs and civil aviation.

In 1936, the Luftwaffe's strength reached nearly 20,000 men and it had 1,000 combat aircraft with 300 aircraft being produced each month. However, even then the German Air Force continued to use civilian aviation as a screen for its military activity.

Aircraft used by the Luftwaffe in 1938 and 1939 had been designed for alternative and 'commercial' purposes. They were easily adapted for military use though, and the military variants included the Heinkel He 111 and the Dornier Do 17. The Messerschmitt Bf 109

Structure of the Opposing Forces:

Royal Air Force	Luftwaffe
Group	Fliegerkorps
Command Wing	Geschwader
Fighter Command	Jagdgeschwader
Bomber Command	Kampfgeschwader
Coastal Command	Stukageschwader
_____	_____
(no equivalent)	GRUPPE
_____	_____
Squadron	Staffel

evolved from a high-performance sports aircraft.

Hitler's Luftwaffe had been given the opportunity to try out these aircraft in a war zone during the Spanish Civil War, when Italy and Germany supported the efforts of General Franco in establishing a government there. During that time, the Luftwaffe tested its entire range of aircraft in action, enabling it to develop the combat efficiency of the aircraft and the skills of its pilots.

By September 1939, Hitler knew he had the world's most powerful Air Force with 4,840 advanced aircraft including 1,750 bombers and 1,200 fighters.

The aircraft forces available to him for the attack on Britain included the same aircraft used in Spain and in Northern Europe, but with the RAF's Fighter Command at the ready, Goering's bombers needed more fighter cover than was necessary in Poland or the Lowlands, and these fighters had limited range, despite having both superior performance and armament.

The Royal Air Force

Only Great Britain had an Air Force equipped with aircraft capable of successfully fighting the Luftwaffe when war was declared in September 1939. However, the number of aircraft ready for action on British soil totalled only 1,500 with a similar number of reserve aircraft.

Under the direction of Lord Beaverbrook, from May 1939 production increased significantly reaching a rate of nearly 700 aircraft per month. These were primarily more modern aircraft designs capable of matching the Luftwaffe's proven technology.

A decisive phase in strengthening the RAF had begun six years earlier when Hitler was elected as the German Chancellor. In that year, the British General Staff had invited aircraft manufacturers to offer commissions for a new single-seat fighter with eight machine guns. The commissioning of two and four-engined bombers followed in 1934 and 1936. Under the leadership of General Hugh Trenchard the British High Command based these commissions on a considered evaluation of the requirements of modern air warfare. Under his leadership, Britain

concluded that the fighter was the most suitable weapon for defending British shores and that the bomber would be a strategic offensive weapon.

In 1937, as a direct result of these efforts the RAF had three main components: Fighter Command, Bomber Command and Coastal Command.

Fighter Command already had the Hurricane, a modern monoplane fighter and was preparing to put the Spitfire into service alongside it. Both had eight wing-mounted machine guns and were agile. Its older fighters included the Gladiator bi-plane, which the RAF already knew would be unsuitable for modern warfare. Its other new fighters, the Blenheim and Defiant were twin-seat fighters which were slower, less manoeuvrable and totally unknown quantities. Both had turret-mounted machine guns.

Bomber Command had the Hampden, Wellington and Whitley bombers at its disposal.

Aircraft production reached 4,000 per year in 1938 and 7,000 in 1939, a tremendous increase and effort due to the dedication and organisational skills of Lord Beaverbrook, who

EQUIVALENT RANKS

RAF	LUFTWAFFE
Royal Air Force Marshal	Generalfeldmarschall
Air Chief Marshal	Generaloberst
Air Marshal	General
Air Vice-Marshal	Generalleutnant
Air Commodore	Generalmajor
Group Captain	Oberst
Wing Commander	Oberstleutnant
Squadron Leader	Major
Flight Lieutenant	Hauptmann
Flying Officer	Oberleutnant
Pilot Officer	Leutnant
Warrant Officer	Hauptfeldwebel
Flight Sergeant	Oberfeldwebel
Sergeant	Feldwebel

was a successful industrialist appointed to the task. (His son was a serving squadron leader during the Battle of Britain, Sqd Ldr J W M Aitken serving with 601 Squadron).

Working alongside Fighter Command was the Fleet Air Arm. This arm of the Royal Navy had predominantly fighter aircraft operating off aircraft carriers. Some of its aircraft became involved in defending the shores of Britain during the Battle of Britain, specifically including the Fairey Fulmar. Some pilots in the Fleet Air Arm transferred to the Royal Air Force for that reason, the ranks for some of the pilots in this book are Naval ranks.

Above: A trio of Spitfire Mk 1s of No. 92 Squadron line up for take-off from Biggin Hill during the Battle of Britain

An RAF Pilot in 1940

By 1934 the British Government was becoming of its need to update and to enlarge its Air Force, alongside other European nations. It was decided that the size of the RAF would be expanded to a total of 128 first line squadrons by 1939. A major recruitment and training campaign followed, during which time the Air Ministry was also starting to commission new aircraft designs. In 1935 the Hawker company displayed its design for the first British high speed monoplane, an aircraft which evolved into the Hawker Hurricane. Production of this new monoplane started so that it could enter service in 1938.

In March 1936, Supermarine's Model 300 made its maiden flight to great acclaim. This aircraft was to evolve into the Spitfire. Four months later in July 1936, the Government announced the formation of the RAFVR. This allowed volunteers to undergo free flying training at weekends and during 15 day annual training camps. To encourage university students to learn to fly, a special training initiative was launched in 1937; the University Air Squadron. The aim of this was to identify and to train men who had the potential

to become fighter pilots. About 100 Oxford and Cambridge students were identified for training within this elite initiative and by the outbreak of the war in 1939 there were approximately 2,500 RAFVR (reserve) pilots.

By September 1939 the world was on the brink of war. All enlisted RAFVR were called up on a permanent basis.

As part of the Government's promotion of air training, private companies were allowed to contract for and provide training for military personnel. One of the many private initiatives for training pilots was the Number 11 Elementary and Reserve Training School, established in 1936. It was set up and run by a private company, Airwork Ltd. J. H (Ginger) Lacey was one of the RAF's most successful fighter pilots during the Battle of Britain. He was one of the pilots who trained with Airwork. Another famous student was George Pinkerton, who was the first pilot to shoot down an enemy aircraft over Britain.

The principal aircraft for pilot training was the DH 82 Tiger Moth which first came into service in 1931 as a two-seated trainer. The Tiger Moth was designed by de Havilland which had built many of the most successful fighters of the First World War. De Havilland took over Airwork in 1939. By 1940 the Number 11 Elementary Flying school was operating 90 Tiger Moths.

Other aircraft used for various stages of training included the Avro Tutor, Gloster Gamelin and Bristol Bulldog.

Typical Training:

Rank: Aircraftsman II
2 Month elementary flying course
First Solo:
After 7 hours flying in Tiger Moth Biplane
Further training:
4 months on Proctors
Before Awarded 'Wings' & Commission
Proceeded to Fighter Training School
Minimum one-year total training, 200 hours total flying plus 'Flying blind' in a Link Trainer

A De Havilland Tiger Moth Trainer

Flying Officer W.P. (Billy) Clyde of 601 Squadron takes a well-earned rest during the Battle. Clyde was a famous pre-war skier and joined the RAF at the outbreak of war

The Profile of an RAF Pilot

As soon as war was declared, the British and Commonwealth countries embarked on an urgent campaign of pilot recruitment.

Trained volunteer pilots came from around the world: from the British Commonwealth countries, from European countries that had already fallen to the might of the Third Reich, from the Middle East and the West Indies. Volunteers even arrived from America, which had declared its neutrality. The RAF also called on the services of the hundred and twenty or so university graduates who had been trained to fly in the 'University Air Squadron' between 1937 and 1939. However, all these pilots needed to be trained to fly the RAF's newest and advanced fighter aircraft and to be taught gunnery skills.

Canada was selected as the base for the establishment of a Commonwealth Fighter Pilot training establishment, and from here new recruits were processed to prevent the RAF's training establishments being swollen with new recruits and being trained to fly and to fight in skies that were to become hostile.

Pilot Profile:

RAF Pilot Officer (lowest commissioned rank)

Physical Details:
Average Height: 5 feet, 8.5 inches
Minimum Age: 18 years
Maximum Age: 35 years
Entry: By written examination
Physical Fitness: Examination
Colour Blindness: Examination

Training Rank: Aircraftsman II
2 Month elementary flying course
First Solo: After 7 hours flying in Tiger Moth Bi-Plane
Further training: 4 months on Proctors before Awarded 'Wings' & Commission
Proceed to Fighter Training School
Minimum one-year total training, 200 hours total flying
Flying 'blind' in a Link Trainer

Pay: 11 shillings per day (£200 per year)
          Plus £25 per year flying pay
          and dependents' allowance

Gunnery Training

For many trainee fighter pilots the main concern was not flying the aircraft but becoming an accurate marksman while flying not in a straight line, but in the middle of a dogfight. Each RAF single-seat fighter had eight wing-mounted machine guns. There was no crew who specialised in gunnery, so the pilot's role was to both fly the aircraft and to shoot down the enemy aircraft.

During training, pilots were taught the physics of a bullet losing both speed and direction as it passed through the air. The further it travelled, the more drag through air and wind resistance had to be allowed for, as well as 'fall'. In other words, the pilot had to consider the trail of the bullet three dimensionally. The further it had to travel, the more allowance had to be made and compensated for. This, while flying evasively to avoid enemy fire and at speeds of around 300 miles per hour.

The fact that RAF fighters only had on average about fifteen seconds of ammunition per sortie also meant that accuracy was essential. The pilots were trained and equipped to shoot down enemy aircraft. Numerically, they were vastly out-numbered on nearly every sortie. The economical and accurate use of their limited ammunition was therefore crucial to their success as a fighter pilot and also, to their survival.

.303 calibre Browning machine guns were the standard armament of Spitfires and Hurricanes. With four guns located in each wing, the guns were usually set to converge the might of the aircraft's firepower at 500 yards. However, in the same way as flying tight formations were based on theoretical battles, the convergence of the firepower of eight machine guns at 500 or even 400 yards was found by pilots to be generally too far. At that distance the bullets would converge but were losing velocity and to a degree, direction. As a result, seasoned fighter pilots soon started to have their guns trained to converge at 200 or 250 yards. At this distance, the firepower was found to be more accurate and the concentration more deadly. The only drawback to this strategy was the requirement of the pilot to get very close to his prey. However, the use of this tactic did mean that the pilot's gunnery was generally more accurate and the physics of 'real bullet trails' and 'ideal bullet trails' became one less consideration during the heat of the battle.

A Mayfly existence

For pilots on both sides during the Battle of Britain a considerable amount of time was spent not killing others, but killing time. Many airfields were little more than landing strips where conditions were often at best primitive and spartan. Time was spent playing cards, chess or reading, others managed to 'get some shut-eye' or 'forty winks' (often sat ready for action in their flying kit). In the summer and early autumn of 1940 it may well have seemed a carefree existence; a case of eat, drink and be merry for tomorrow we die. Pilots would often venture off to their local pub and seemed as if they hadn't a care in the world and yet their phlegmatic approach was often just a way of dealing with imminent danger.

Both German and Allied propaganda made much of the seemingly debonair knights of the sky. Pilots were lionised and their wartime role made to seem supremely glamorous. British pilots appeared to pepper their language with words and phrases that soon passed into popular usage or memory. With the pilot's war cry of *'Tally-ho!'* and their old adage *'Beware the Hun in the sun'* they were widely admired by the civilian population. RAF slang was soon in general conversation:

Pilot 'Speak'

'a piece of cake' – easy
'gone for a Burton' – killed
'prang' – crash
'erks' - ground crew
'wizard' – excellent
'snog' – a lengthy kiss
'round the bend' – crazy

Pilots playing chess to calm their nerves between sorties

Above: A Wartime poster recruiting aircrew volunteers

Flight Formations

Pilots were quickly taught the importance of flight formations. These enabled them to act as a single efficient unit able to protect each other.

Squadrons generally flew in formations of twelve aircraft, divided into 'flights' of three. These flights were identified by colours. The colour sections were then numbered from one to three. Each flight had a Flight Leader, who would be one of the more senior pilots.

Flying in formation, pilots were expected to be within 100 yards of his nearest aircraft. In practice this meant that too much time was taken checking the position of friendly aircraft as opposed to scanning the skies for hostile aircraft. Tight formation flying also meant that in the event of attack by enemy fighters, the closeness of the RAF fighters presented a singular large target to the enemy, enabling early hits to be registered before the formation had broken.

German pilots flew the 'finger of four' formation, which gave three groups of four fighters different heights and lateral spacing. The RAF adopted this formation during the summer of 1940.

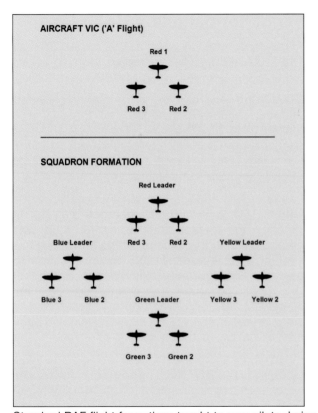

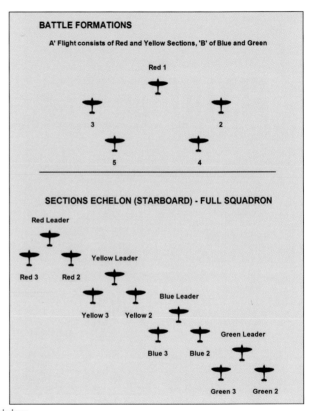

Standard RAF flight formations taught to new pilots during training.

Although pilots tried to stay close to a second aircraft, known as the wingman, when confronted with aerial warfare of the type and hostility that developed during the summer of 1940, most found they were engaged in a personal fight for survival and were looking for victories.

The Aircraft They Flew

Although the main force of Fighter Command, the Hurricane and Spitfire were fine aircraft for their day, the Luftwaffe pilot had the better aircraft from many perspectives during the summer of 1940 in the Messerschmitt Bf 109F.

This variant of the Bf 109 was an advanced fighting machine, incorporating a fuel-injected carburettor, cannons, as well as machine guns, and ammunition indicators, all of which the Hurricane Mark 1 and Spitfire Marks 1 and 1a did not yet have. Pilots therefore had to be aware of their fuel, but more so, their armament. A Hurricane or Spitfire each armed with eight .303 Browning machine guns in their wings had only about fifteen seconds of ammunition. On average this was a quarter of the amount of ammunition carried by the Messerschmitt Bf 109F.

Right:
Hawker
Hurricane
mark 1

Left:
Supermarine
Spitfire
mark 1

Right:
Messerschmitt
Bf 109F

The Luftwaffe utilised all three of its Command 'wings' during the Battle of Britain; Bomber Command, Dive-Bomber and Fighter Command.

Initially, the Bf 110 twin-engine fighter provided the fighter escort for its main combat aircraft which were three medium range bombers, the Heinkel He 111, Dornier Do 17 and Junkers Ju 88. The Messerschmitt Bf 109 single-seat fighter was intended solely to engage fighters that had been scrambled to intercept incoming bombers. The Junkers Ju 87 'Stuka' dive-bomber played a significant role during the early weeks of the Battle, but like the Bf 110, was outclassed by the Hurricanes and Spitfires of RAF Fighter Command.

RAF Fighter Command bore the brunt of the hostilities during the Battle of Britain, though Coastal Command and Bomber Command were involved to a limited degree. For that reason, the main aircraft employed by the RAF were its new single-seat fighters, the Spitfire and Hurricane, with some activity also for the twin-engined multi-role Blenheim and the twin-seat Defiant, the Gladiator and the Fleet Air Arm's Fulmar.

The main objective of the German forces during the Battle of Britain was simply to engage the inferior numbers of RAF fighters in battle and to erode the defence capability of the nation. This was a prerequisite of 'Operation Sea Lion', Hitler's plan for the invasion of Britain.

Above: The Boulton Paul Defiant, an aircraft of mixed fortunes

It was against this backdrop, and with these aircraft, that the 2,533 pilots who engaged in combat in the Battle of Britain fought, died or survived . . .

RAF 'SPEAK'
The Pilot's Dictionary

Some of the codes and language used by the RAF

Abbeville Kids	A particularly aggressive bunch of Luftwaffe fighter units based at Abbeville
Ace	Pilot credited with five or more enemy aircraft
Ack-ack	Anti Aircraft fire
Airmaids	Crew of an Air Sea Rescue boat
Angels	Altitude in units of 1000 feet e.g. Angels 20
Arse end Charlie	The man who weaves above and behind the fighter squadron to protect them
Attaboy	Air Transport Auxiliary (ATA) member, many from US
Bags of swank	Pride in a job
Bail out	Or bale out, forced departure by parachute
Banana-boat	Aircraft carrier
Bandit	Enemy aircraft
Beam	(On the) - be right, understand
Beat up	To fly very low over those who are watching
Beehive	Bombers (hive) with fighter escort (bees)
Beer-lever	Joystick
Blighty	The UK
Blood-wagon	Ambulance
Blotto	Drunk as in "he was completely blotto"
Blower	Aircraft supercharger; telephone
Blue	(The) - the desert
Bluebird	WAAF
Body-snatcher	Stretcher bearer
Boffins	Scientific types working on new equipment
Bogey	Unidentified aircraft
Bolshie	A crewman taking a dim view of service 'bull'
Boomerang	Returning early from an uncompleted sortie
Bought it	(Buy a packet). Be shot down, with carelessness
Bounce	Surprise attack
Brass	(The) or brasshats, senior Wing or Group officers with gold braid "brass" on their hats
Brassed off	Or browned off, cheesed off. Fed up/angry
Brolly, Umbrella	Parachute
Brown jobs	The Army - also "pongos" and "squaddies"
Bull	Formalities of the service (square bashing, saluting the King's Commission etc.) e.g. "He's full of bull"
Bumf	Useless paperwork
Burton	"Gone for a Burton" - killed in action - maybe from old beer commercial for Burton Ale
Buy	(To) - as in "to buy it" "to buy the farm"; be killed or lost
Cabbage	Also cookie, egg, visiting card - Bomb
Camp Comedian	Camp Commandant
Canteen cowboy	Ladies' man
Chair-borne division	RAF personnel working in offices
Char	Tea, from Hindustani borrowing from Chinese, *tchai*: "char and a wad"
Chocks away	Let's make a start
Civvies	Civilian clothing
Civvy	A civilian
Civvy street	The non military world outside the RAF
Clobber	Flying gear worn in a wartime bomber

Close the hangar doors	Stop talking shop (i.e. about RAF)
Cockup	A chaotic situation (from "cocked hat")
Collect a gong	Receive a medal
Coming to town	Enemy aircraft approaching
Conservatory	Plane cabin (from the perspex on three sides)
Cooler	Guardroom
Corker	(A) - mine, also very attractive woman
Court a cat	Take a girlfriend out
Crabbing along	Flying near the ground or water
Crate	Aircraft, particularly one which is obsolescent
Cricket	German night fighter plane
Crown	(Get your) - promotion to Flight Sergeant, who wore a crown badge above the sergeant's three stripes
Curtains	Killed
Crump Dump	The Ruhr
Dead stick	Engine failed - e.g. dead stick landing
Deck	The ground
Desert lily	Urinal made from tin can
Dicey do	Or shakey do. A hair-raising operation
Ditch	To force land on water
Dobhi	One's laundry
Doggo	(Lie) - remain quiet/hidden
Drink	(In the) - to come down in the sea
Dust-up	Heated action/fight/altercation
Egg-whisk	An autogyro
Erb	Any airman
Erk	Junior ground crew - from the Cockney pronunciation of aircraftman
Eyetie	An Italian (plane)
Finger	(To remove one's) - hurry up and/or pay attention
Fishheads	Navy
Fireproof	Invulnerable
Fireworks	Heavy anti aircraft fire
Fizzer	(Disciplinary) charge
Flak	*Fliegerabwehrkanonen* - anti-aircraft gun, "getting some flak" - being criticised
Flaming onions	Anti aircraft tracer
Flap	"There's a flap on" - rush to do something
Flicks	Searchlights or cinema.
Fling one up	Or throw one up. Salute
Flip	Short flight, esp. as a favour to a friend
Flying Pencil	Dornier bomber
Flying Suitcase	Handley Page Hampden
Flying Tin-Opener	Hurricane in tank busting role
Football feet	Make excessive use of rudder
Frozen on the stick	Paralysed with fear
Full bore	Flat out, at top speed
Gardening	Sea/coastal mine-laying by aircraft
Gen	Information, good "pukka" or bad "duff"
Gerry or Jerry	German
Get cracking	Get on with it, get going
Get some flying hours in	Get some sleep
Gong	A medal, specifically a decoration
Gravel basher	Drill or Physical Training Instructor
Gravy	(The) - Atlantic: gravy - fuel
Greenhouse	Cockpit windows
Grocer	Equipment Officer
Groceries	Also cabbages, cookies, eggs - Bombs

Ground wallah	An officer who did not fly	**Odd bod**	Crew member with lost crew or whose crew could not fly because of illness etc
Gubbins	Necessary equipment (eg: "has that kite got the gubbins for dropping a cookie?")	**Office**	Cockpit of aircraft
Half-section	Mate, companion, even wife	**Old lag**	Experienced airman - often Regular Airforce
Happy Valley	The Ruhr, often bombed and heavily defended	**Old Man**	(The) - Squadron CO
Hedge-hopping	Flying very low	**Pack up**	Cease to function - "My engine packed up"
Hip-flask	Revolver	**Packet**	(Catch a) - be on the receiving end of offensive fire
Hit the deck	To land	**Pansy**	Effeminate
Homework	Sweetheart or girlfriend	**Party**	Air battle
Hop the twig	Crash fatally (Canadian)	**Passion wagon**	WAAF transport
Huffy	WAAF disdainful of approaches	**Peel off**	(To) - break formation to engage enemy
Humdinger	Very fast plane	**Penguin**	Ground officers with no operational experience
Hun	German	**Pickled, Pie eyed**	Drunk
Iron lung	Nissen Hut	**Piece of nice**	Any pleasant entertainment
Jankers	To be put "on a charge" for violating service discipline	**Play pussy**	Hide in the clouds
Jink away	Sharp manoeuvre, sudden evasive action	**Plonk**	Cheap wine
Keen as mustard	Eager, pun on Kean's mustard powder	**Plug away**	Continue to fire, keep going for target
King	NCO in charge of, e.g. bowser king	**Plumber**	Armourer
Kite	An aircraft (in the US also called a "ship")	**Pond life**	Lowest of the low
Ladybird	WAAF Officer	**Pukka**	Genuine as in "pukka gen"
Lose your wool	Lose composure	**Pulpit**	Cockpit of aircraft
Low down	(The) - inside information	**Queen Bee**	Officer in charge of the WAAF unit/camp
Mahogany Spitfire	Desk "flown" by penguins and ground wallahs	**Quick squirt**	Short sharp burst of machine-gun fire, "quickie"
Meat wagon	Ambulance	**Rocket**	A reprimand
Mickey Mouse	Bombing panel with clockwork distributor and switches (like a Mickey Mouse watch)	**Ropey**	Uncomplimentary adjective "A ropey landing"
Mob	Royal Air Force	**Sardine-tin**	Torpedo carrying plane
Muscle in	(On) - to take advantage of something	**Sawn-off**	Short in stature
Nickels	Propaganda leaflets	**Scarlet slugs**	Bofors tracer fire
No joy	No enemy contact	**Schooly**	Education Officer
		Scramble	Immediate operational take off

Scrambled egg	Gold braid on senior officer's hat
Scream downhill	Execute a power dive
Screw	Propeller
Scrounge	Obtain illicitly
Shed	Hangar
Shot down in flames	Crossed in love - severely reprimanded
Shot to ribbons	Totally incapable through drink
Shufti	(Have a) - take a look
Silver sausage	Barrage balloon
Skirt patrol	Search for a female companion
Sky pilot	Padre
Snake	Lively or noisy party
Snake-charmers	Dance band
Snoop	Service Policeman; SP about his duties
Snow Drops	RAF/Military Police
Soggy	Aircraft with unresponsive controls
Soup	Fog; "tangled in the soup"
Spawny	Very lucky
Sprog	A "new boy" fresh from training
Square bashing	(Marching) drill on the parade ground
Steam	Work hard and effectively
Stooge	Deputy, i.e. second pilot or any assistant
Strip	(Tear off a) - to be severely reprimanded; rank badges were torn off upon demotion
Sunray	Code for any CO
Supercharged	In a drunken state
Swede	Green recruit/countrified
Tail end Charlie	Rear gunner or rear aircraft of a formation
Tap in	Have a good time: "enemy ahead, tap in!"
Target for tonight	Girl friend

Taters	(Sack of), bombs dropped at same address
Taxi-driver	Instructor at a school of air navigation
Ticket	Pilot's certificate
Tiggerty-boo	(tickety-boo) all in order (from Hindustani *teega*)
Tin fish	Torpedo
Toy	A training aircraft or Link Trainer
Turn up the wick	Open the throttle
Turnip bashing	Drill on the square or in fields
Twitch	Body tremors developed by aircrew after a number of operations - "he's got the twitch" - sign of operational stress
Vic	Aircraft formation in the shape of a "V"
Waafize	The substitution of WAAF for male members of a unit
Wad	Cake or bun or scone "char and a wad"
Waffle/waffling	Out of control or cruising indecisively
Wallah	Chap or fellow
Wallop	Beer
Weaving	(Get), get going, hurry up
Week-End Air Force	Auxiliary Air Force, 1925 to outbreak of war
Whiff	Oxygen
Whistle	(To), depart hurriedly e.g. scramble
Whistled	State of intoxication
Wizard, Wizzo	First class, superlative, attractive
Woof	To open the throttle very quickly
Wrap up	Crash
Yellow doughnut	Collapsible dinghy carried on aircraft
Yellow peril	Training aircraft

Phases of the Battle

Opinions vary as to when the Battle of Britain started and ended. The most widely accepted dates are that it commenced on July 10th 1940, and ended on October 31st 1940.

Phase 1 - July 10th to August 7th

This first phase was predominantly attacks on coastal towns and convoys passing through the English Channel. There were isolated bombing raids on inland towns and cities. These raids tested the response times of the RAF, who the Germans knew were using Radar.

Dowding was aware that this opening phase was not the real battle, so would not commit large numbers of fighters to defend the shipping in the Channel where the response time was small and the Germans held the advantage.

Phase 2 - August 8th to 23rd

Phase 2 marked incorporated 'Adlertag' (Eagle's Day), the day assigned to commence a four day assault on Fighter Command's airfields and aircraft factories along with other establishments crucial to the fighting efficiency of the RAF. August 13th, Eagle's Day, was simply designated to the destruction of the RAF both on the ground and in the air and by doing so, prepare the way for Operation Sea Lion.

The weather remained unhelpful to Goering though, with cloud being a dominant factor and a hindrance to his bombers.

Phase 3 - August 24th to September 6th

Phase 3 comprised of further sustained attacks on Sector airfields, with the intention of finishing the job which had been commenced during the previous weeks. Bombing raids escalated daily while inaccurate German intelligence reports showed that the sustained raids of early August had successfully reduced the defence capability of the RAF.

Phase 4 - September 6th to 30th

Phase 4 marked the commencement of daylight bombing raids on London and other major cities. Goering believed this would bring all of the RAF's fighters into the air in defence of its capital city. In fact this change of strategy created a period of respite for the RAF's airfields, giving them the opportunity to regroup and to repair the damage. The Luftwaffe's attacks were having a far greater effect on the airfields than Goering had known and this change of tactics acted in Britain's favour.

Phase 5 - October 1st to 31st

Phase 5 included the day on which Hitler was forced to concede that Operation Sea Lion would not be launched until 1941.

Goering reverted to using the efficiency of his bombers at high operational ceilings, to avoid searchlights, anti-aircraft fire and to a degree, the fighter aircraft, which he believed could not climb to such altitudes quickly enough to intercept his bombers. High-level raids were less accurate but did also reduce the percentage of losses. Operating at such height also gave Radar less than 20 minutes in which to get RAF fighters ready to intercept before the bombs were released.

Aircraft spotter on the roof of a building in London. St Paul's Cathedral is in the background.

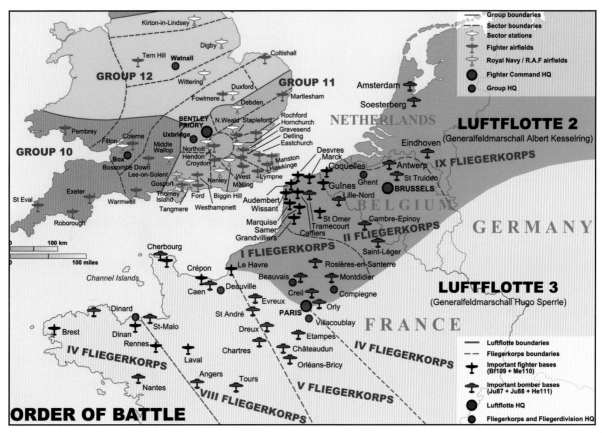

Group boundaries
Sector boundaries
Sector stations
Fighter airfields
Royal Navy / R.A.F airfields
Fighter Command HQ
Group HQ

Luftflotte boundaries
Fliegerkorps boundaries
Important fighter bases (Bf109 + Me110)
Important bomber bases (Ju87 + Ju88 + He111)
Luftflotte HQ
Fliegerkorps and Fliegerdivision HQ

Kirton-in-Lindsey
Digby
Tern Hill   **Watnall**
GROUP 12
Coltishall
Wittering
Duxford
Fowlmere
Martlesham   GROUP 11
Debden
Amsterdam
BENTLEY PRIORY
N.Weald Stapleford
Rochford
Hornchurch
Gravesend
Detling
Eastchurch
Soesterberg
NETHERLANDS
LUFTFLOTTE 2
(Generalfeldmarschall Albert Kesselring)
Pembrey
Colerne
Filton
Uxbridge
Middle
Wallop
Northolt
Hendon
Croydon
West
Malling
Manston
Hawkinge
Lympne
Desvres
Marck
Coquelles
Eindhoven
IX FLIEGERKORPS
Antwerp
St Truiden
GROUP 10
Box
Boscombe Down
Lee-on-Solent
Gosport
Kenley
Ford
Biggin Hill
Guînes
Ghent
Lille-Nord
BRUSSELS
BELGIUM
GERMANY
St Eval
Exeter
Warmwell
Thorney
Island
Tangmere
Westhampnett
Audembert
Wissant
St Omer
Tramecourt
Caffiers
Cambre-Epinoy
II FLIEGERKORPS
Roborough
Marquise
Samer
Grandvilliers
I FLIEGERKORPS
Saint-Léger
Cherbourg
Crépon   Le Havre
Rosières-en-Santerre
Montdidier
Channel Islands
Caen
Deauville
Beauvais
Creil
Compiegne
LUFTFLOTTE 3
(Generalfeldmarschall Hugo Sperrle)
Evreux
St André
PARIS
Orly
Villacoublay
FRANCE
Dinard
Brest
St-Malo
Dinan
Rennes
Dreux
Chartres
Etampes
Châteaudun
Orléans-Bricy
IV FLIEGERKORPS
IV FLIEGERKORPS
Laval
Angers
Tours
V FLIEGERKORPS
Nantes
VIII FLIEGERKORPS

ORDER OF BATTLE

100 km
100 miles

45

RAF Order of Battle: 10th July 1940

11 GROUP

Sector Station	Sqd	Airfield	Aircraft
Biggin Hill	32	Biggin Hill	Hurricane
	141	Biggin Hill	Defiant
	610	Gravesend	Spitfire
	600	Manston	Blenheim
North Weald	56	North Weald	Hurricane
	151	North Weald	Hurricane
	85	Martlesham	Hurricane
	25	Martlesham	Blenheim
Kenley	64	Kenley	Spitfire
	615	Kenley	Hurricane
	111	Croydon	Hurricane
	501	Croydon	Hurricane
Hornchurch	65	Hornchurch	Spitfire
	74	Hornchurch	Spitfire
	54	Rochford	Spitfire
Tangmere	43	Tangmere	Hurricane
	145	Tangmere	Hurricane
	601	Tangmere	Hurricane
Debden	17	Debden	Hurricane
Northolt	1	Northolt	Hurricane
	604	Northolt	Blenheim
	257	Hendon	Hurricane

10 GROUP *(Part of 11 Group until July 21st)*

Sector Station	Sqd	Airfield	Aircraft
Filton	92	Pembrey	Spitfire
	87	Exeter	Hurricane
	213	Exeter	Hurricane
	234	St Eval	Spitfire
Middle Wallop	609	Middle Wallop	Spitfire
	238	Middle Wallop	Hurricane

12 GROUP

Sector Station	Sqd	Airfield	Aircraft
Duxford	264	Duxford	Defiant
	19	Fowlmere	Spitfire
Coltishall	66	Coltishall	Spitfire
	242	Coltishall	Hurricane
Kirton in Lindsey	222	Kirton	Spitfire

Digby	46	Digby	Hurricane
	611	Digby	Spitfire
	29	Digby	Blenheim
Wittering	229	Wittering	Hurricane
	266	Wittering	Spitfire
	23	Collyweston	Blenheim

13 GROUP

Sector Station	Sqd	Airfield	Aircraft
Church Fenton	73	Church Fenton	Hurricane
	616	Church Fenton	Spitfire
	249	Leconfield	Hurricane
Catterick	41	Catterick	Spitfire
	219	Catterick	Blenheim
Usworth	607	Usworth	Hurricane
	72	Acklington	Spitfire
	152	Acklington	Spitfire
Turnhouse	79	Turnhouse	Hurricane
	253	Turnhouse	Hurricane
	245	Turnhouse	Hurricane
	603	Turnhouse	Spitfire
	602	Drem	Spitfire
	605	Drem	Hurricane

Dyce	263	Grangemouth	Hurricane
Wick	3	Wick	Hurricane
	504	Castletown	Hurricane

A restored Hurricane belonging to the Historic Aircraft Collection (picture courtesy of Air Displays International) and an original Mark 1 Spitfire (the 'Duxford' Spitfire). Picture courtesy of IWM Duxford

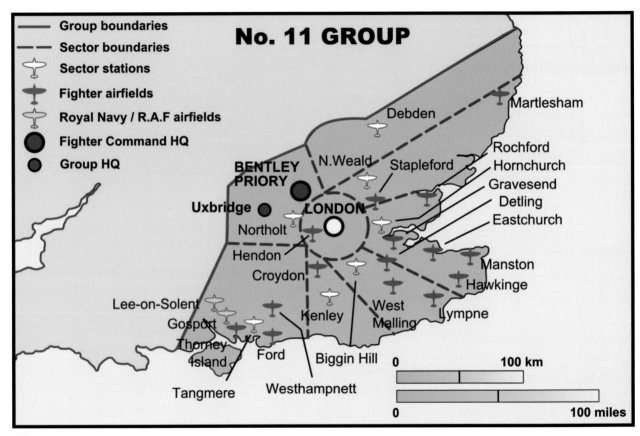

No. 11 GROUP

- Group boundaries
- Sector boundaries
- Sector stations
- Fighter airfields
- Royal Navy / R.A.F airfields
- Fighter Command HQ
- Group HQ

BENTLEY PRIORY
Uxbridge
LONDON
Northolt
Hendon
Croydon
Debden
N.Weald
Stapleford
Rochford
Hornchurch
Gravesend
Detling
Eastchurch
Manston
Hawkinge
Martlesham
Lee-on-Solent
Gosport
Thorney Island
Ford
Kenley
West Malling
Lympne
Biggin Hill
Westhampnett
Tangmere

0   100 km
0   100 miles

The Few – Some of the Pilots and Their Stories

The pages that follow tell in part, the story of some of the thousands of pilots who lived and fought during the battle of Britain. It is designed to be a 'representative' list, featuring some of the men who died and some who lived. Men from all social backgrounds and classes and men from many of the nationalities represented in the RAF's records of those who fought under Fighter Command's control during the Battle of Britain between July 10th and October 31st 1940.

Squadron Leader George Blackwood

George Blackwood was educated at Eton before joining the RAF on a short service commission in 1933. He was recalled when war was declared on Germany in 1939, and initially posted to No. 213 Squadron in June 1940 as its Squadron Leader, just weeks before the Battle of Britain commenced.

At the end of June 1940, he was posted to Duxford to help form the first completely Czech fighter squadron, No. 310. The pilots he took responsibility for were primarily experienced Czech pilots who had escaped the German occupation of their country. They had all seen combat defending their country and some had also fought during the battle for France.

George was often frustrated by not being able to properly communicate with his pilots in the English language but his men were skilled and eager to enter combat.

The squadron finally received 'operational status' on 17 August 1940.

George claimed a Dornier Do 17 on August 26th but his aircraft was shot down during the same sortie. He bailed out, unhurt, while his Hurricane (number P3887) crashed near to Maldon in Essex.

He ended the Second World War as Wing Commander, in charge of the Czech Fighter Wing of the RAF Second Tactical Air Force.

He was awarded the Defence Medal, George Star, Aircrew Europe Star, Czech War Cross, Czech Military Medal and some years after the war, the Czech Medal of George of Podebrady.

Above: Squadron Leader George Blackwood's medals, displayed at the Imperial War Museum, Duxford

Squadron Leader Robert Stanford Tuck in his 257 Squadron Hurricane

Squadron Leader Robert Stanford Tuck

Robert Stanford Tuck was one of Britain's top fighter aces, having been accredited with 29 'kills' before he was shot down by German flak over France and taken as a prisoner of war in 1942.

His first posting was to No. 62 Squadron, flying Gloster Gladiators.

He joined the RAF in 1935 and mostly flew the standard RAF biplane fighter, the Gladiator. In one of these aircraft, he narrowly avoided death in 1938 while involved in a flying accident with two of his friends. The accident was caused by the three aircraft flying too close together while flying in a standard formation during heavy turbulence. One of the three pilots was killed but

Tuck bailed out with only a long scar on his right cheek as a reminder of this incident.

In May 1940 Tuck was transferred to 92 Squadron, flying Spitfires out of Hornchurch. Tuck scored his first victory over France as part of the RAF's effort in defending the evacuating troops. A Messerschmitt Bf 109 fell into Tuck's gun-sights and he soon saw it crash into a field near St. Omer. Minutes earlier, Tuck had seen his colleague Pat Learmond's Spitfire shot down in a fireball. His squadron were scrambled three times that day in defence of the retreating British Expeditionary Force, and Tuck scored his first 3 kills.

One of Tuck's kills that day was a Bf 110 which he had forced down. He circled the aircraft as the German pilot climbed out of the cockpit. Sliding open his canopy, he waved at the German pilot who responded by shooting at him with a hand-held machine gun. One of the bullets cracked Tuck's canopy, having narrowly missed his already scarred face.

Days later, 92 Squadron lost their commanding officer, Roger Bushell, and Tuck took over as the Squadron Leader C.O.

The first thing he did as Squadron Leader C.O. was to order his pilots to make more space between them while flying in formation.

On his first day as 92's Squadron Leader C.O., Tuck shot down 2 Dornier bombers.

Tuck was one of just a few pilots who flew a Bf 109 in late May 1940 as an evaluation exercise. It had been rebuilt having crash landed in Britain. From this test, Tuck could report the aircraft's weak and strong points, which helped fighter command create tactics for facing such a fine fighter aircraft as its main opposition.

Tuck was awarded the Distinguished Flying Cross (DFC) by King George VI for his "initiative" and "personal example" over Dunkirk on June 28th, 1940.

92 Squadron were drawn back from the front line to Wales during July and August 1940. While chasing a lone German bomber he shot it down, but later found that the crashed aircraft had killed his brother-in-law, as it crashed into an army camp.

92 Squadron pilots during the Battle of Britain

While visiting colleagues stationed at North Weald in August, a German raid started. Instead of taking cover, Tuck took off in a Spitfire, catching up with 2 Junkers Ju 88 bombers over the Channel. He shot down both, but his Spitfire engine was damaged by return fire and he had to bail out and await rescue.

In September, Tuck was transferred to No. 257 Squadron which were flying Hurricanes. This

squadron had suffered heavy losses and the pilots were demoralised. Within days he had turned the squadron around.

On September 15th, he led this squadron and two other Hurricane squadrons towards a huge number of incoming bombers. Without the time to gain altitude or a tactical advantage, Tuck led his squadrons in for the attack, ignoring attacking Bf 109s which were coming out of the sun. While attacking a Heinkel bomber, Tuck was jumped by a Bf 109. He sent his wingman after the Messerschmitt and continued shooting at the Heinkel. This day would later in history be known as **"Battle of Britain day".**

Tuck was awarded a bar to his DFC for his bravery during his attack on the German formations. Surprised, he replied "I've just been bloody lucky, that's all". He was later awarded the Distinguished Service Order (DSO) - a decoration second only to the Victoria Cross for his leadership of No. 257 Squadron with "great success".

On one occasion, Tuck was flying alone over the east coast of England when he was jumped by three Bf 109s. The first Bf 109 fired at Tuck and passed him. Ignoring the other two Bf 109s, he fired at the one in front sending it into the sea below. He then banked around sharply and found one of the other Bf 109s. Letting it pass beneath him he dived after him and after a second quick burst, the second Messerschmitt also went down. Before he could recover his height, fire from the third Bf 109 shot the joystick out of his hand and shot the cockpit to bits. Despite this, he turned his Hurricane around, firing with everything he had against the last Messerschmitt, damaging it severely before he had to bail out. He was later picked up from the sea and treated for minor injuries.

In mid-July 1941 Tuck was given command of the Duxford wing, flying Airacobras, Spitfires and Typhoons. However, it was air-to-ground fire that finally brought Tuck down over France in January 1942. Doing a low "Rhubarb" sweep over France, together with his wingman he found himself in heavy flak coming from both sides of a shallow valley. Tuck's Spitfire was damaged but he managed to crash land it in front of a squad of German soldiers.

Tuck was taken to Stallag Luft 3 where he met many of his old friends, including Douglas Bader, a former leader of the Duxford wing and his old C.O., Roger Bushell. Tuck managed to escape his captors in 1945 when the whole camp was moved ahead of the Russian advance.

Robert Stanford Tuck settled in Kent with his wife Joyce after the war, dying in 1987.

Sergeant Kenneth 'Dutchy' Holland

Sergeant Kenneth 'Dutchy' Holland was one of the pilots who fought and died during the Battle of Britain, aged just 20. Holland was born in Sydney, Australia in 1920. His mother was from Cork (Ireland) and despite moving to New South Wales, family retained friends in Britain, which is why Kenneth was living in England in 1935. He had come to England as a ward of Hugh Ripley, a First World War comrade of Kenneth's father. Although living in Cornwall, he joined the Airspeed Aeronautical College in Portsmouth.

He enrolled at the Airspeed Aeronautical College in Portsmouth while Ripley was living in Camelford. The College was part of the Airspeed Company, founded in 1931. One of the co-founders of Airspeed was Nevil Shute, the acclaimed author. Holland stayed with Airspeed until 1939. He did not complete his aeronautical engineering course but instead joined the RAF.

Holland was assigned to 152 Squadron at Warmwell as part of No. 10 Group. Warmwell was originally constructed in 1937 as part of an air gunnery training facility. During 1939 it became a busy airfield, being home to 33 squadrons between 1939 and 1941. Squadrons based at Warmwell were given defence of areas which included Portland Naval base and West Country cities including Southampton and Exeter.

Holland joined a squadron under the leadership of Squadron Leader P K Divitt. Recognising the need for pilots 'on the edge' to have short breaks from the intense activity during the summer of 1940, Divitt found a pub in the small seaside town of Swanage which he used for his pilots to get rest and recreation. The squadron stayed at Warmwell throughout the Battle of Britain and its Spitfires were in action during all four months of the Battle. There were constant pilot casualties. On two occasions the squadron suffered the loss of two pilots in the same day (August 12th and September 25th) which was a significant blow to morale.

The last days of Holland's life are well documented in combat reports and Battle of Britain diaries. From 17th September to the 25th, Holland was involved in the destruction of three German aircraft. Holland's plane was hit in three places by return fire during one sortie. Two days later, he was scrambled during the late afternoon to investigate a radar contact near Swanage. A Junkers Ju 88 was sighted and engaged by Holland and his wingman, bringing it down into the sea.

On Wednesday September 25th, there were reports of large aircraft movements along the French coast and an incoming raid of over sixty German bombers and escorts heading towards Bristol. Three squadrons including 152 were scrambled. Although the bombers reached their target, on turning home they met waves of British fighters. Holland was part of Blue section which attacked a Heinkel bomber over the city of Bath. As the bomber emitted smoke, Holland ceased firing and went closer to inspect the damage but was hit by a German gunner who was still at his post, taking a bullet in the head. His plane lurched and dropped towards the ground. Both planes crashed in the fields of

Church Farm near the village of Woolverton, Somerset.

Although reports state that Holland was found in the cockpit of his crashed plane, a local newspaper article suggested that he bailed out and he is officially listed as having died of his wounds.

He is permanently remembered on a memorial on the A36 at Woolverton near Bath.

Flying Officer 'Dal' Russel

Canadian born Russel was on board a passenger liner with a contingent of Canadian troops on their way to England on June 17th 1940 when the news came that France had fallen. As soon as he arrived in Britain, he was posted to the No. 1 Canadian Squadron (401) at Middle Wallop, an airfield near the south coast of England. At 23, Russel was one of the youngest flying officers in his squadron.

His basic training had been in a de Havilland Gypsy Moth single-engine biplane, the standard training aircraft of the Montreal Light Flying Club throughout the 1930s. When Canada declared war on Germany on September 10th 1939,

Russel, together with three other pilots at the club joined the Royal Canadian Air Force and were commissioned with 115 Fighter Squadron stationed at the airfield. This squadron evolved to become No. 1 Squadron (and was renamed 401 in 1941).

The pilots of No. 1 Squadron trained in Canadian-built Hurricanes. The aircraft were crated and shipped overseas with them, but were soon replaced with later marks. Training continued at Middle Wallop, then Croydon, before being transferred to Northolt, which would be their main base for eight key weeks during the Battle of Britain.

August 18th was No. 1 Squadron's first day of action as they intercepted and destroyed three Dornier bombers. After that, Russel, along with his comrades were in action nearly every day, sometimes flying up to four or five sorties a day.

By the time the squadron's last air battle was fought on October 5th, exhaustion was taking a heavy toll. The pilots had been in the front line of the battle for 53 days. No. 1 Squadron had destroyed and damaged over 70 enemy aircraft; they had lost sixteen Hurricanes in action; three of their pilots had been killed, and ten wounded.

Russel was awarded the Distinguished Flying Cross.

Sergeant J R 'Frank' Toombs (Turret Gunner)

'Two-pint' Toombs joined the RAF Volunteer Reserve and was commissioned in May 1940 at the age of 29. He was posted to Duxford's satellite airfield of Fowlmere to join No. 264 Defiant Squadron as a Defiant turret-gunner. The Defiant units had mixed fortunes during the Battle of Britain although their unique design gave them great success during the defence of the evacuating troops while fighting over in France.

Over four days of combat in late May 1940, No. 264 Squadron lost ten aircraft and eleven aircrew were killed. 'Two-pint' Toombs was a popular member of the squadron's aircrew and was known on a regular occasion to go to his gun-turret to read a daily newspaper.

The Defiant's shortcomings meant that it was withdrawn as a day fighter in the South and used instead as a night fighter. In the darkness of evening on November 15th 1940, 'Two-pint' took-off from Rochford Aerodrome in Essex for a Night Patrol but after only a few minutes the aircraft mysteriously caught fire in mid-air. The pilot immediately turned his night fighter round for an emergency landing, but approaching from downwind he was not successful in his first attempt to land the stricken fighter. Aware of how difficult it could be for an air-gunner to get out of the turret in an emergency, he quickly made a second attempt at landing the Defiant, but in doing so, struck a tree and crashed on a nearby golf course. The aircraft burst into flames, but while the pilot managed to quickly crawl away from his blazing cockpit, 'Two-pint' was seen by soldiers who had initially run to assist him struggling inside the gun-turret as flames licked around him. They felt they were unable to help him escape, but when the Station Medical Officer arrived on the scene, showing incredible courage, he pulled Toombs from the burning aircraft.

'Two-pint' was hospitalised immediately but he died from his horrific wounds two days later.

Sergeant Pilot Trevor Guest Oldfield

Trevor Oldfield joined No. 92 Squadron at RAF Biggin Hill in mid-September 1940, having spent the previous few weeks with No. 64 Squadron at RAF Leconfield in Yorkshire to gain operational experience on the Spitfire.

Trevor had originally joined the Auxiliary Air Force in 1938 serving as an Air-gunner at RAF Kenley with No. 615 'County of Surrey' Squadron. The following year, he qualified as an armourer and with the approaching war was called up in August 1939.

Having been recognised for aptitude and all-round ability he was recommended for pilot training which took place at No. 5 Elementary Flying Training School at RAF Meir in Staffordshire. In early August he completed his flying training and was awarded his pilot wings brevet. He was posted to fly Spitfires at an Operational Training Unit and then flew his first operational sortie with No. 92 Squadron on Saturday 21st September 1940.

The following Thursday afternoon, he stalked a lone Dornier bomber with his wingman while on patrol over Tenterden, Kent. The enemy aircraft was brought down despite dodging in and out of cloud.

On the morning of the 27th, he was involved in ferocious sorties in which the Squadron lost two pilots to enemy fighters. Just before midday, the Squadron was scrambled again and Sgt Oldfield, flying as Green 4, found himself in the position known as 'weaver'.

Oldfield reported: *"I was Green 4 detailed to weave above the Squadron formation. When in the Canterbury area I was weaving approximately 1000 feet above the Squadron when the Squadron split up and engaged the enemy (Bf 109s). Owing to my being above the Squadron I was able to turn sharply to the left and attacked a Bf 109 from quarter astern. I saw pieces fly off the enemy aircraft near to the wing roots after I had given him a 3 second burst. I had only time to see him half roll and dive away before I spun out. I could not see whether the aircraft crashed but about 2 minutes later I saw someone making a parachute descent."*

Ninety minutes later, the Squadron was scrambled again. Oldfield jumped into his Spitfire (R6622) along with ten others from the

Squadron to patrol above base. As Junkers Ju 88s approached, escorted by Messerschmitt Bf 109s, the Squadron racked up a good number of claims against the bombers but only nine Spitfires returned to Biggin Hill. Trevor Oldfield however, never returned. He had fatally crashed onto Hesketh Park in Dartford at about 15:15 hours, after becoming a victim of the German fighter-escorts.

Witnesses on the ground said that he had flown his aircraft into the ground to prevent it crashing into houses. The aircraft exploded and spread debris all over the park. The Merlin engine landed in a nearby garden.

Flying Officer John C. Mungo-Park

John Colin Mungo-Park was born in Wallasey, Cheshire in 1918. He joined the RAF in 1937.

He was posted to 74 Squadron at RAF Hornchurch on 4th September 1939 and fought with this squadron throughout the Battle of Britain. By the end of November 1940 he had twelve confirmed victories and had been awarded the Distinguished Flying Cross.

He had taken the leadership of 'A' Flight of the squadron on 8th September 1940 and was promoted to command the squadron in March 1941 when the existing commander, 'Sailor' Malan, was posted to another appointment.

On 16th June 1941 he shot down two Messerschmitt Bf 109s over the French coast but his own aircraft was damaged and he glided back with a dead engine to crash land at Hawkinge near Folkestone.

On 27th June 1941 he was shot down and killed at Adinkerke, Belgium and is buried there.

Pilot Officer Roy Marchand

Roy Achille Marchand was born in Bromley, Kent in 1918, and after leaving Westminster School in 1936, began to study medicine at King's College, London University. Two years later, at the age of 20, Roy joined the RAF on a Short Service Commission and began his ab-initio training towards becoming a fighter pilot. He was awarded his 'Wings' in August 1939 and became a reserve 'Ferry Pilot' for France.

His desire to be a fighter pilot was realised in early 1940 when he was posted to fly Hawker Hurricane fighters with No. 73 Squadron at

Rouvres, one of RAF Fighter Command's few fighter units based in France.

Roy claimed early kills in the occasional skirmishes of the 'phoney war' in March and April, 1940. During this period he married. After the German invasion of the Lowlands on May 10th 1940, combat against a numerically superior Luftwaffe became a reality. Roy's next claim was unconfirmed - a Dornier Do 17 bomber on May 13th, but on the same day fire from Bf 109s hit his aircraft and he was wounded in the shoulder and beneath his left eye.

While recovering from his injuries, Roy missed the Allied retreat from Dunkirk. However, in early July 1940 he returned to his Squadron, which was now stationed at Church Fenton in Yorkshire, where it was re-equipping for its new role as a night defence squadron.

As the Battle of Britain raged through July and August, 73 Squadron did not experience much contact with the enemy as night raids were not common. However, at the beginning of September, the Squadron were sent further south, ending up at Castle Camps in Cambridgeshire. Here, the 73 Squadron Hurricanes were soon in action and by nightfall had lost three of their fighters and a further three had been damaged.

The next day, Marchand found himself in the thick of activity as the Squadron diarist recorded:

"... P/O MARCHAND destroyed a 109, 10 miles N.E. of MAIDSTONE, thus opening the Squadron's score in that category. He landed at PENSHURST having run short of petrol and rather lost his way. He got back in the evening his smiles even as large as if his wife had walked suddenly into Freddie 1 (Castle Camps). It was a tonic to see him but when he came to make out his individual combat report, the I.O. noticed that he had only claimed a 'probable'. Even more pleased was he when told it obviously came into the 'destroyed' class and he was the first to get a definite kill for 73 Sqdn."

Aerial activity was generally quiet for the Squadron over the next few days, but during the afternoon of Wednesday 11th September, Roy Marchand engaged in combat with enemy fighters again over North Kent where he claimed a 'probable' Bf 110.

On Saturday 14th September, three Hurricanes of 73 squadron were shot down in combat with one pilot killed and two others wounded including the C.O., Squadron Leader Maurice Robinson. Five Hurricanes sustained damage. Roy's Hurricane (P2869) was one of the few which made it back to Castle Camps relatively unscathed, though he had a bullet hole through his port main fuel tank, port aileron, main spar, and had suffered another bullet go clean through his radio mast just over his head.

On Sunday 15th September 1940 the Squadron was ordered to patrol Chelmsford at 15,000 feet. One of the Squadron pilots who took to the skies on what was to become the most decisive day of the Battle of Britain was 22 year-old Pilot Officer Roy Marchand.

Marchand was flying Hurricane P3865 TP-K when he took up his position as a 'lookout'. At around 11:30am a large force of free-hunting Messerschmitt Bf 109s crossed the English coastline high over Dover ahead of a formation of Dornier Do 17 bombers whose target was London.

With this large enemy raid building up over Kent, 73 Squadron was vectored south of the Thames Estuary to intercept the raiders. The Hurricane pilots soon joined in combat near Maidstone just after midday, and it was against a strong number of the deadly Bf 109s that a swirling dogfight ensued. As ammunition and fuel became exhausted, the Hurricane pilots gradually broke off and returned to Castle Camps with claims for 3 enemy fighters destroyed. All the 73 Squadron pilots were accounted for except one pilot who had reportedly force-landed at Biggin Hill. It was wrongly assumed to be Marchand, who had in fact crashed at Teynham near Sittingbourne and been killed.

The Squadron diarist paid tribute:

"P/O Marchand was an excellent pilot and a charming and unassuming boy who was never ruffled by anybody or anything. We will sorely miss him."

The record for the day was closed with the words, *"The Squadron feels that to some extent the death of gallant MARCHAND today has been avenged by the day's good work."*

Flying Officer Ian L McGregor Hallam

Ian 'Toddy' Hallam was born in Edinburgh at the very end of World War One. His nickname "Toddy" came from being named after his Uncle Ian, who had been killed in the trenches during that war. He was educated at Repton School and eagerly learnt to fly at the Phillips and Powis Aircraft Ltd Training School.

His first solo flight was in early April 1937 in a Hawk Trainer. After further training he was posted to No. 2 Squadron based at Hawkinge (Kent). When the British Expeditionary Force left for France in September 1939, No. 2 Squadron was posted to the Abbeville / Senon / Labiusuere region of Northern France. His action in France was simply reconnaissance flights until the Squadron was sent back to Britain on May 19th due to the speed of the Germans' advance.

His reconnaissance skills were such that in July 1940, he was sent to the Photographic Reconnaissance Unit (PRU) at Heston, Middlesex for training. In August he was posted to No. 225 (A.C.) Squadron at Tilshead, Wiltshire, where he was trained in the flying of fighter aircraft, including the Spitfire.

At the beginning of October 1940 he was posted to No. 222 Squadron at Hornchurch. He was one of just a few experienced pilots available to replace existing front line Battle of Britain pilots. With 222 Squadron he flew up to 4 sorties a day. On 17th October he claimed damage to a Bf 109 and between the 2nd and 25th October he claimed a further Bf 109 destroyed, 2 damaged and 1 probable.

On 27th September he was posted to No.73 Squadron at Castle Camps, Suffolk during which time of service he experienced a crash landing on 3rd November 1940 near Redhill, Surrey due to poor visibility.

After several more postings within the UK he was placed at No. 21 Air School of the South African Air force based in Kimberley and then moved to Cranbourne in Southern Rhodesia. He remained with this unit until June 1942 when he was promoted to Squadron Leader and returned to active flying as a photo - reconnaissance pilot.

While flying unarmed Hurricanes on Tactical Photo-Reconnaissance missions on 24 August 1942 he failed to return from a mission over the El Alamein battlefield. On 26th September 1942 the Germans broadcast his name as being a Prisoner of War.

He remained at Stalag Luft III until 11 February 1945 when the prisoners were freed from their captivity by advancing Americans.

Following further courses he was appointed to become the CO of the Aberdeen University Air Squadron. He died in a flying accident on 10th May 1952.

Flying Officer Brendan 'Paddy' Finucane

Brendan Fergus FINUCANE was born in Dublin in October 1920. His family moved from Dublin to Richmond, Surrey in 1936, and after leaving school Brendan found work as a clerk, potentially leading to a career in accountancy.

As war loomed in 1938, Brendan applied to join the RAF. He began his flying training in August just prior to his 18th birthday.

Brendan initially struggled in his career and was officially rated as 'below average'. However, he did eventually achieve operational status and was assigned as a fighter pilot in July 1940, being posted to No. 65 Squadron at Hornchurch,

equipped with Supermarine Spitfires.

Brendan was soon in the thick of the action shooting down his first enemy plane, a Messerschmitt Bf 109, on August 12th together with a 'probable'. He did the same again the next day. At the end of the month the squadron was 'rested' and transferred away from the frontline to RAF Turnhouse in Scotland.

It was not until January 1941 that Brendan achieved another kill, which led to the award of a Distinguished Flying Cross (DFC) in May, the citation stating:

"This officer has shown great keenness in his efforts to engage the enemy and he has destroyed at least 5 of their aircraft. His courage and enthusiasm have been a source of encouragement to other pilots of the squadron."

This award coincided with his promotion to Flight Commander of a newly formed unit in April 1941 that was to become the first full Australian squadron in England. Soon after the squadron (No.452 Royal Australian Air Force) became operational, Paddy scored the unit's first kill on July 11th, 1941.

He became friends with Australian Flight Lieutenant Keith 'Bluey' Truscott, with whom he planned to set up in business in Australia after the war.

Between early August and mid-October 1941 Paddy claimed sixteen enemy fighters destroyed. His achievements led to the award of two more DFCs in September followed by the award of a Distinguished Service Order (DSO) in October. The citation for the DSO stated:

"Recently, during two sorties on consecutive days, Flight Lieutenant Finucane destroyed 5 Messerschmitt 109s bringing his total victories to at least 20. He has flown with this squadron since June, [sic] *1941, during which time the squadron has destroyed 42 enemy aircraft of which Flight Lieutenant Finucane has personally destroyed 15. The successes achieved are undoubtedly due to this officer's brilliant leadership and example."*

Paddy was later promoted to command of No. 602 Squadron at RAF Redhill in early 1942.

Pilot Officer Billy Fiske

Billy Fiske was born in New York, USA in 1911, the son of a New England banking magnate. He attended school in Chicago, moved to France in 1924 and then attended Cambridge University. He settled in England, where he did weekend flying in the 1930s.

Billy Fiske excelled in winter sports and driving fast cars. When bobsledding became an Olympic sport in 1924, 16 year-old Fiske talked some of his American friends into trying for the US team. Olympic history tells the rest: Fiske became the youngest gold medalist in the sport, at just 16 years old during the 1928 Winter Olympics.

Fiske was also a Cresta Run Champion and drove the first Stutz car to be entered in the Le Mans 24 hour race when he was just 19.

Before he joined his father's firm, he had won his second Gold at the 1932 Olympics at Lake Placid. He then worked at the London office of Dillon, Reed & Co, the New York bankers. Fiske drove a British racing green Bentley. When asked to lead the American bobsled team in the 1936 Winter Olympics, which was to be held in

Germany, he declined due to 'disdain' for Adolf Hitler, and his anti-Semitic policies.

Fiske met and married an English woman in 1938 but was recalled to the New York offices of his father's bank just before the start of the war. However, an English friend, working in New York, who was an RAF reservist talked him into sailing back to England with him in late August 1939 to join the RAF.

In his diary Fiske recorded, *"I believe I can lay claim to being the first US citizen to join the RAF in England after the outbreak of hostilities"*.

Two weeks after the outbreak of the war Fiske volunteered to join the RAF. Although Britain needed pilots badly, the RAF only took British citizens or subjects at that time. In order to get round the issue of America's neutrality which prevented him from serving, Billy pretended to be Canadian. Despite this, it was only by knowing 'the right people' that he got an interview and was accepted.

He was promoted to the rank of Pilot Officer on 23rd March 1940, pledging his life and loyalty to King George VI. During his training, he and his wife lived in Wiltshire. In July however, he was posted to No. 601 Air Force Squadron at Tangmere - a unit known as the 'Legionnaires and Millionaires Squadron' because its original members had been at White's Club, St. James in 1924 and were handpicked by Lord Grosvenor in that year.

During the first month of the Battle of Britain, as a member of 601 he flew Hurricanes and was counted to have destroyed six enemy aircraft, the first being a Heinkel He 111.

Fiske's Flight Commander, Sir Archibald Hope, claimed: *"Unquestionably Billy Fiske was the best pilot I've ever known. It was unbelievable how good he was. He picked up so fast it wasn't true. He'd flown a bit before, but he was a natural as a fighter pilot. He was also terribly nice and extraordinarily modest, and fitted into the squadron very well."*

On August 16th 1940, the Squadron were scrambled to intercept a squadron of German dive-bomber Junkers Ju 87s which had crossed the coast east of Selsey Bill. The raiders were intercepted as they attacked Tangmere Aerodrome. During one of the subsequent dogfights, a German gunner put a bullet into

Fiske's fuel tank. He nursed the Hurricane back to base but it caught fire on landing burning his ankles, face and hands. He was puilled out before the aircraft exploded but had suffered severe burns.

Two days later he died of his wounds, aged 29.

Fiske was the man whom Lt Col J T C Moore-Brabazon (later Baron Brabazon of Tara) honoured with the words in a newspaper tribute, *"We thank America for sending us the perfect sportsman. Many of us would have given our lives for Billy."*

Pilot Officer Ronald J.W. Brown

Ronald Brown was born in March 1914 and was educated at John Ruskin Central School, Croydon. He joined the Royal Air Force in 1929 as an Aircraft Apprentice but volunteered for pilot training in 1935. He was originally posted on fly bombers, but was transferred to 111 Squadron at Northolt in February 1937, the first to be equipped with Hurricanes and Ronald Brown flew the Hurricane in a number of technical trials.

He remained with Hurricanes when they became operational in December 1938. On May 31st 1940 Brown shot down a Bf 109 over Dunkirk but was shot down during the same campaign a few days later near Abbeville. He bailed out and was picked up by a retreating Guards unit which helped him onto a hospital ship evacuating troops back to England.

He rejoined the Squadron in mid August and on the 18th, had a shared kill of a Dornier 17 which crashed near Biggin Hill.

He served throughout the war testing captured enemy aircraft alongside new British and US types. He later worked on developing the original Martin-Baker ejector seat before retiring from British Aerospace in 1979 with an MBE.

Wing Commander Douglas Robert Bader

Perhaps one of the most well known fighter pilots who fought in the Battle of Britain was Douglas Bader. His achievements before, during and after the war earned him a knighthood, alongside his previously awarded CBE, DSO and bar, DFC and bar, FRAeS and DL. As a young man he was an outstanding all-round sportsman and played first class cricket.

Bader joined the RAF in 1928 as an officer cadet at Cranwell (Lincolnshire). He was commissioned to No. 23 Squadron in July 1930 flying Gloster Gamecocks and Bristol Bulldogs. However, he was involved in a serious air accident while flying a Bulldog in 1931, in which he lost both of his legs. The accident was as a result of his trying to execute a slow barrel roll, in violation of orders. Despite opposition from every quarter, his persistence and tenacity enabled him to successfully retake all aspects of his training with artificial legs. He was successful, but his attitude and disregard for authority continued and contributed to his being unable to stay in an active flying role within the RAF. He was therefore retired in 1933.

The needs of the RAF during 1939 and 1940 enabled him to rejoin the RAF at his existing rank of Pilot Officer. His early encounters flying a Spitfire proved that he had an advantage over other pilots in that with no legs (into which the blood would normally rush), the effect of negative 'G's in these high performance aircraft were significantly reduced and he could stay conscious much longer than his colleagues. He flew with No. 19 Squadron from Duxford (Cambridgeshire) from February to April 1940, after which he was appointed Wing Leader of 222 Squadron, also based at Duxford. He scored his first 'kills' during the battle of France, over Dunkirk, the first being a Messerschmitt Bf 109 and the second a Dornier bomber. Within days, 222 Squadron was relocated further north to Kirton in Lindsey but in June, Bader was promoted to Squadron Leader, taking command of 242 Squadron at Coltishall. 242 had suffered significant losses during the battle of France and had been rendered inoperable. Bader's role was to inspire the young pilots, many of whom were Canadian, and to bring the squadron back to operational status, which he did with flying colours. Once operational again, the squadron was transferred to Duxford.

In July and August, Bader shot down a Dornier bomber and then two Bf 110s. In early September, two Bf 109s and later in the month two further bombers. During September 1940, Air Vice Marshals Leigh Mallory and Keith Park were reported to be at loggerheads over the concept of a 'big wing'. This concept intended to assemble large numbers of fighters to intercept the opposing raiders instead of attacking squadron by squadron. As Fighter Command's resources were built, the 'Duxford Wing' evolved from 12 Group with Bader leading up to five squadrons to simultaneously attack incoming bomber formations as a single fighting unit.

In 1941 Bader was promoted to Wing Commander and given the role of 'Wing Leader' with 616 Squadron, based at Tangmere, West Sussex. From here, he particiapted in fighter 'sweeps' over Europe but on one mission in August, was forced to bail out over occupied France and spent the rest of the war as a Prisoner of War. By now, he had accumulated 22 victories (kills).

His eventual escape and recapture in 1942 led to him being sent to Colditz, a castle from which it was thought that escape was not possible. Together with other 'troublesome prisoners' further escape attempts were constantly made. During his imprisonment, he was visited by Adolf Galland, a German fighter ace who had learned of and respected Douglas' achievements. They remained friends for many years. He was liberated in 1945 and left the RAF in 1946.

Douglas Bader was an inspirational British hero

of the era, having overcome the loss of both of his legs yet still returning to the RAF to become an inspirational leader and fighter ace.

Left:
Wing Commander Douglas Bader pictured in 1940 at RAF Duxford. Picture courtesy of IWM Duxford

Squadron Leader J W M Aitken

John 'Max' Aitken was born in 1910, the son of a politician and successful press entrepreneur, Baron Beaverbrook. Although born in Montreal, John was educated in England at Westminster School before moving to Cambridge University. It was here that his talent for sports became evident, embracing both soccer and golf. He also learnt to fly as a young man before travelling throughout Europe and the USA. He joined the Royal Auxiliary Air Force in 1935.

During the early part of the war, 'Max' flew Blenheim bombers before becoming a fighter pilot with 601 Squadron, which was newly equipped with Hurricanes.

He became the Commanding Officer of 601 Squadron in June 1940, just before the commencement of the Battle of Britain, aged 30. This was older than the average pilot who fought in this conflict.

By February 1941, he had been accredited with eight 'kills' leading to his being awarded the Distinguished Service Order and Distinguished Flying Cross.

He then transferred to command 68 Squadron, a night fighter squadron, where he claimed another four victories.

1943 saw 'Max' serving in the Middle East as a Wing Commander, and although technically not holding a 'flying role' he managed to account for two Junker Ju 52s while flying Beaufighters with No. 46 Squadron.

Aitken became Wing Leader of the Banff Strike Wing of RAF Coastal Command in 1944, where he stayed until the war ended. He reached the rank of Group Captain achieving a total of 14 confirmed kills and one shared before leaving the RAF.

In 1945 he entered politics and became the Conservative Member of Parliament for Holborn with a small majority for five years. Aitken also entered the family newspaper business in 1946 and became a Director of the Express Group before finally becoming Chairman of Beaverbrook Newspapers Ltd. He also served as Chancellor of the University of New Brunswick.

Flying Officer Jack Rose

Jack joined the Royal Air Force reserve in October 1938, and completed his training as a fighter pilot just before war broke out in September 1939.

Jack fought in the Battle of France and returned to fight in the Battle of Britain, during which he was shot down.

In France, he flew Hurricanes with No 3

Squadron, one of 6 squadrons that initially supported the British Expeditionary Force. He arrived in France on May 14th and shared in the kill of a Bf 109 on the 15th.

On May 18th, he shot down a Bf 110. On the 19th, he attacked a Heinkel He 111 bomber and closed to within a few yards during the attack so that oil from its engine covered his windscreen. Jack had to climb and take the Hurricane down to near stalling speed so that he could remove his harness and stand up to wipe the oil away, restoring his vision. As he was standing, tracer fire from the Heinkel nearly hit him and the Heinkel, assuming he was trying to bail out, claimed him as a 'kill'. However, Jack broke away and managed a forced landing at a nearby forward airfield.

On May 20th, orders were given to withdraw and his aircraft was destroyed where it stood.

In the 10 days of the Air War over France, No. 3 Squadron lost seven pilots, killed or taken prisoner. A further nine Hurricanes were destroyed.

Jack's brother Tommy flew Hurricanes in 56 Squadron. He was shot down and killed on May 18th, 1940.

Returning to England, Jack joined No. 32 Squadron, which was moved to Biggin Hill on August 22nd, as the Battle of Britain intensified.

On August 25th, before being scrambled, Jack's squadron was issued with fluorescent water-dye packs to be sewn onto their life jackets. These were designed to stain the sea around any pilot forced down into the English Channel and help the rescue operation. After Jack had sewed his pack on, six Hurricanes from No. 32 Squadron were scrambled to intercept incoming Dornier bombers. During their attack, Jack was shot down by an escort Messerschmitt Bf 109 and was forced to bail out over the English Channel from where he was picked up after two hours. A pilot who had not had the opportunity to sew a pack onto his life jacket that day was lost to the sea.

Jack remained convinced that his rescue was due to the timely distribution of this new aid, which remains in use to this day.

In 1942, Jack was awarded a DFC and was appointed as the Squadron Leader of No. 184 Squadron. This squadron was also equipped with Hurricanes until 1943 when it was re-equipped with Typhoons.

In 1944, 184 Squadron was involved in the build up to the D-Day landings. Soon after, Jack was sent to Burma to take command of a Hurricane squadron based there.

He left the RAF in 1946 to join the Colonial Service. He was awarded an MBE in 1954 and a CMG in 1963. He retired in 1979 with the rank of Wing Commander, and was finally laid to rest in late 2009.

15th September 1940:
A Day To Be Remembered

The battle experiences and the fate of the pilots varied from day to day. Just what they each experienced can best be summarised by analysing the activity, events and casualties on just one day during this epic air battle.

More pilots and more aircraft were involved in aerial battles over England on September 15th than any other day. It was also a day in which for both Air Forces, there were more incidents and casualties.

This is an account of how on that day alone, 56 aircraft were destroyed and 13 pilots lost their lives and another was taken as a prisoner of war.

The activity indicates different circumstances and differing events causing casualties during that one day:

Throughout the day there were heavy attacks on London, successfully broken up by Fighter Command. German losses became the highest since 18th August [185 claimed by the RAF].

The enemy delivered two major attacks on London with smaller formations attacking Portland and targets in the Southampton area.

RAF fighters destroyed 177 enemy aircraft (124 bombers and 53 fighters) plus 41 probables and 72 damaged. RAF casualties were 25 aircraft destroyed and 13 pilots killed or missing.

The Battles:

11:00 hours   First Major Attack: Enemy aircraft began to mass in the Calais/Boulogne area.

11:30 hours   The leading wave of about 100 aircraft crossed the coast between Dover and Dungeness, followed by a second wave of 150 aircraft. Targets appeared to be London.

11 Group sent up 16 squadrons to meet the attack, and 12 Group provided 5 squadrons to patrol Debden and Hornchurch.

Approximately 100 enemy aircraft succeeded in reaching Central London.

P/O R.E.Jones. Shot down in combat with Do 17s and Bf 109s. Jones bailed out of damaged aircraft before it crashed & landed unhurt.
Hurricane L2122. 605 Squadron Croydon

P/O G.L.D.Doutrepont. Aircraft crashed onto Staplehurst Railway Station after being shot down by Bf 109 fighters. Pilot Killed.
Hurricane N2537. 229 Squadron Northolt

P/O R.R.Smith. Pilot wounded in leg during exchange of fire with Do 215 and Bf 110s. Pilot

bailed out of aircraft and landed safely.
Hurricane V6616. 229 Squadron Northolt

F/O A.D.Nesbitt. Shot down by Bf 109. Bailed out wounded but landed safely.
Hurricane P3080. 1 RCAF Squadron Northolt

F/O R.Smither. Attacked and shot down by Bf 109. Pilot failed to bail out.
Hurricane P3876. 1 RCAF Squadron Northolt

Sgt R.T.Holmes. Unhurt - bailed out after aircraft damaged by Bf 109. Aircraft crashed in Buckingham Palace Rd.
Hurricane P2725. 504 Squadron Hendon

Fl/Sgt C.Sydney. Unhurt - returned to base with damage to wing after combat with Bf 109s.
Spitfire R6767. 92 Squadron Biggin Hill

P/O R.A.Marchand. Killed - crashed into farm at Teynham after being shot down by Bf 109s.
Hurricane P3865. 73 Squadron Debden

F/O M.E.A.Royce. Unhurt – returned to base with oil cooler problem after combat action.
Hurricane L1913. 504 Squadron Hendon

P/O C.F.A.Capon. Unhurt - made forced landing

at Croydon after combat action.
Hurricane P3642. 257 Squadron Debden

P/O G.N.Gaunt. Killed - crashed in flames near Kenley after being hit by gunfire from Bf 110.
Spitfire R6690. 609 Squadron Warmwell

Sgt C.A.L.Hurry. Unhurt – returned to base with damage to aircraft.
Hurricane N2599. 46 Squadron North Weald

P/O G.A.Langley Killed – crashed into building after being shot down by Bf 109s.
Spitfire P9324. 41 Squadron Hornchurch

P/O E.Q.Tobin Unhurt – crashed into airfield truck during landing approach.
Spitfire K9997. 609 Squadron Warmwell

Fl/Lt P.M.Brothers. Unhurt - landed at Biggin Hill for safety check after sustained damage in combat.
Hurricane P3620. 257 Squadron Debden

S/L H.A.V.Hogan. Unhurt – damaged in cooling system after combat with Bf 109s. Made forced landing.
Hurricane V7433. 501 Squadron Kenley

Fl/Lt G.E.Ball. Unhurt – made forced landing with damaged aircraft after combat action.
Hurricane V6576. 242 Squadron Coltishall

P/O A.E.A von den Hove d'Ertsenrijck. Killed – aircraft exploded in mid-air after hit by gunfire from Bf 109.
Hurricane P2760. 501 Squadron Kenley

P/O W.Lokuciewski. Leg wounds – returned to base after receiving damage from Bf 109.
Hurricane P2903. 303 Squadron Northolt

P/O J.T.Gurteen. Killed – shot down by enemy aircraft and crashed at full speed into a private home.
Hurricane N2481. 504 Squadron Hendon

14:00 hours Second Major Attack: A wave of approximately 150 enemy aircraft crossed the coast near Dover, followed by a second wave of 100 aircraft. These formations spread over South-East and South-West Kent and the Maidstone area, and about 70 penetrated Central London.

11 Group sent up 16 squadrons and 12 Group 4

squadrons. Targets in South London and railways in London and Kent appeared to be the chief objectives.

P/O T.P.M.Cooper-Slipper. Injured - hit by gunfire from Do 17. Collided with enemy aircraft losing wing. Pilot bailed out
Hurricane L2012. 605 Squadron Croydon

Sgt J.Hubacek. Slight injuries – bailed out after aircraft was hit by Bf 109 gunfire.
Hurricane R4087. 310 Squadron Duxford

P/O K.T.Lofts. Unhurt – crash landed at West Malling after being attacked by Bf 109 while intercepting Heinkel He 111 bomber.
Hurricane V6566. 249 Squadron North Weald

Fl/L G.ff Powell-Sheddon. Slight injuries – shot down by Bf 109 while attacking Do 17. Pilot bailed out.
Hurricane P2884. 242 Squadron Coltishall

Fl/Lt T.P.Chlopik. Killed – shot down by enemy aircraft. Bailed out, died on landing.
Hurricane P2954. 302 Squadron Duxford

P/O A.Hess. Unhurt – shot down in flames by enemy aircraft. Pilot bailed out safely.
Hurricane R4085. 310 Squadron Duxford

F/O M.Jebb. Died of injuries 19.9.40 – crashed at Dartford after combat with enemy aircraft.
Hurricane N2705. 504 Squadron Hendon

F/O A.Yuile. Wounded – returned to base with severe damage after combat with He 111 and poss Bf 109s.
Hurricane L1973. 1 RCAF Squadron Northolt

P/O R.H.Holland. Slight injuries – injuries sustained on landing after bailing out of damaged aircraft.
Spitfire R6606. 92 Squadron Biggin Hill

F/O T.D.Williams. Unhurt – returned to base with severe damage after combat with He 111.
Spitfire II P7303. 611 Squadron Digby

Sgt T.Andruszkow. Unhurt – bailed out after being hit by gunfire from Bf 109.
Hurricane P3939. 303 Squadron Northolt

P/O A.C.Bartley. Unhurt – returned to base with damage after combat with Do 17.
Spitfire P9513. 92 Squadron Biggin Hill

Sub/Lt A.G.Blake. Unhurt – made forced landing in Kent after combat action
Spitfire R6991. 19 Squadron Duxford

Sub/Lt R.J.Cork. Unhurt – made landing at Rochford. Damage to cockpit and wings in combat with Bf 109.
Hurricane P3515. 242 Squadron Coltishall

P/O M.Feric. Unhurt – returned to base after aircraft damaged by gunfire from Bf 109s.
Hurricane R2685. 303 Squadron Northolt

S/L R.G.Kellett. Unhurt – returned to base with damaged aircraft after action with Bf 109s.
Hurricane V7465. 303 Squadron Northolt

Sgt R.T.Llewellyn. Badly wounded – shot down in combat with Bf 110s and bailed out.
Hurricane P3113. 213 Squadron Tangmere

Sgt L.Pidd. Killed – bailed out after being shot down by enemy aircraft. Found dead on landing.
Hurricane P2836. 238 Squadron Middle Wallop

P/O V.C.Simmonds. Unhurt – returned to base with damage to aircraft tailplane after combat.

Hurricane L2089. 238 Squadron Middle Wallop

Sgt M.Wajciechowski. Unhurt – returned to base after aircraft damaged by gunfire from Bf 109s.
Hurricane V6673. 303 Squadron Northolt

Fl/Lt M.V.Blake. Unhurt – aircraft damaged in combat and had to make a forced landing.
Hurricane P3920. 238 Squadron Middle Wallop

Sgt M.Brzezowski. Listed as missing – believed crashed in Thames Estuary after combat with Bf 109s.
Hurricane P3577. 303 Squadron Northolt

Sgt J.Kowalski. Unhurt – aircraft damaged by enemy aircraft and returned to base.
Hurricane P3935. 302 Squadron Duxford

F/O A. P.Pease. Killed – shot down by unknown enemy aircraft. Pilot did not bail out.
Spitfire X4324. 603 Squadron Hornchurch

Sgt J.A.Potter. Taken POW – ditched damaged aircraft off French coast and captured by

German military
Spitfire X4070. 19 Squadron Duxford

F/O W.Urbanowicz. Unhurt – returned to base after aircraft damaged by gunfire from Bf 109s.
Hurricane V6684. 303 Squadron Northolt

F/O W.Zak. Unhurt – returned to base after aircraft damaged by gunfire from Bf 109s.
Hurricane L2099. 303 Squadron Northolt

F/O C.T.Davis. Unhurt – returned to base with damaged aircraft.
Hurricane P3462. 238 Squadron Middle Wallop

S/L G.L.Denholm. Unhurt – hit by gunfire from Do 17. Bailed out of damaged aircraft.
Spitfire R7019. 603 Squadron Hornchurch

F/O J.D.Dundas. Unhurt – returned to base with severe damage after combat with Do 17.
Spitfire R6922. 609 Squadron Warmwell

Sgt H.A.C.Roden. Slight injuries – crash landed after combat with Bf 109.
Spitfire P9431. 19 Squadron Duxford

P/O P.J.T.Stephenson. Injured – collided with enemy aircraft after attacking Do 17. Pilot bailed out.
Hurricane, 607 Squadron Tangmere

Sgt C.F.Babbage. Unhurt – made forced landing at Shoreham with damage caused by gunfire from Do 17.
Spitfire X4412. 602 Squadron Westhampnett

P/O A.R.H.Barton. Unhurt – damaged in combat with Do 215s. Forced landing at Hawkinge.
Hurricane V6698. 253 Squadron Kenley

15:30 hours Attack on Portland: A formation of 25 enemy aircraft intercepted by and driven off by RAF fighters.

P/O A.R.Covington. Unhurt – exhausted fuel tank. Forced landing made near East Grinstead.
Hurricane P3833. 238 Squadron Middle Wallop

Sgt T.R.Tweed. Killed – failed to come out of spin during practice dogfight over base.
Hurricane P3660. 56 Squadron Boscombe Down

17:25 hours   Attack on Southampton: About 50 enemy aircraft flew over the Isle of Wight and attacked objectives in the Southampton district. This formation was intercepted and driven off by 6 squadrons.

20:00 hours   The first hostile raids were plotted leaving the French Coast at Le Havre. They crossed the Coast at Shoreham and penetrated to the London area which appeared to be the main objective throughout the night.

22:30 hours   Raids to London started to come from the Dieppe area crossing the coast between Selsey Bill and Dover.

Overnight   Two raids were plotted in the Digby and Church Fenton areas and two were plotted in the Irish Channel. Ten raids were suspected of mine laying between Montrose and Flamborough Head. During the night a He 111 was destroyed (plus one probable) by a Defiant of 141 Squadron.

01:00 – 03:00 Raids were coming in via the Thames Estuary and Essex. About fifteen raids were plotted out of the Cherbourg area to South Wales and the Bristol Channel, some of which penetrated to the Midlands and Liverpool.

Summary:

Pilots Killed in Aircraft	5
Pilots died while crash landing	4
Pilots died during parachute descent	2
Aircraft exploded in mid air	1
Pilots killed during flying accident	1
————————	
Aircraft collisions (pilots bailed out wounded)	2
Enemy action wounded (bailed out)	2
Aircraft crashed, pilots survived	3
Pilot run out of fuel	1
Aircraft forced to land, pilots survived	7
Aircraft returned damaged, pilots wounded	3
Aircraft returned to base damaged	14

Invaluable Support from the 'Erks' and ATA

A number of pilots recall forging firm friendships with their ground crew, men who worked tirelessly to repair damaged craft and to keep them in working order. Teams of engineers often put up with rushed meals and sleep deprivation (often getting what sleep they could in the very hangars where aircraft were kept). It was a herculean task to keep planes ready for action; many had been riddled with machine gun holes, others had cannon shell damage, and some had damage sustained during near crash landings.

The engineers, fitters and riggers, armourers and Radio Transmission specialists were collectively known as 'Erks'.

The role of this veritable army has often been overlooked. Many of these men had served apprenticeships at the RAF Technical College, Halton in Hertfordshire and quite a number dreamt of one day being pilots themselves. The work was arduous and dangerous; aircraft had a wealth of hazards from aviation fuel and pressurized glycol to hot oils and explosives.

> Almost a third of pilots during the Battle of Britain were Sergeants, many of whom had originally been dubbed 'Erks'.

When war was imminent, many technicians applied for pilot training, and on acceptance, became one of 'the few'.

Another important contribution was made by the Air Transport Auxiliary (ATA). The ATA was a civilian organisation set up by Gerard d'Erlanger, Director of British Overseas Airways Corporation, under the auspices of the Air Ministry. It began operation in 1939.

The original plan was for the ATA to ferry people and messages in light aircraft to relieve the RAF pilots who could get on with the job of fighting. Over the course of the war the ATA was responsible for ferrying over 300,000 aircraft between factories and front-line airfields, freeing RAF pilots for operational duty. Many of these pilots who delivered aircraft through all weathers were women.

Amy Johnson, the legendary aviatrix flew as a part of the ATA . On Sunday 5th January 1941, she is believed to have drowned when the plane which she was ferrying, crashed into the Thames Estuary during bad weather. Although a more famous name than any of the other female pilots who ferried aircraft to the front line, her life and eventual sacrifice epitomises a generation and spirit of the 'unsung heroes' whose support of the front line pilots made their efforts possible.

Aircrew working on the Merlin Engine of Mark 1 Hurricane

Tragedies and Triumphs

With British industry responding to the demands of war, aircraft could be replaced. The loss of pilots in the context of battle was unavoidable. However, the loss of pilots in unusual circumstances was tragic. By reviewing the casualty lists, it can be seen that many pilots' lives were lost in the most unexpected and unusual ways.

In most cases, pilots whose lives were lost during training accidents during the summer of 1940 are not recorded in the Roll of Honour of pilots who died during the Battle of Britain. This is especially the case for pilots who had not been brought up to operational status. However, some accidents occurred during aerial combat including occasional instances of two British aircraft colliding with each other and more numerous instances of an RAF fighter colliding with an enemy aircraft. In some cases, this was deliberate; an injured pilot and one whose aircraft was too badly damaged to return to base might in the heat of battle consider the necessity of bringing down the aircraft he was attacking a sacrifice worth making and deliberately used his fighter as a projectile to down the incoming aircraft. In one instance, a pilot of an Avro Anson, **Sergeant B Hancock**, of No 6. SFTS (Service Flight Training School) crashed his aircraft headlong into a Heinkel He 111 which was attacking his airfield in Gloucestershire.

The loss of more than one member of aircrew at any time was particularly tragic, and on very few occasions did the gunner of a Defiant or the additional aircrew in a Blenheim survive if the aircraft were to be shot down.

Instances of a pilot bailing out and finding his parachute would not open were rare, but did occur. This was also the case where pilots might be unable to bail out at a safe height. Surviving an aerial battle was therefore not a guarantee of survival. Landing safely on the ground was.

There were reports of instances where pilots had bailed out and were machine-gunned as they descended with their parachutes. These instances were very rare but did unfortunately occur.

Aircraft being successfully returned to base by an injured pilot were common occurrences. In many cases the pilot would survive and be returned to operational duties when they had recovered from their wounds. Frequently though the converse happened, with pilots dying from their wounds the next day or perhaps many weeks later.

Unlike the Luftwaffe, the RAF had a policy of resting pilots and squadrons to help reduce losses as a result of fatigue. That period of rest may have been a deployment to a less active field of combat such as No. 13 Group, or for successful, experienced pilots, assignment to training squadrons where they could pass on their knowledge to new young pilots. This was the case for **Peter Ayehurst**, whose success as a fighter pilot during the Battle of France had him assigned to train young pilots in June 1940. As a result, he was not formally a front line fighter pilot during the Battle of Britain although he had been before and was again soon after. Conversely, the Luftwaffe's strategy was to maximise the skills of their key pilots for as along as possible and very successful pilots were rested. They were expected to fight and to survive – or to die in the cause of advancing the Third Reich. For that reason, many German pilots became fighter aces accruing large numbers of 'kills' before they eventually fell foul of the effects of battle exhaustion.

On more than one occasion before, during and after the Battle of Britain RAF aircraft were shot down by friendly fire. The most common occurrence of this was Blenheim bombers being mistaken for Messerschmitt Bf 109s. On one occasion, friendly fire from anti-aircraft guns aimed at an enemy bomber, hit the fighter pursuing the bomber instead.

Other occurrences of friendly fire being responsible for the loss of aircraft and pilots included an incident earlier in the war where a flight of unidentified aircraft were intercepted and shot down by Spitfires of No. 74 Squadron. These, the first aircraft to be shot down by the guns of a Spitfire in the war were subsequently found to be Hurricanes. Such events were tragic but a reality of war when aircraft were intercepting each other at high speeds and adrenalin was running high in the bloodstream of the young pilots on whose shoulders the survival of the free world existed.

Stories of pilots who deliberately flew their aircraft into the ground instead of bailing out and leaving the aircraft to fall uncontrollably to the ground were also common. This heroism was demonstrated to avoid the aircraft falling into residential areas and potentially killing civilians. Such was the case in Dartford, where the pilot, unable to return his aircraft to base, crashed it into the town's Hesketh Park to avoid the aircraft falling into the residential areas all around. The loss of his life may have saved dozens and the sacrifice he displayed was representative of the courage displayed by many pilots who knew their role included the protection of the civilian population below.

The Tragedy of Barking Creek

At 06.15 hours a searchlight battery reported unidentified aircraft approaching from high altitude over West Mersea on the Essex coast.

This message was relayed to 11 Group headquarters at Bentley Priory. At 06.27 hours on 6th September 1939, the third day of the war, one flight of six Hurricanes from 56 Squadron stationed at North Weald were ordered to scramble to meet reported enemy aircraft incoming from the North Sea. The Squadron's Commanding Officer, Group Captain Lucking decided to send up his entire unit. In addition to these, and unbeknown to the rest of the pilots,

Pilot Officers Frank Rose and Montague Hulton-Harrop managed to take up a pair of reserve aircraft and followed at a distance.

Other aircraft were also scrambled:- 151 Squadron's Hurricanes (also from North Weald), and Spitfires from 54, 65, and 74 Squadrons based at Hornchurch. All the aircraft were vectored (directed) to the eastern part of Essex between the Blackwater and Stour Estuaries.

As they converged on the area in which the unidentified aircraft had been reported, 'A' Flight from 74 Squadron spotted what they believed to be two Bf 109s and were given permission to engage them. Three Spitfires peeled off to attack. They were piloted by Flying Officer Byrne, Pilot Officer Freeborn and Sergeant Flinders.

The 'bandits' were in fact the two reserve aircraft from 56 Squadron, flown by Pilot Officers M. L. Hulton-Harrop and F.C. Rose. Byrne and Freeborn were the only pilots to actually open fire. Hulton-Harrop was hit in the back of the head killing him instantly. At this stage of the war Hurricanes were not fitted with armour plating behind the pilot's head. His aircraft crashed at Manor Farm, Hintlesham, Suffolk. P/O Rose crash landed but was not injured and was taken to the airfield at Martlesham Heath (Rose later returned to RAF North Weald where he remained with 56 Squadron, being promoted to Flying Officer. He was later shot down and killed over France on 18th May 1940).

Byrne and Freeborn were placed under arrest on their return to Hornchurch. They later stood trial but were acquitted. Group Captain Lucking was removed from his post as CO of 56 Squadron.

At the time of this incident, 74 Squadron was being led by **Adolph 'Sailor' Malan** who was reputed to have given the order to attack. Malan always denied this accusation though and unlike the pilots who opened fire on the Hurricanes, was not court martialled. Malan went on to become one of Britain's premier fighter aces.

This tragic affair became known throughout Fighter Command as The Battle of Barking Creek.

26 year-old Pilot Officer Hulton-Harrop was buried with full military honours in the graveyard of St Andrew's Church in North Weald Bassett, a

village adjoining the aerodrome. He was the first of the 50 RAF personnel based at North Weald to be buried in that graveyard in the months and years that followed.

The Guinea Pig Club

In war much is made of victories and defeats, yet very little is spoken of its cost, especially the human cost. In the midst of horror, a remarkable New Zealander did what he could to rebuild those disfigured by war.

Sir Archibald McIndoe (1900-1960) was one of those few individuals who can be said to have literally transformed lives. McIndoe (born in Dunedin, New Zealand) was one of the early pioneers of Plastic Surgery. The work done by McIndoe in both physically and psychologically rehabilitating badly burned pilots and aircrew, earned him an international reputation. He did not just care about their physical health, he also campaigned tirelessly to improve their pay and conditions.

McIndoe started working at the now famous Blond-McIndoe Research Centre based at the Queen Victoria Hospital in East Grinstead, West Sussex, at the start of the war. The nature of aircraft meant that once hit or damaged the highly inflammable fuel could ignite and spread rapidly through the plane causing horrific injuries.

The pilots McIndoe and his team worked with were nick-named 'Guinea Pigs' because the treatment and operations being carried out were so new. Plastic surgery was in its infancy and often patients had to undergo dozens of painful operations and skin grafts. Those pilots who underwent such treatment soon became known as the Guinea Pig club and formed a close bond.

It was common at that time for those disfigured by war to be hidden away, but McIndoe believed that it was for the good of all that such patients be allowed to engage with the local community, something the people of East Grinstead were prepared to do.

Many pilots came under the care of McIndoe and his team after 'exploits' in burning aircraft. It was not uncommon for pilots to be burned in their cockpits while trying to bail out and the damage to their hands and faces left them in need of both physical and psychological care for months or even years as they tried to re-adapt to a life as near to normal as possible while horribly disfigured.

Pilot Stories *(Continued)*

Flying Officer Richard Hillary

Among the pilots who were badly burned while trying to escape from the cockpits of burning aircraft was Richard Hillary, a young pilot of 603 Squadron.

Hillary was one of the pilots whose initial training had been with the University Air Squadron and at the time of his training coming to a successful conclusion, was posted to 603 (City of Edinburgh). In June 1940, 603 were stationed in Dyce, Scotland. Hillary's initial battle experiences were therefore in intercepting bombers flying from Norway. However, on August 10th, as the ferocity of the Battle of Britain increased, 603 were transferred from 13 Group to 11 Group at Hornchurch.

The realities of the battle hit on the very first day the squadron arrived at Hornchurch. It had already been bombed when they arrived that morning and one of the squadron's most popular figures, MacDonald was shot down during their very first sortie.

Hillary was shot down on September 3rd over the English Channel. His Spitfire cockpit hood had been damaged by the heat of a bomb blast while it was on the ground the day before and on the 3rd Hillary was having difficulty sliding it.

During an intense dogfight he was shot down and unable to quickly escape the cockpit of his burning aircraft, suffered severe burns to the hands and face before managing to bail out.

After many months of operations and reconstructive surgery, Hillary was returned to operational duties in 1942 but died in combat on January 7th 1943. During his time in hospital he wrote several books recounting his early life and the friendships he made in 603 Squadron. The first of these entitled "The Last Enemy" was published in 1942.

Flying Officer AG 'Zulu' Lewis

Albert Lewis was born in Kimberley, South Africa in April 1918. He joined the Royal Air Force in 1938 on a four-year Short Service Commission, being gazetted as an Acting Pilot Officer with effect from 29th October, 1938.

He was awarded his 'wings' on 14th March, 1939. On June 15th he was posted to No. 754 Squadron Fleet Air Arm and became a Staff Pilot at HMS Daedalus at Lee-on-Solent, flying Walrus, Magister, Mentor, Sea Fox and Swordfish aircraft. On 20th June he crashed a Walrus, the machine being a complete write-off. He was briefly hospitalised. The outbreak of war on 3rd September found him as Sea Duty Pilot and he received the signal for the Commanding Officer of the unit which directed: "Commence hostilities against Germany at once".

Later that month, on 18th September 1939, he was posted to No. 616 (South Yorkshire) Squadron Auxiliary Air Force, which had been formed on 1st November 1938, for bombing, with Hinds, Tutors and Avro 504Ns. When he arrived, however, the Squadron had Gauntlets, Tutors and Battles. He flew all three aircraft before being posted to No.12 Group Ferry Pool, where he spent most of his time ferrying Gladiators, and practising Fighter Attacks on unescorted bombers worked out by the Air Fighting Development Unit.

On 16th December 1939, he was posted to No. 504 "City of Nottingham" Squadron, at Debden. The Squadron was equipped with Hurricanes.

Lewis flew Hurricane L1912, lettered N, to test the variable pitch airscrew. Up till then all Hurricanes had fixed-pitch two-bladed propellers. The fixed pitch propeller aircraft had a speed range from about 80 mph stalling speed to 350 mph top speed which was an almost impossible com-promise between top speed

performance and take-off performance. If the top speed were very good, the take-off was correspondingly poor.

Left:
Flying Officer 'Zulu' Lewis climbing off his Hurricane after returning from a sortie

The two-pitch (coarse and fine) propeller was something like a two-speed gear box which could give full engine power and efficiency at the low end of the speed range in fine pitch, and at the top end in coarse pitch. A constant speed unit was added, rather like an infinitely variable gearbox (the motorist's dream) and controlled the pitch of the propeller to keep the engine at whatever speed the pilot selected. The result was maximum propeller efficiency over the whole speed range.

In addition to testing the new propeller, he flew 306 hours and 45 minutes on convoy patrols, formation practices and night flights before being posted to No. 87 Squadron in France and then almost immediately to No. 85 Squadron under Squadron Leader "Doggie" Oliver.

From 10th May, 1940 during the Battle for France, and for nearly two weeks, the Squadron flew around the clock. Losses were heavy with aircraft being shot up on the ground by Messerschmitt Bf 109 fighters and bombed by Heinkel He 111 bombers. Lewis's first 'kill' was on 9th May, 1940 when he shot down a Messerschmitt Bf 109E and a Heinkel He 111. On the 19th he got five confirmed kills in one day

(he was to surpass even this later), two Bf 109s on the first patrol in the morning, and three more on the evening patrol, this fight having been witnessed by his CO and the Squadron.

He returned to England on May 21st in one of only 66 Hurricanes to be returned from France.

On June 28th he flew Hurricane VY-Z to Castle Camps from Debden; this satellite airfield (originally known as Freddie I) became 85 Squadron's flying base for the early part of the Battle of Britain. It was at this time that Squadron Leader (later Group Captain) Peter Townsend was posted to the Squadron to command. He soon christened Albert Lewis "Zulu".

On 26th June "Zulu Lewis" was awarded a DFC.

From July, activity over Britain intensified and three or four sorties a day were becoming common. Lewis usually patrolled from Martlesham Heath. On 18th August, he destroyed a Bf 110 before the Squadron moved down to Croydon.

On 31st August he got another Bf 109e after being scrambled in a hurry. The combat report reveals that 9 Hurricanes took off at 19:17 hours to patrol Hawkinge. They were then ordered to intercept Raid 18c. The first indication of position of enemy aircraft was given by anti-aircraft fire from Dover and then nine Bf 109s were seen flying at about 15,000 feet. The squadron circled out to sea as enemy aircraft were on the left, and then wheeled in and caught them by surprise when individual combats ensued. It goes on: "Pilot Officer Lewis fired a four-second burst at enemy aircraft from 150 yards on the beam and from slightly below. Black smoke billowed out and enemy aircraft dived steeply. P/O Lewis followed it down to 5,000 feet making sure it was done for and rejoined Squadron. Position then above sea near Eastbourne. Nine Hurricanes landed at Croydon 20:05 hours to 20:22 hours. Enemy Casualties: 4 Bf 109s destroyed. Our losses: Nil."

On 15th September Lewis downed a Heinkel He 111 bomber and shared in the probable destruction of another. On the 18th he got his twelfth confirmed enemy aircraft.

On September 27th, he got nine ... six confirmed and three probables. His eleven kills in the two days of 19th May and 27th September 1940 set a record for pilots of single-engined British fighters. However, the next day while in combat over Maidstone, Lewis was shot down in flames after being jumped by a Heinkel He 113. He recorded it at the time as a He 113, but there were no He 113s in the Battle of Britain, although there were many combat reports for the period August-October 1940 making reference to sightings and combats with such aircraft. The mythical He 113 was in fact the He 100D, first flown in January 1938. Very few of these aircraft were built, but none were accepted by the Luftwaffe for operational use. In fact, it was a Bf 109 that had shot him down, as were all the other reputed He 113s.

Although he could not initially get clear of the aircraft he eventually managed it, and his descent was followed by Jimmy Crossey who circled the parachute to prevent any danger of his being shot at.

Lewis landed safely, but was severely burned and was taken to Faversham Cottage Hospital, blind for two weeks, and with shrapnel in his legs, and severe burns on the face, throat, hands and legs. He received his little golden caterpillar with his name engraved on the back while he was in hospital, which confirmed his membership of the select band who had their lives saved by a parachute.

After two months in hospital and convalescing, Zulu returned to the Squadron in December 1940, having been promoted to Flying Officer.

In January 1941 he became "A" Flight Commander, and was awarded a bar to the DFC. He flew local, night, enemy and routine patrols and sweeps and then in June he was posted to No. 52 OTU as an instructor commanding "C" Flight and was promoted to Flight Lieutenant. At 52 OTU (Debden) he flew Spitfires for the first and only time in his career.

Lewis continued with the RAF flying around Africa and then became involved in fighting the Japanese off Ceylon. On 9th April 1942, the day before his 24th birthday, Zulu led his Squadron to intercept a Japanese raid and as he was taking off, his aircraft was hit by fire from one of the Japanese Zeros. He was wounded in the left shoulder and his arm became useless. On fire, he bailed out at 200 feet, his parachute opening just in time. He could see his base being heavily attacked, and for six hours lay suffering from shock until he was found by natives, who revived him with coconut milk.

In June 1942, he returned to Britain via his home country of South Africa. In Britain he was made Chief Flying Instructor at Tealing in Scotland and then went to 10 Group HQ at Box in Wiltshire in 1944-45 and then to 11 Group HQ. He left the RAF on 16th February 1946, having been an Acting Squadron Leader since 22nd April 1943.

Lewis was a brave and resourceful pilot but was also a deeply religious man. He recalled many years later, "*As my mind reflects on the Battle of Britain and on the many wonderful characters who formed a part of that scene and died a quarter of a century ago in order that the world might be a better place to live in, as did those in the First World War and indeed all righteous people from the beginning of time - I wonder, have we achieved lasting peace? If we are not to disappoint ourselves and all those who have come before, we need a plan - one that is practical and embraces all mankind . . . I sincerely believe that the Gospel of Jesus Christ is the only plan which can embrace the world so that all who desire to may live in peace.*"

Flight Lieutenant 'Pete' Brothers

Pete was born in Lancashire in 1917. He took his civil pilot's licence in 1936, so was already a pilot of some experience when he joined the RAF. After gaining his wings he was posted to 32 Squadron which at that time was operating Gloster Gauntlet biplane fighters. By 1938 he was a Flight Commander, and No. 32 was equipped with the Hurricane.

Peter Brothers shot down a confirmed number of 16 enemy aircraft during World War Two and had considerably more 'probables'. He was awarded the DSO and two DFCs. His period of active service encompassed both the Battle of France and Battle of Britain. As a perfectionist and strong believer in the need for speed, he had the drag-inducing external rear-view mirror removed from his Hurricane and had his crew install a curved car mirror inside the cockpit instead. He also had the wing rivets filed right down further to eliminate potential drag, and was reknown for assisting the ground crew between sorties.

When war broke out in 1939 the squadron was based at Biggin Hill from where it flew sorties across the Channel to France. In a single week in May, Brothers shot down two enemy fighters, a Bf 109 and a Bf 110, over Cambrai and Ypres.

During the Battle of Britain, Biggin Hill was in the thick of the action and Brothers shot down eight more enemy aircraft, being posted to the relatively young 257 Squadron in September, in which he flew with Bob Stanford Tuck. On September 15th 1939, the climax of the fighting and celebrated as Battle of Britain Day, Brothers shot down two more German raiders.

Rested early in 1941, he returned to operations in March 1942 in command of 457 (Spitfire) Squadron, a Royal Australian Air Force Unit which he had formed and trained. With this and 602 Squadron, also a Spitfire unit, he had considerable success in sweeps into enemy-occupied France and took part in air operations during the ill-fated Dieppe Raid.

His final combat victory was in August 1944, in the skies over a Europe which was by then being liberated by Allied forces after the Normandy invasion.

This victory was scored over a Focke-Wulf FW 190.

His next command was of the famous Tangmere Wing which he led from October 1942 to June 1943, claiming an FW 190 off the French coast in January.

After a further "rest" from operations as CO of an operation training unit, he was back on operations again as Wing Leader of the Exeter Wing and then, during the Normandy invasion, of the Culmhead Wing with which he scored his last combat victory over Blois, on the River Loire, on August 7th 1944.

The citation for his DSO spoke of "his courage and brilliant leadership".

In retirement he formed a consultancy. He was master of the Guild of Air Pilots and Navigators, 1973-74, and was for many years chairman of the Battle of Britain Fighter Association. He died on December 18th 2008, aged 91.

Pilot Officer D Clayton Shepley

Douglas Clayton Shepley was born in July 1918, in Carlton-in-lindrick. He moved to Woodthorpe Hall, Holmesfield when he was eight years old.

He joined his father's business before following his older brother George into the RAF in 1938. He entered RAF College Cranwell as a flight cadet and received his commission in late 1939. He was posted to 152 Squadron at RAF Acklington. The squadron received their first Spitfire Mark 1s in December of that year and were operational by early 1940. 152 Squadron flew south to RAF Warmwell in Dorset with the task of protecting the naval base at Portland. Douglas was married on the 29th June 1940 at St John's Church in Sidcup, Kent to Frances, a young nurse.

During the Battle of Britain he claimed two confirmed victories, both Bf 109s, on the 8th and the 11th of August 1940. On the 12th, Douglas Shepley and F/L Latham Withall were both reported missing after a sortie off the Isle of Wight. Douglas was flying Spitfire K9999, and Latham Spitfire P9456. Both pilots were reported lost at sea.

After Douglas' death, his mother Emily and his widow Frances started raising money to buy a Spitfire for the RAF. They both worked energetically towards their target and with the help of the citizens of North Derbyshire and South Yorkshire, they organised a variety of fund raising events such as dances, concerts, jumble sales and house to house collections, also collections in public houses, theatres, and cinemas. Contributions came in from the Sheffied A.R.P who gathered donations from all their local posts. After 15 weeks of hard work, they had achieved their target of 5,700 pounds.

Spitfire W3649 was selected for the family, and the name 'SHEPLEY' was placed on the panel below the cockpit. Spitfire W3649 was a Mark Vb and was issued to 602 Squadron on the 16th August 1941, just over a year after the death of Douglas. The aircraft also served with 303 (Polish) Squadron before ending up with 485 (New Zealand) Squadron, and became the personal aircraft of Group Captain Victor Beamish, DSO, DFC; carrying the code FV-B. Beamish was reported missing in the aircraft on the 28th March 1942 over the Channel.

Group Captain Victor Beamish

Group Captain Beamish was born in 1903 in Ireland and was educated at Coleraine Academical Institute.

He was commissioned from Cranwell in 1923 and although technically retired from the RAF in 1933, returned to the service when pre-war expansion began. He was awarded the AFC in 1936, the DSO in July 1940, and the DFC in November 1940.

Beamish took over command of 151, 249 & 56 Squadrons during the Battle of Britain and personally led them on many patrols against the enemy. In June 1940 during an offensive mission over France, six Messerschmitt Bf 109s were destroyed, two of them by Wing Commander Beamish himself. He assisted in the destruction of a Messerschmitt, whilst leading the escort to a convoy, and three days later he shot down a Dornier Do 17. He was later appointed as Group Captain with 485 (RNZAF) Squadron.

Beamish demonstrated outstanding leadership and courage and inspired the young pilots placed under his command.

He was killed in action on March 28th 1942 in the 'Shepley' Spitfire.

Squadron Leader Geoffrey Wellum DFC

Geoffrey Wellum joined the RAF with a Short Service Commission in August 1939. He was posted to 92 Squadron flying Spitfires in June 1940 at the time of the evacuation of the BEF from Dunkirk. He flew throughout the Battle of Britain, later completing over 50 fighter sweeps and escorts over Northern France and Belgium before August 1941. He joined 65 Squadron as Flight Commander in March 1942 operating over northern France and flew off aircraft carrier HMS Furious as a Flight Lieutenant on Operation Pedestal, to Malta.

He returned to the UK as a test pilot for Gloster Aircraft and finished the war as a Pilot Attack Instructor.

Geoffrey was accredited with three enemy aircraft destroyed, four probables and several damaged. He was awarded the DFC in July 1941.

Wing Commander Tom Neil DFC, AFC

Tom Neil joined 249 Squadron flying Hurricanes just before the start of the Battle of Britain flying from North Weald. His first victory was on 7th September 1940, when he shot down a Bf 109, followed in quick succession by 10 others and 1 probable.

On 7th November he collided in mid-air with Wing Commander Francis Beamish and his aircraft lost its tail. He bailed out of his Hurricane unhurt, Beamish force-landing unscathed. Tom was awarded a Bar to his DFC in November 1940. He also served in Malta where he gained another victory, over a Macchi MC.200 Saetta. In September 1942 he was given command of 41 Squadron flying Spitfires before moving to the 9th USAF, 100th Fighter Wing in January 1944, flying P51 Mustangs before and after D-Day.

He is believed to be the first English pilot to land on French soil after D-Day. Tom Neil finished the war with 12 confirmed 'kills' and 4-shared victories.

Fighter Aces

Successful pilots were recognised as becoming a 'Fighter Ace'. The criteria for becoming one of these elite pilots was simply having destroyed five enemy aircraft during aerial battles.

During the First World War there were very few 'Aces' on either side. This was because the life expectancy of a pilot was very low, with unreliable aircraft, a distinct lack of speed, poor armament and defensive armour culminating to the disadvantage of even the very best pilots.

From the start of the Second World War, it was clear that with speed, superior armament and armour plating, the number of elite fighter pilots could be very high.

The very first fighter aces of World War Two were pilots who fought over Poland, the Lowland countries and France during the early months of the war. These included Polish and Czechoslovakian pilots, who became renowned for their tenacity in the air. By the time the Battle of Britain had commenced, many British and German pilots too were reaching or had already reached five kills and throughout the Battle of Britain, others joined their ranks.

The number of factors that came into play in each and every sortie was great. Each contributed to whether or not a pilot was able to score a 'kill', survive, and perhaps become an 'ace'.

In many cases, potential 'aces' were prevented from joining that elite group of pilots by factors outside their control. It could be said that 'luck', or 'fate' had its part to play in the final outcome of every engagement.

During the Battle of Britain, another factor that became significant for the crews of both opposing air forces was pilot fatigue. During the early months of the war, the shortage of trained pilots meant that the same pilots had to take their aircraft up time and time again on the same day, irrespective of their fitness to do so. The wearying effect of minor ailments was no reason to be excused of flying duty in such dire national circumstances.

During the height of the Battle of Britain, pilots may have fought up to six sorties a day. Any one of those would have stretched the pilot to the edge of his ability, and by the second or third sortie, fatigue would have become a major factor in his performance.

Another defining factor was the number of the opposition being faced. Many fine pilots were lost simply because they had to engage too many opposing aircraft. There are countless records of RAF pilots engaging incoming Luftwaffe forces who outnumbered them three or four to one.

So to sum up, factors that defined who might win an individual 'dogfight' included:

- Who has the best performing aircraft?
- Who is the most experienced pilot?
- Who has the most effective armament?
- Who has the most defensive armour to withstand the firepower of the opposition?
- Who has sufficient ammunition left after any previous encounters?
- Who has not fought already in the day, therefore bringing in the accountability of fatigue?
- Who has the necessary fuel and range to enable pushing the aircraft to its limits for as long as necessary and still be able to return safely to base?
- Who has the least opposing aircraft to contend with at the same time?

Not all pilots who died during the Battle of Britain were lost in the battle zone. Air accidents were not uncommon. As an example of this, three experienced pilots were lost in one incident when a transport plane crashed while transporting them to another airfield. Two of those pilots had already become aces. The cumulative loss of their experience was very costly to the RAF.

Verification of Claims

The number of 'kills' registered had to be verified to enable the victory to be officially counted. Initially, the evidence of aircraft that crashed and the testimony of other pilots or witnesses on the ground did this. By late 1940, cameras were starting to be fitted to aircraft to help establish whether claimed victories were legitimate. However, the cameras were in a fixed position, following the line and angle of the guns, so although it recorded the 'attack', when the aircraft pulled up, the camera images were of the sky, not of the aircraft which had been shot at.

British & Allied Top Fighter Aces

Name	Rank	Squadron(s)	Aircraft Flown	V	Awards / Medals	Notes
Johnson, James. E. ('Johnnie')	Pilot Officer	616 & 610	Spitfire	38	DSO**, DFC*, CBE, CB	
Braham, John.R.D. ('Bob')	Flying Officer	29	Hurricane / Blenheim	29	DSO*, DFC*, AFC	
Tuck, Robert. R.S.	Flight Lieutenant	92 & 257	Spitfire / Hurricane	29	DFC**,DSO, AFC	
Carey, Frank.R.	Pilot Officer	43	Hurricane	28	DFC**,AFC, DFM	
Lacey, James H. ('Ginger')	Sergeant	501	Hurricane	28	CdeG, DFM*	
Moore, Arthur.R.	Sergeant	245, 615 & 3	Hurricane	28		
Locke, Eric. S. ('Sawn-off Lockie')	Pilot Officer	41	Spitfire	26	DSO, DFC*, MiD	MIA (Killed) 1941
Drake, Billy.	Flight Lieutenant	213	Hurricane	25	DSO, DFC*	
Gilroy, George.K. ('Sheep')	Pilot Officer	603	Spitfire	25	DFC	
Allard, Geoffrey. ('Sammy')	Pilot Officer	85	Hurricane	24	DFC, DFM*	KIFA 1941
Berry, Ronald. ('Ras')	Pilot Officer	603	Spitfire	24		
Bader, Douglas. R.S.	Squadron Leader	242	Hurricane	23	DSO*, DFC*	Captured - taken POW 1941
Kingaby, Donald E.	Sergeant	266 & 92	Spitfire	23	DSO, AFC, DFM	
Stephens, Maurice.M. ('Mike')	Flying Officer	232 & 3	Hurricane	23	DFC**,DSO	
Crossley, Michael. N.	Flight Lieutenant	32	Hurricane	22	DSO, DFC	
McMullen, Desmond.Anthony.P	Flying Officer	222 & 54	Spitfire	22		
Boyd, Robert. F.	Flight Lieutenant	602	Spitfire	21		
Rabagliati, Alexander. C. ('Sandy')	Flight Lieutenant	46	Hurricane	21		KIA Post Battle of Britain
Edge, Gerald.R.	Flight Lieutenant	253 & 605	Hurricane	20	DFC	
McKellar, Archibald.A	Flight Lieutenant	605	Hurricane	20	DSO, DFC*	KIA Post Battle of Britain
Robinson, Michael.L. ('Mike')	Flight Lieutenant	601, 238 & 609	Hurricane / Spitfire	20	DSO.DFC	MIA (Killed) 1942
Shepherd, John.B.	Sergeant	234	Spitfire	20	DFC**	KIA 1946

MIA = Missing in Action   KIA = Killed in Action   POW = Prisoner of War   'V' denotes Victories

BRITISH

Aitken, Sir John
Squadron Leader

Allard, Geoffrey
Pilot Officer

Bader, Douglas
Squadron Leader

Bamberger, Cyril
Sergeant

Barclay, Richard
Flying Officer

Beamont, Roland
Flying Officer

Bennions, George
Pilot Officer

Braham, John
Flying Officer

Brothers, Peter
Flight Lieutenant

Carey, Frank
Pilot Officer

Crook, David
Pilot Officer

Crossley, Michael
Flight Lieutenant

Crowley-Milling, Denis
Pilot Officer

Currant, Christopher
Pilot Officer

Denholm, George
Squadron Leader

Doe, Robert
Pilot Officer

Donaldson, Edward
Squadron Leader

Drake, Billy
Flight Lieutenant

Fokes, Ronald
Sergeant

Hope, Sir Archibald
Flight Lieutenant

Johnson, James
Pilot Officer

Johnstone, Alexander
Squadron Leader

Kayll, Joseph
Squadron Leader

Kellett, Ronald
Squadron Leader

Kingaby, Donald
Sergeant

Lacey, James
Sergeant

Lock, Eric
Pilot Officer

Mason, Ernest
Squadron Leader

McKellar, Archibald
Flight Lieutenant

Melville-Jackson, George
Pilot Officer

O'Meara, James
Pilot Officer

Page, Alan
Pilot Officer

Rhodes-Moorhouse, William
Flying Officer

Stephens, Maurice
Flying Officer

Thompson, John
Squadron Leader

Tuck, Robert
Flight Lieutenant

Unwin, George
Flight Sergeant

Wright, Allan
Flight Lieutenant

Irish

Finucane, Brendan
Flying Officer

Harkness, H
Squadron Leader

New Zealand

Carbury, Brian
Pilot Officer

Deere, Alan
Flight Lieutenant

Gray, Colin
Flying Officer

Mackie, Evan
Sergeant

South African

Malan, Adolphus
Flight Lieutenant

Stapleton, Gerald
Pilot Officer

Czechoslovakian

Fejfar, Stanislav
Flying Officer

Furst, Bohumil
Sergeant

Frantisek, Josef
Sergeant

Kuttelwascher, Karel
Sergeant

Kucera, Jiri
Sergeant

Mansfeld, Miloslav
Sergeant

Stehlik, Josef
Sergeant

Vasatko, Alois
Pilot Officer

Polish

Pisarek, Marian
Flying Officer

Skalski, Stanislaw
Pilot Officer

Zumbach, Jan
Pilot Officer

Belgian

Le Roy du Vivier, Daniel
Pilot Officer

Philipart, Jacques
Pilot Officer

Offenburg, Jean
Pilot Officer

Ortmanns, Victor
Pilot Officer

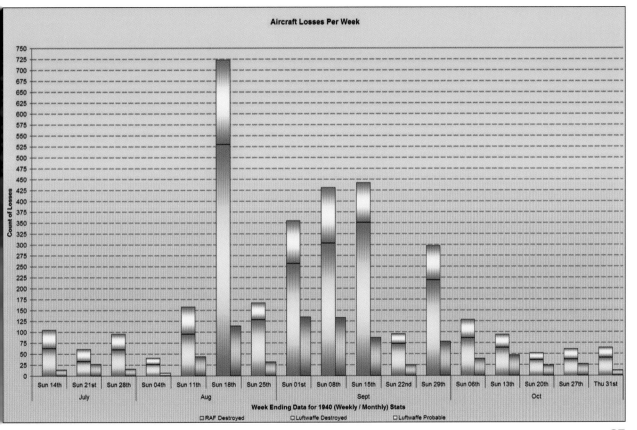

Aircraft Losses Per Week

RAF Order of Battle:
3rd November 1940

11 GROUP

Sector Station	Sqd	Airfield	Aircraft
Biggin Hill	92	Biggin Hill	Spitfire
	74	Biggin Hill	Spitfire
	141	Gravesend	Defiant
	66	West Malling	Spitfire
	421	West Malling	Hurricane
North Weald	249	North Weald	Hurricane
	46	Stapleford	Hurricane
	17	Martlesham	Hurricane
	257	North Weald	Hurricane
Kenley	501	Kenley	Hurricane
	253	Kenley	Hurricane
	605	Croydon	Hurricane
	219	Redhill	Blenheim
Hornchurch	41	Hornchurch	Spitfire
	222	Rochford	Spitfire
	603	Hornchurch	Spitfire
	264	Hornchurch	Defiant
Tangmere	145	Tangmere	Hurricane
	23	Ford	Blenheim
	213	Tangmere	Hurricane
	602	Westhampnett	Spitfire
	422	Tangmere	Hurricane
Debden	25	Debden	Blenheim
	73	Castle Camps	Hurricane
Northolt	302	Northolt	Hurricane
	615	Northolt	Hurricane
	229	Northolt	Hurricane

10 GROUP

Sector Station	Sqd	Airfield	Aircraft
Pembrey	79	Pembrey	Hurricane
Filton	601	Exeter	Hurricane
	504	Filton	Hurricane
	87	Exeter	Hurricane
Middle Wallop	152	Warmwell	Spitfire
	56	Boscombe Down	Hurricane
	604	Middle Wallop	Blenheim
	609	Middle Wallop	Spitfire
	238	Middle Wallop	Hurricane

Sector Station	Sqd	Airfield	Aircraft

10 GROUP (cont)

Sector Station	Sqd	Airfield	Aircraft
St Eval	234	St Eval	Spitfire
	247	Robourgh	Gladiator

12 GROUP

Sector Station	Sqd	Airfield	Aircraft
Duxford	19	Duxford	Spitfire
	310	Duxford	Hurricane
	19	Duxford	Spitfire
Coltishall	72	Coltishall	Spitfire
	64	Coltishall	Spitfire
Kirton in Lindsey	85	Kirton	Hurricane
	616	Kirton	Spitfire
Digby	151	Digby	Hurricane
Wittering	1	Wittering	Hurricane
	266	Wittering	Spitfire
	29	Wittering	Blenheim
Church Fenton	303	Leconfield	Hurricane

13 GROUP

Sector Station	Sqd	Airfield	Aircraft
Catterick	54	Catterick	Spitfire
	600	Catterick	Blenheim
Usworth	43	Usworth	Hurricane
	32	Acklington	Hurricane
	610	Acklington	Spitfire
Turnhouse	1	Prestwick	Hurricane
	65	Turnhouse	Spitfire
	607	Turnhouse	Hurricane
	263	Drem	Hurricane
	232	Drem	Hurricane

9 GROUP

Sector Station	Sqd	Airfield	Aircraft
Speke	312	Speke	Hurricane
Ternhill	611	Ternhill	Spitfire
	29	Ternhill	Blenheim

14 GROUP

Sector Station	Sqd	Airfield	Aircraft
Wick	3	Castletown	Hurricane

Ground Crew re-arm a Hurricane between sorties

NOTES ON THE STATISTICS

The 2,927 pilots and aircrew who fought in the Battle of Britain were awarded the Battle of Britain Clasp.

An additional estimate of 500 pilots were wounded during the conflict.

In addition to the 510 recorded as killed in action, others received injuries they would later die from.

To enable pilots to be able to join the RAF, some were not truthful about their nationalities. Some American pilots became 'Canadian' to get around their country's neutrality and to enable them to enlist without renouncing their citizenship.

The Battle of Britain Clasp, awarded to aircrew who were assigned to an operational unit between July 10th and October 31st 1940

Pilot Casualties During the Battle of Britain

KEY:

Pilot's Name & Rank
Date and Location of Action
Aircraft & Squadron details
Details of action (where known)

Single Seat Fighter Pilots

P/O H.C. Adams British, Killed,
6 Sep, Ashford
Hurricane, 501 Sqn Gravesend
Aircraft shot down during combat and crashed at Eltham

P/O R.A.C. Aeberhardt British, Killed,
31 Aug, Fowlmere
Spitfire, 19 Sqn Duxford
Aircraft crashed and burnt out on landing due to damage to flaps during combat

P/O H.J. Akroyd British, Died of injuries,
7 Oct, Lyme Regis
Spitfire, 152 Sqn Warmwell
Shot down on 7th October, died of injuries on 8th October

F/O J.H.L. Allen New Zealander, Missing believed drowned, 12 Jul, Off Burnham
Hurricane, 151 Sqn North Weald
Aircraft lost at sea after being hit in the engine by gunfire from a raiding Dornier 17 off Orfordness. Aircraft crashed into sea.

Pilot's body never found

F/O J.L.Allen British, Killed,
24 Jul, Margate
Spitfire, 54 Sqn Rochford
Aircraft engine damaged in combat with Bf 109, and losing height crashed into town

Sgt H.H. Allgood British, Killed,
10 Oct, Maidstone
Hurricane, 254 Sqn Kenley
Crashed into houses at Albion Place, Maidstone, cause unknown

Sgt L.C. Allton British, Killed,
19 Oct, Smarden
Spitfire, 92 Sqn Biggin Hill
Crashed on Tuesnoad Farm, Smarden. Cause unknown

P/O R. Ambrose British, Killed,
4 Sep, RAF Digby
Hurricane, 151 Sqn Digby
Aircraft crashed into a crane during take off (ferry flight)

P/O C.J.D. Andreae British, Listed as missing, 15 Aug, Dungeness
Spitfire, 64 Sqn Kenley
Aircraft last reported as seen in combat with Bf 109s over the Channel

Sgt S. Andrews British, Killed,
11 Sep, Stapleford
Hurricane, 46 Sqn Stapleford
Aircraft crashed and burnt out for reasons unknown after an uneventful patrol

Sgt. T. Andruszkow Polish, Killed,
27 Sep, Horsham
Hurricane, 303 Sqn Northolt
Shot down by H. Kopperschager from I Gruppe of JG 53

P/O D.G.Ashton British, Killed,
12 Aug, South of Portsmouth
Spitfire, 266 Sqn Tangmere
Aircraft burst into flames from gunfire from enemy aircraft

P/O H.D. Atkinson British, Listed as missing, 25 Aug, Hampshire
Hurricane, 213 Sqn Exeter
Aircraft last seen in combat over Warmwell. Failed to return to base

P/O R. Atkinson British, Killed,
17 Oct, Egerton
Hurricane, 213 Sqn Tangmere
Shot down in combat with Bf 109s, crashed at Weeks Farm, Egerton near Pluckley

Sgt D.H. Ayers British, Listed as missing, 23 Oct, Over Channel,
Spitfire, 74 Sqn Coltishall
Pilot chased a Bf 109 to the French coast but was shot down and crashed into sea

Sgt C.A.H. Ayling British, Killed,
11 Oct, Hawkinge
Spitfire, 421 Flight Gravesend
Crashed near Newchurch during combat with enemy aircraft over Hawkinge

P/O C.H. Bacon British, Killed,
30 Oct, Alnmouth Beach
Spitfire, 610 Sqn Acklington
Crashed on beach due to flying accident

S/L J.V.C. Badger British, Died of injuries, 30 Aug, Woodchurch
Hurricane, 43 Sqn Tangmere
Aircraft shot down by Bf 109 over Romney Marshes. Pilot died of wounds sustained 30th June 1941

P/O J.C.L.D. Bailey British, Killed,
2 Sep, Thames Estuary
Hurricane, 46 Sqn Stapleford
Aircraft was shot down while engaged in combat with enemy. Pilot did not bail out

Sgt E.D. Baker British, Listed as missing,
8 Aug, South of Isle of Wight
Hurricane, 145 Sqn Westhampnett
Last seen in combat with Ju 87s and Bf 110s, over the Channel. Aircraft failed to return to base

Sgt R.D. Baker British, Killed,
11 Aug, East Coast
Hurricane, 56 Sqn North Weald
Aircraft mistakenly shot down by unknown Spitfire while on convoy patrol. Crashed into sea.

Sgt. E.S. Bann British, Killed,
28 Sep, Fareham
Hurricane, 238 Sqn Middle Wallop
Bailed out after a dogfight but parachute failed to open.

Sgt J.K. Barker British, Killed,
4 Sep, South of Bognor
Spitfire, 151 Sqn Warmwell
Possibly shot down by Dornier Do 17 over Channel. Pilot's body washed up on French coast

F/L P.H. Barran British, Killed,
11 Jul, Off Portland
Spitfire, 609 Sqn Warmwell
Aircraft lost at sea after being shot down by Bf 109 over convoy in Channel off Portland. Pilot bailed out and was rescued but died of wounds on rescue boat

F/O N.J.M. Barry South African, Killed,

7 Oct, Wrotham
Hurricane, 501 Sqn Kenley
Shot down over Wrotham in Kent

Sgt S. Baxter British, Killed,
14 Sep, Rochford
Spitfire, 222 Sqn Hornchurch
Aircraft badly damaged by gunfire from Bf 109s. Pilot crashed attempting to land

Sgt E.A. Bayley British, Killed,
10 Oct, Cooling Marsh
Hurricane, 249 Sqn North Weald
Crashed during routine patrol, believed due to oxygen failure

P/O W. Beaumont British, Listed as missing, 23 Sep, Over Channel
Spitfire, 152 Sqn Warmwell
Aircraft and pilot listed as missing in action over the Channel

P/O J.J.I. Beedham British, Killed,
7 Oct, Aldergrove
Hurricane, 245 Sqn Aldergrove
Killed in flying accident

P/O W.G. Beley Canadian, Killed,
12 Aug, Off Ramsgate
Hurricane, 151 Sqn North Weald
Aircraft shot down by Bf 109. Crashed into sea and rescued. Pilot taken to Manston but died of wounds

F/O J.S. Bell British, Killed,
30 Aug, West Malling
Spitfire, 616 Sqn Kenley
Aircraft shot down during attack on Bf 109. Crashed and burnt out

P/O N.J.V. Benson British, Killed,
28 Aug, Tenterden
Spitfire, 603 Sqn Hornchurch

Shot down by Bf 109 and crashed in flames

P/O J. Benzie Canadian, Killed,
7 Sep, Thames Estuary
Hurricane, 242 Sqn Coltishall
Killed while on patrol

Fl/L H.R.A. Beresford British, Killed,
7 Sep, Thames Estuary
Hurricane, 257 Sqn Debden
Aircraft crashed on Isle of Sheppey. Pilot's body buried with aircraft

F/Sgt F.G. Berry British, Killed,
1 Sep, Ruckinge
Hurricane, 1 Sqn Northolt
Aircraft shot down by Bf 109s during combat over Kent

P/O J.L.Bickerdyke New Zealander, Killed, 22 Jul, Castle Camps
Hurricane, 85 Sqn Martlesham Heath (Aircraft destroyed) Aircraft crashed on approach to Castle Camps airfield

Sgt R.R.G. Birch New Zealander, Killed,
13 Jul, Balsham
Spitfire, N/A
Aircraft destroyed. Stalled while attempting steep turn during dogfight practice

Sgt H.E. Black British, Died of injuries,
29 Oct, Ashford
Hurricane, 32 Sqn Biggin Hill
Shot down in combat with Bf 109s. Believed crashed in Hothfield Park near Ashford. Died of injuries 9th November

Sub-Lt A.G. Blake British, Killed,
29 Oct, South London
Spitfire, 19 Sqn Duxford
Believed picked off by Bf 109 whilst acting

as weaver during squadron patrol. Crashed and burned at 216 London Rd, Chelmsford

P/O J.W. Bland British, Killed,
18 Aug, Canterbury
Hurricane, 501 Sqn Gravesend
Aircaft shot down by Gerhard Schopfel of III Gruppe (JG 26) in a Bf 109

Sgt H.A. Bolton British, Killed,
31 Aug, Kenley
Hurricane, 79 Sqn Biggin Hill
Aircraft crashed making for a forced landing with battle damage after combat

P/O C.R. Bon Seigneur Canadian, Killed,
3 Sep, Ingatestone
Hurricane, 257 Sqn Debden
Aircraft shot down. Pilot bailed out but found dead soon after landing

Sgt G.B. Booth British, Died of injuries,
1 Sep, Tunbridge Wells
Hurricane, 85 Sqn Croydon
Pilot bailed out of burning aircraft but burnt parachute failed to fully open. Died of injuries 7th February 1941

F/O J. Borowski Polish, Killed,
18 Oct, Kempton Park Race Course
Hurricane, 302 Sqn Northolt
Crashed returning from routine patrol in deteriorating weather conditions

F/O J.E. Boulton British, Killed,
9 Sep, Croydon
Hurricane, 310 Sqn Duxford
Aircraft collided with Hurricane of 310 Sqn during attack on enemy

F/Lt C.E. Bowen British, Killed,
1 Oct, Isle of Wight
Hurricane, 607 Sqn Tangmere

Shot down during combat with Bf 110s

P/O N.G. Bowen British, Killed,
16 Aug, Adisham
Spitfire, 266 Sqn Hornchurch
Aircraft shot down and aircraft burst into flames during combat with Bf 109

F/O J.G. Boyle Canadian, Killed,
28 Sep, Charing
Spitfire, 41 Sqn Hornchurch
Shot down over Charing, Kent

F/O G.R. Branch British, Listed as missing,
11 Aug, Swanage
Hurricane, 145 Sqn Westhampnett
Believed to be shot down by Bf 109s off the coast. Crashed into sea

Sgt J.S. Brennan New Zealander, Killed,
21 Aug, N/A
Blenheim, 23 Sqn Collyweston

Sgt J.J. Brimble British, Killed,
14 Sep, Tonbridge
Hurricane, 73 Sqn Debden
Aircraft shot down by enemy aircraft and crashed at Parkhurst Farm, Chart Sutton

P/O H.W.A Britton British, Killed,
6 Aug, Debden
Hurricane, 17 Sqn Debden
Crashed after taking off from Debden and burnt out

P/O J.W. Broadhurst British, Killed,
7 Oct, Salehurst
Spitfire, 222 Sqn Hornchurch
Killed when bailed out after attacking a bomber

P/O D.O.M. Browne British, Listed as missing, 16 Aug, Harwich
Hurricane, 1 Sqn Northolt

Aircraft last seen in combat with enemy fighters over North Sea

F/Lt D.C. Bruce British, Listed as missing,
4 Sep, 5 miles east of Folkestone
Hurricane, 111 Sqn Croydon
Crashed into the Channel after combat with Bf 109

Sgt N. Brumby British, Killed,
1 Oct, Isle of Wight
Hurricane, 607 Sqn Tangmere
Shot down during combat with Bf 110s

P/O J.S. Bryson Canadian, Killed,
24 Sep, North of Epping Forest
Spitfire, 92 Sqn Biggin Hill
Aircraft shot down by Bf 109s over Essex and crashed in flames near North Weald

Sgt M. Brzozowski Polish, Listed as missing, 15 Sep, Thames Estuary
Hurricane, 303 Sqn Northolt
Missing following action with Bf 109s over Thames Estuary

P/O J.R. Buchanan British, Listed as missing, 27 Jul, Weymouth
Spitfire, 609 Sqn Warmwell.
Aircraft shot down over Weymouth

P/O M.S.H.C. Buchin Belgian, Listed as missing, 15 Aug, Portland
Hurricane, 213 Sqn Exeter
Aircraft failed to return to base after combat over the Channel

Sgt J.A.Buck British, Drowned,
19 Jul, Off Selsey Bill
Hurricane, 43 Sqn Tangmere
Aircraft hit by gunfire from Bf 109. Pilot bailed out over Channel but drowned

P/O F.W. Buckland British, Killed, 8 Oct,

Gillingham
Spitfire, 74 Sqn Coltishall
Killed when collided with P/O D. Hastings during practice. Disintegrated upon impact at a Norfolk farmyard

Sub/Lt G.G.R. Bulmer British, Listed as missing, 20 Jul, Off Dover
Hurricane, 32 Sqn Biggin Hill
(Aircraft lost at sea) Aircraft hit by gunfire from Bf 109 and crashed into the Channel

P/O E. Burgoyne British, Killed,
27 Sep, Canterbury
Spitfire, 19 Sqn Duxford
Shot down by a Bf 109

F/O P.R.F Burton South African, Killed,
27 Sep, Redhill
Hurricane, 249 Sqn North Weald
Killed due to collision with a Bf 110 over Redhill area

P/O J. Bury-Burzymski Polish, Killed,
24 Oct, Practice
Hurricane, 303 Sqn Leconfield
Crashed during dogfight practice

Sgt S.I Butterfield British, Killed,
11 Aug, Off Portland
Hurricane, 213 Sqn Exeter
Aircraft shot down over Channel. Crashed into sea

P/O F.W. Cale Australian, Killed,
15 Aug, Teston (Kent)
Spitfire, 266 Sqn Hornchurch
Pilot bailed out over the River Medway but was dead when found in the river

F/Lt W.P. Cambridge British, Killed,
6 Sep, Kingsnorth (Kent)
Hurricane, 253 Sqn Kenley

Circumstances unknown. Pilot bailed out of aircraft but dead when found

P/O K.C. Campbell British, Killed,
29 Jul, Dover Area
Hurricane, 43 Sqn Northolt
Aircraft crashed and burnt out

P/O N.N. Campbell Canadian, Killed,
17 Oct, Yarmouth
Hurricane, 242 Sqn Coltishall
Presumed damaged by returned fire from Do 17 and crashed in sea

P/O P.M. Cardell British, Killed,
27 Sep, Over Channel
Spitfire, 603 Sqn Hornchurch
Bailed out of Spitfre after combat but parachute failed to deploy

Sub/Lt J.C. Carpenter British, Killed,
8 Sep, Isle of Sheppy
Hurricane, 46 Sqn Stapleford
Aircraft shot down. Pilot bailed out but killed. Aircraft crashed at Maidstone

P/O P.E.G. Carter British, Killed,
18 Oct, Kempton Park Race Course
Hurricane, 302 Sqn Northolt
Crashed returning from routine patrol in deteriorating weather conditions

P/O H.R. Case British, Killed,
12 Oct, Capel-le-Ferne
Spitfire, 72 Sqn Croydon
Lost formation and crashed at Capel-le-Ferne, near Folkestone, cause unknown

P/O F.N. Cawse British, Killed,
11 Aug, Weymouth
Hurricane, 238 Sqn Middle Wallop
Aircraft shot down in combat by Bf 109 off the coast, crashed into sea

F/O A. Cebrzynski Polish, Died of injuries,
11 Sep, South London
Hurricane, 303 Sqn Northolt
Aircraft shot down during combat. Pilot made a failed attempt at a crash landing and died of injuries 19th September

P/O H.H. Chalder British, Killed,
28 Sep, Charing
Spitfire, 41 Sqn Hornchurch
Shot down during combat. Pilot bailed out seriously wounded, landed at Garlinge Green. Admitted to Chartham hospital but died 10th November 1940

P/O P. Chaloner Lindsey British, Listed as missing, 26 Jul, St Catherines Point
Hurricane, 601 Sqn Tangmere
Aircraft shot down by Bf 109 over Channel and crashed into sea

P/O S.J. Chalupa Polish, Killed,
16 Oct, Ely
Hurricane, 310 Sqn Duxford
Crashed during routine training flight, cause unknown

F/Lt T.P. Chlopik Polish, killed,
15 Sep, North Weald
Hurricane, 302 Sqn Duxford
Aircraft shot down by enemy aircraft. Pilot bailed out but died on landing

P/O J.A.G. Chomley Rhodesian, Listed as missing, 12 Aug, South of Portsmouth
Hurricane, 257 Sqn Northolt
Aircraft last seen engaging Bf 109s.
Failed to return to base

Sgt J.M. Christie British, Killed,
26 Sep, Swanage
Spitfire, 152 Sqn Warmwell

Attacked and shot down by Bf 109

P/O A.W. Clarke British, Listed as missing, 11 Sep, Romney Marsh
Hurricane, 504 Sqn Hendon
Aircraft crashed and burnt out near Newchurch after combat over coast

Sgt I.C.C. Clenshaw British, Killed, 10 Jul, Unknown Location
Hurricane, 253 Sqn Kirton in Lindsey
Aircraft destroyed. Pilot lost control in bad visibility

P/O J.K.G. Clifton British, Killed, 1 Sep, Dungeness
Hurricane, 253 Sqn Kenley
Aircraft shot down in combat with Do 215 and Bf 110s. Pilot failed to bail out

P/O D.G. Cobden New Zealander, Killed, 11 Aug, East Coast
Spitfire, 74 Sqn Hornchurch
Aircraft believed to be shot down by Bf 110 off Harwich, crashed into sea

F/O J.H. Coghlan British, Killed, 17 Aug, N/A
Hurricane, 56 Sqn North Weald

F/O P. Collard British, Killed, 14 Aug, Dover
Hurricane, 615 Sqn Kenley
Aircraft shot down over the Channel. Body of pilot believed to have been washed ashore in France

Sgt G.R.Collett British, Killed, 22 Aug, Deal
Spitfire, 54 Sqn Hornchurch
Aircraft shot down into the sea. Body subsequently washed up on beach on Dutch coast

P/O P.W. Comely British, Listed as missing, 15 Aug, Portland
Hurricane, 87 Sqn Exeter
Aircraft shot down by Bf 110 off the coast and crashed into the sea

F/Lt S.D.P. Connors British, Killed, 18 Aug, Wallington
Hurricane, 111 Sqn Croydon
Hit by anti-aircraft fire directed at a Dornier Do 17 pilot was engaging

F/Sgt C.J. Cooney British, Killed, 29 Jul, Dover
Hurricane, 56 Sqn Nth Weald
Aircraft exploded in mid air over the Channel off Dover

P/O A.M. Cooper-Key British, Killed, 24 Jul, Derby
Hurricane, 46 Sqn Stapleford
Engine failure caused pilot to attempt to land in a park at Normanton, but children playing caused him to divert and he crashed into a nearby railway embankment.

P/O J.H.H. Copeman British, Killed, 11 Aug, Margate
Hurricane, 111 Sqn Croydon
Aircraft shot down in combat over the Thames Estuary, crashed into sea

P/O G.H. Corbett Canadian, Killed, 8 Oct, Chatham
Spitfire, 66 Sqn Gravesend
Shot down by Bf 109

F/O W.H. Coverley British, Died of injuries, 7 Sep, Biggin Hill
Spitfire, 602 Sqn Westhampnett
Aircraft shot down and crashed in flames. Pilot bailed out with severe burns, dying as a result

Sgt J.R.Cowsill British, Listed as missing, 13 Jul, Calais
Hurricane, 56 Sqn North Weald
Aircraft last seen in combat with Bf 109. Pilot believed to have ditched in the Channel. Pilot's body not recovered

F/O P.AN. Cox British, Killed, 27 Jul, Dover
Hurricane, 501 Sqn Gravesend

P/O K.H. Cox British, Killed, 28 Aug, Dover
Spitfire, 610 Sqn Biggin Hill
Aircraft shot down by Bf 109 and crashed into a house in a village outside Dover

F/O P.G. Crofts British, Killed, 28 Sep, Over Sussex
Hurricane, 605 Sqn Croydon
Shot down by Bf 109. Bailed out but parachute failed to open

P/O J.D. Crossman Australian, Killed, 30 Sep, Forest Row
Hurricane, 46 Sqn Stapleford
Shot down at Forest Row, Sussex

P/O J. Cruttenden British, Listed as missing, 8 Aug, South of Isle of Wight
Hurricane, 43 Sqn Tangmere
Aircraft hit by enemy gunfire and crashed into the sea

Sgt J.H. Culverwell British, Killed, 25 Jul, Hullavington
Hurricane, 87 Sqn Exeter
Killed whilst on night flying practice

F/Lt J.L.G. Cunningham British, Listed as missing, 28 Aug, Dover
Spitfire, 603 Sqn Hornchurch
Aircraft failed to return to base. Possibly shot down into sea

P/O J.W. Cutts British, Killed,
4 Sep, Maidstone
Spitfire, 222 Sqn Hornchurch
Aircraft shot down by Bf 109. & crashed at Sutton Farm

F/O B.W.J D'Arcy-Irvine British, Listed as missing, 8 Aug, St Catherines Point
Hurricane, 257 Sqn Northolt
Last seen in combat with Bf 109s over Channel. Aircraft failed to return to base. Presumed crashed into Channel

P/O J.A.J. Davey British, Killed,
11 Aug, Sandown
Hurricane, 1 Sqn Northolt
Aircraft hit by gunfire during combat with Bf 110. Attempted forced landing but aircraft burnt out

P/O A.E. Davies British, Killed,
30 Oct, Crowhurst
Spitfire, 222 Sqn Hornchurch
Wing shot off during combat with Bf 109s. Crash and burned on Upper Wilting Farm, Crowhurst

F/O P.J.Davies-Cooke British, Killed,
27 Sep, Sevenoaks
Spitfire, 72 Sqn Croydon
Shot down by Bf 109. Bailed out but was dead upon landing

F/Lt C.R. Davis American, Killed,
6 Sep, Tunbridge Wells
Hurricane, 601 Sqn Tangmere
Aircraft shot down by Bf 109 & crashed and burnt out in back garden of a cottage

P/O R.A. De Mancha British, Listed as missing, 21 Jul, South of Isle of Wight
Hurricane, 43 Sqn Tangmere

Aircraft collided with Bf 109 and crashed into the Channel

F/O R.S. Demetriadi British, Killed,
11 Aug, Portland
Hurricane, 601 Sqn Tangmere
Aircraft shot down by enemy aircraft over the Channel. Pilot's body recovered and buried at Cayeux-sur-Mer, (France)

W/C J.S. Dewar British, Killed,
12 Sep, Over Channel
Hurricane, 213 Sqn Tangmere
Circumstances unknown. Pilot's body washed ashore at Kingston Gorse (Sussex) on September 30th

P/O R.B. Dewey British, Killed,
27 Oct, Maidstone
Spitfire, 603 Sqn Hornchurch
Shot down in surprise attack by Bf 109s, crashed into tree at Apple Tree Corner, Chartham Hatch

P/O W.G. Dickie British, Listed as missing,
11 Aug, Portland
Hurricane, 601 Sqn Tangmere
Aircraft failed to return to base after combat over the Channel

Sgt. J.H. Dickinson British, Killed,
30 Aug, Dungeness
Hurricane, 253 Sqn Kenley
Aircraft shot down by Bf 109. Pilot bailed out but was dead on landing

F/O I.B. Difford South African, Killed,
7 Oct, Collision
Hurricane, 607 Sqn Tangmere
Killed in mid-air collision with another Hurricane flown by I.M.W. Scott

Sgt F.J.P Dixon British, Killed,

11 Jul, Off Portland
Hurricane, 501 Sqn Middle Wallop
Aircraft lost at sea after being hit by gunfire from Bf 109 of 11 /JG27 ten miles off Portland. Pilot bailed out but body not found

P/O M.D. Doulton British, Listed as missing, 31 Aug, Thames Estuary
Hurricane, 601 Sqn Debden
Aircraft shot down by Bf 109 and crashed into sea

P/O G.L.J. Doutrepont Belgian, Killed,
15 Sep, Sevenoaks
Hurricane, 229 Sqn Northolt
Aircraft crashed onto Staplehurst Railway Station after being shot down by Bf 109s

P/O A.R.Downer British, Died of injuries,
20 Jul, Grangemouth
Hurricane, 263 Sqn Grangemouth
Aircraft crashed while making a forced landing at airfield. Died of Injuries 21st July

P/O G.J. Drake South African, Killed,
9 Sep, Goudhurst
Hurricane, 607 Sqn Tangmere
Engaged in combat with enemy aircraft and shot down over Mayfield

F/O J.F. Drummond British, Killed,
10 Oct, Tangmere
Spitfire, 92 Sqn Biggin Hill
Mid-air collision with P/O D.G. Williams. Crashed and burned when bailed out too low

Sgt S. Duszynski Polish, Listed as missing, 11 Sep, Romney Marshes
Hurricane, 238 Sqn Middle Wallop
Aircraft seen pursuing Junkers Ju 88 over

Romney. Aircraft found crashed at Lydd

Sgt L.A.Dyke British, Listed as missing,
27 Sep, Patrol
Spitfire, 64 Sqn Kenley
Failed to return from routine section patrol.
Cause unknown

Sgt. W.L. Dymond British, Listed as
missing, 2 Sep, Thames Estuary
Hurricane, 111 Sqn Debden
Aircraft shot down while in combat. Pilot's
body never recovered

P/O H.P.M. Edridge British, Killed,
30 Oct, Ewhurst
Spitfire, 222 Sqn Hornchurch
Severely damaged in combat with Bf 109s,
crashed in flames attempting to land at
Longwood Farm, Ewhurst. Died from
injuries after being pulled from wreckage

F/O R.L. Edwards Canadian, Killed,
26 Aug, Essex
Hurricane, 1 RCAF Sqn Northolt
Aircraft shot down by gunfire from Do 17
during attack on Debden Airfield

P/O H.D. Edwards Canadian, Killed,
11 Sep, Smeeth (Kent)
Spitfire, 92 Sqn Biggin Hill
Aircraft shot down by Bf 109 during
combat and crashed into woodland

Sgt G.H. Edworthy British, Listed as
missing, 3 Sep, River Crouch
Hurricane, 46 Sqn Stapleford
Aircraft believed to have crashed into River
Crouch following combat over the Essex
coast

Sgt E.J. Egan British, Killed,
17 Sep, Ashford

Hurricane, 501 Sqn Kenley
Aircraft shot down during surprise attack
by Bf 109. Aircraft burst into flames. Pilot
did not bail out

Sgt D.W. Elcome British, Listed as
missing, 26 Oct, Patrol
Spitfire, 602 Sqn Westhampnett
Failed to return from routine squadron
patrol

Sgt F.W. Eley British, Killed,
31 Jul, Folkestone
Spitfire, 74 Sqn Hornchurch.
Aircraft shot down off Folkestone

Sgt. J.H.M. Ellis British, Listed as missing,
1 Sep, Kenley
Hurricane, 85 Sqn Croydon
Aircraft reported in combat action with Bf
109s. Failed to return to base

P/O C.E. English British, Killed,
18 Jul, Westerham
Hurricane, 605 Sqn Croydon
Shot down by Bf 109. Bailed out but
parachute caught on tail plane

Sgt P.R. Eyles British, Listed as missing,
20 Sep, Dungeness
Spitfire, 92 Sqn Biggin Hill
Aircraft crashed into the Channel after
being shot down by Major Moelders in a Bf
109

Sgt J.R. Farrow British, Killed,
8 Oct, Bovingdon
Hurricane, 229 Sqn Northolt
Lost formation in cloud and fell out of
control, disintegrating at 200 feet

Sgt A.N. Feary British, Killed,
7 Oct, Yeovil
Spitfire, 609 Sqn Warmwell

Shot down in surprise attack over Yeovil.
Unable to regain control and bailed out too
low

P/O E. Fechtner Czech, Killed,
29 Oct, Near Base
Hurricane, 310 Sqn Duxford
Mid-air collision whilst getting into
formation during wing patrol

Sgt S.A. Fenemore British, Killed,
15 Oct, Redhill
Hurricane, 501 Sqn Kenley
Following action with Bf 109s crashed at
Postern Gate Farm, Godstone

F/Lt H.M. Ferriss British, Killed,
16 Aug, Marden
Hurricane, 111 Sqn Croydon
Aircraft collided with Do 17 during a head-
on attack on enemy formation

P/O A. Finnie British, Killed,
25 Jul, Dover
Spitfire, 54 Sqn Rochford
Aircraft hit by gunfire from Bf 109 and
crashed at Kingsdown (Dover)

F/O B.M. Fisher British, Killed,
15 Aug, Selsey Bill
Hurricane, 111 Sqn Croydon
Aircraft shot down by Ju 88 and exploded.
Pilot bailed out of burning plane but did not
survive

P/O W.M.L Fiske American, Killed,
16 Aug, Bognor Regis
Hurricane, 601 Sqn Tangmere
Aircraft damaged by gunfire from Ju 87 and
crashed on landing. Pilot died of injuries
next day

P/O R.D.S .Fleming British, Killed,
7 Sep, Maidstone

Hurricane, 249 Sqn North Weald
Aircraft shot down by Bf 109s during combat

P/O G.M. Forrester British, Killed,
9 Sep, Farnborough
Hurricane, 605 Sqn Croydon
Aircraft caught in enemy crossfire and collided with He 111 losing part of wing

P/O C.D. Francis British, Killed,
30 Aug, West of Maidstone
Hurricane, 253 Sqn Kenley
Aircraft shot down during combat with Bf 109

Sgt J. Frantisek Czech, Killed,
8 Oct, Ewell
Hurricane, 303 Sqn Northolt
Crashed during routine patrol, cause unknown

Sgt R.H.B. Fraser British, Killed,
22 Oct, Folkestone
Hurricane, 257 Sqn North Weald
Shot down in combat with Bf 109s.
Crashed and burned at Moat Farm, Shadoxhurst

Sgt E.T.G. Frith British, Killed,
9 Oct, Smeeth, Ashford
Spitfire, 92 Sqn Biggin Hill
Believed shot down by Bf 109s. Bailed out badly burned but died in hospital 17th October

F/O D.R. Gamblen British, Listed as missing, 29 Jul, Dover
Spitfire, 41 Sqn Manston
Aircraft failed to return after action near Dover

Sgt L.A. Garvey British, Killed,

30 Oct, Ashford
Spitfire, 41 Sqn Hornchurch
Shot down in combat with Bf 109s.
Believed crashed on Church Farm, Stanford

P/O G.N. Gaunt British, Killed,
15 Sep, London
Spitfire, 609 Sqn Warmwell
Aircraft crashed in flames near Kenley after being hit by gunfire from Bf 110

F/O J. Gillan British, Listed as missing,
11 Aug, Portland
Hurricane, 601 Sqn Tangmere
Failed to return to base. Aircraft believed shot down over Channel during combat

F/Lt K.M. Gillies British, Killed,
4 Oct, Over East Coast
Spitfire, 66 Sqn Gravesend
Failed to return from interception of He 111 off east coast. Crashed into sea, body recovered on 21st October

P/O K.R. Gillman British, Listed as missing, 25 Aug, Dover
Hurricane, 32 Sqn Biggin Hill
Aircraft failed to return to base after combat over the Channel

Sgt A.G. Girdwood British, Killed,
29 Oct, Take-off
Hurricane, 257 Sqn North Weald
Caught taking-off during low-level bombing attack on airfield by Bf 109s of LG2.
Crashed and burned

Sgt G. Gledhill British, Killed,
11 Aug, Weymouth
Hurricane, 238 Sqn Middle Wallop
Aircraft shot down over Channel during

combat with unknown enemy aircraft

Sgt W.J. Glowacki Polish, Killed,
24 Sep, Over Channel
Hurricane, 605 Sqn Croydon
Aircraft shot down during combat with Bf 109 over French coast. Pilot killed

F/O R.L. Glyde Australian, Listed as missing, 13 Aug, Selsey Bill
Hurricane, 87 Sqn Exeter
Aircraft hit by gunfire from Ju 88 and crashed into the sea

Sgt F. Gmur Polish, Killed,
30 Aug, Thames Estuary
Hurricane, 151 Sqn Stapleford
Shot down and killed, crashing at Epping Green, Essex

F/O C.W. Goldsmith South African, Killed,
28 Oct, Maidstone
Spitfire, 603 Sqn Hornchurch
Shot down in surprise attack by Bf 109s, crashed near Waltham. Died 28th October

F/O H. Goodwin British, Killed,
14 Aug, Bournemouth
Spitfire, 609 Sqn Warmwell
Aircraft shot down off coast by unknown enemy aircraft

P/O W.H.G. Gordon British, Killed,
6 Sep, Hadlow Down (Kent)
Spitfire, 234 Sqn Middle Wallop
Aircraft shot down by Bf 109 and crashed on farm at Hadlow Down

F/Lt W.E. Gore British, Listed as missing,
28 Sep, East of Selsey
Hurricane, 607 Sqn Tangmere
Shot down in action with Bf 109s. Believed crashed in sea.

P/O V. Goth Czech, Killed,
25 Oct, Tenterden
Hurricane, 501 Sqn Kenley
Mid-air collision with another 501 Squadron
aircraft during combat with Bf 109s.
Crashed in orchard at Manor Farm,
Staplehurst

P/O G.K. Gout British, Killed,
25 Jul, Porthtowan (Cornwall)
Spitfire, 234 Sqn St Eval
Aircraft crashed near to town.
Circumstances unknown

Sgt M. Gray British, Killed,
25 Sep, Eltham
Spitfire, 72 Sqn Croydon
Crashed after combat with Bf 109s into
Eltham Park Wood

Sub/Lt H.L. Greenshields British, Killed,
16 Aug, Calais (France)
Spitfire, 266 Sqn Hornchurch
Pilot pursued a Bf 109 across the Channel.
Crashed and burnt in suburb of Calais

Sgt E. Greenwood British, Listed as
missing, 21 Oct, Loch Neagh
Hurricane, 45 Sqn Turnhouse
Dived into Loch Neagh and exploded,
cause unknown

P/O F.S.Gregory British, Killed,
13 Aug, Eastway
Spitfire, 65 Sqn Hornchurch
Accident during night flying practice. Pilot
bailed out too low for reasons unknown

F/O F. Gruszka Polish, Killed,
18 Aug, Stodmarsh (Canterbury)
Spitfire, 65 Sqn Hornchurch
Shot down in unknown circumstances

P/O H.R.Gunn British, Killed,
31 Jul, Folkestone
Spitfire, 74 Sqn Hornchurch
Aircraft shot down over Channel off
Folkestone

P/O P.S. Gunning British, Killed,
15 Oct, Thames Estuary
Hurricane, 46 Sqn Stapleford
Shot down in combat with Bf 109s,
crashed and burned in chalk pit at Little
Thurrock

P/O E.M.Gunter British, Killed,
27 Sep, Sittingbourne
Hurricane, 501 Sqn Kenley
Bailed out after combat but parachute
failed to open

P/O J.V. Gurteen British, Killed,
15 Sep, South London
Hurricane, 504 Sqn Hendon
Aircraft shot down and crashed at full
throttle into residential house

Sgt L.N. Guy British, Killed,
18 Aug, Sussex Coast
Hurricane, 601 Sqn Tangmere
Aircraft took fatal fire from Bf 109 during
combat

F/Lt N.M. Hall British, Killed,
8 Aug, St Catherines Point
Hurricane, 257 Sqn Northolt
Aircraft hit by gunfire from Bf 109 and
crashed into the sea

Sgt D.W. Halton British, Listed as missing,
15 Aug, Deal
Hurricane, 615 Sqn Kenley
Aircraft crashed and burnt out. No sign of
pilot

P/O J.R. Hamar British, Killed,
24 Jul, North Weald
Hurricane, 151 Sqn North Weald
Aircraft stalled at 500ft and crashed nose
first onto airfield

F/Lt H.R. Hamilton Canadian, Killed,
29 Aug, Rye
Hurricane, 85 Sqn Croydon

Sgt B. Hancock British, Killed,
18 Aug, Gloucester
Avro Anson, No. 6 SFTS Gloucester
Crashed aircraft headlong into Heinkel
attacking airfield

F/O D.H.W. Hanson British, Killed,
3 Sep, Foulness Island
Hurricane, 17 Sqn, Debden
Aircraft shot down. Pilot bailed out at only
100 feet. Killed on impact

Sgt O. Hanzlicek Czech, Killed,
10 Oct, River Mersey
Hurricane, 312 Sqn Speke
Caught fire during routine patrol, cause
unknown. Crashed into mud of River
Mersey, bailed out into river at Oglett

F/O J.R. Hardacre British, Killed,
30 Sep, Weymouth
Hurricane, 504 Sqn Hendon
Shot down in combat off Weymouth,
Dorset

P/O F.N. Hargreaves British, Listed as
missing, 11 Sep, Dungeness
Spitfire, 92 Sqn Biggin Hill
Aircraft failed to return after combat.
Presumed crashed into the sea

P/O D.S. Harrison British, Killed,
28 Sep, Over the Solent

Hurricane, 238 Sqn Middle Wallop
Shot down in combat with Bf 109s and crashed into the sea. Body washed ashore Brighton 9th October 1940.

P/O J.H.Harrison British, Listed as missing, 12 Aug, South of Isle of Wight
Hurricane, 145 Sqn Westhampnett
Shot down over Channel during combat with Ju 88s and Bf 109s

P/O F.C. Harrold British, Killed,
28 Sep, Deal
Hurricane, 501 Sqn Kenley
Shot down by a Bf 109 near Deal in Kent

P/O D. Hastings British, Killed,
8 Oct, Gillingham
Spitfire, 74 Sqn Coltishall
Killed in a mid-air collision with P/O F.W. Buckland during practice attacks over base

Sgt R.P. Hawkings British, Killed,
18 Aug, Sussex
Hurricane, 601 Sqn Tangmere
Unknown circumstances during patrol over Sussex

Sgt F.B. Hawley British, Listed as missing, 15 Aug, Dunkirk
Spitfire, 266 Sqn Hornchurch
Aircraft believed crashed into Channel after destroying He115

F/O J.F.J. Haworth British, Listed as missing, 20 Jul, South of Isle of Wight
Hurricane, 43 Sqn Tangmere
Aircraft shot down while investigating enemy intruder. Pilot bailed out over Channel

Sgt D.A. Helcke British, Killed,
17 Sep, Faversham

Hurricane, 504 Sqn Hendon
Pilot lost control during dog fight practice and failed to bail out

P/O D.A. Hewitt Canadian, Missing believed drowned, 12 Jul, Off Portland
Hurricane, 501 Sqn Middle Wallop
Aircraft hit by gunfire while attacking Do 17 off Portland and crashed into sea. Pilot's body never found

P/O N.B. Heywood British, Killed,
22 Oct, Folkestone
Hurricane, 257 Sqn North Weald
Came under anti-aircraft fire during combat with Bf 109s. Crashed near Lydd Church

Sgt W.B. Higgins British, Killed,
14 Sep, Bredgar
Hurricane, 253 Sqn Kenley
Aircraft shot down in flames after combat with Bf 109. Pilot did not bail out

F/O T.P.K. Higgs British, Killed,
10 Jul, Folkestone
Hurricane, 111 Sqn Croydon
Aircraft destroyed after colliding with Dornier Do 17 off Folkestone. Pilot bailed out but drowned in English Channel. (Body found off Norwegian Coast 15th August)

P/O C.H. Hight New Zealander, Killed,
15 Aug, Bournemouth
Spitfire, 234 Sqn Middle Wallop
Shot down and crash landed. Pilot collapsed and died by his aircraft

P/O H.P. Hill British, Killed,
20 Sep, West Hougham
Spitfire, 92 Sqn Biggin Hill
Aircraft shot down by Major Moelders in Bf 109 and burst into flames on crashing

F/Lt H.B.L. Hillcoat British, Listed as missing, 3 Sep, Unknown
Hurricane, 1 Sqn Northolt
Failed to return from patrol

Sgt J Hlavac Czech, Killed,
10 Oct, Wareham
Hurricane, 56 Sqn Boscombe Down
Shot down in combat with Bf 109s and crashed at Manor Farm, Worgret

P/O R.M. Hogg British, Listed as missing, 25 Aug, Portland
Spitfire, 152 Sqn Warmwell
Aircraft shot down by Bf 109s over Channel and crashed into sea

Sgt R. Holder New Zealander, Killed,
26 Oct, Take-off
Hurricane, 151 Sqn Digby
Crashed attempting left turn shortly after take-off from Coleby Grange

P/O D.F. Holland British, Killed,
20 Sep, Canterbury
Spitfire, 72 Sqn Croydon
Pilot bailed out after being shot down by Bf 109s. Died of wounds shortly after admission to hospital

Sgt K.C. Holland Australian, Killed,
25 Sep, West of Bristol
Spitfire, 152 Sqn Warmwell
Shot down while attacking a He 111

F/O M.G.Homer British, Killed,
27 Sep, Sittingbourne
Hurricane, 242 Sqn Coltishall
Shot down by Bf 109

S/L H.R.L. Hood British, Listed as missing, 5 Sep, Thames Estuary
Spitfire, 41 Sqn Hornchurch (Manston)

Collided with Spitfire R6635. Aircraft disintegrated over Wickford

F/O R. Hope British, Killed,
14 Oct, South Norwood
Hurricane, 605 Sqn Croydon
Flew into the Inner Artillery Zone during routine patrol and believed collided with balloon cable, but possible victim of AA defences

Sgt V. Horsky Czech, Killed,
26 Sep, Solent
Hurricane, 238 Sqn Middle Wallop
Shot down by Bf 110 over the Solent

Sgt O.V. Houghton British, Killed,
6 Sep, Ashford
Hurricane, 501 Sqn Gravesend
Aircraft shot down during combat. Crashed at Charing

P/O P. Howes British, Killed,
18 Sep, Ashford
Spitfire, 603 Sqn Hornchurch
Aircraft shot down in combat with Bf 109s. Pilot did not bail out

F/Lt D.P. Hughes British, Listed as missing, 11 Sep, Tunbridge Wells
Hurricane, 238 Sqn Middle Wallop
Aircraft last seen intercepting Junkers Ju 88s. Failed to return to base

F/Lt P.C. Hughes Australian, Killed,
7 Sep, Bessels Green
Spitfire, 234 Sqn Middle Wallop
Believed to have crashed into wreckage of a Dornier 17 pilot had destroyed during combat

F/Lt C.B. Hull South African, Killed,
7 Sep, South London

Hurricane, 43 Sqn Tangmere
Aircraft shot down in combat with Bf 109 and crashed in grounds of Purley High School

P/O R.R. Hutley British, Killed,
29 Oct, Patrol
Hurricane, 213 Sqn Tangmere
Abandoned aircraft during squadron patrol, reason unknown

Sgt S. Ireland British, Killed,
12 Jul, Biggin Hill
Spitfire, 610 Sqn Biggin Hill
Believed that aircraft went out of control during diving practice

F/Lt M.M. Irving British, Listed as missing,
28 Sep, Selsey
Hurricane, 607 Sqn Tangmere
Shot down into the sea by a Bf 109 South East of Selsey. Reported missing

Sgt L.R. Isaac British, Listed as missing,
5 Aug, Folkestone
Spitfire, 64 Sqn Kenley
Presumed shot down by Bf 109 over Channel. Failed to return to base

P/O W. Januszewicz Polish, Killed,
5 Oct, Stowting
Hurricane, 303 Sqn Northolt
Shot down and killed by Bf 109 over Stowting, Kent

F/Lt F. Jastrzevski Polish, Killed,
25 Oct, Over Channel
Hurricane, 302 Sqn Northolt
Failed to return from patrol, last seen gliding towards enemy coast

P/O D.T. Jay British, Killed,
24 Oct, Patrol

Hurricane, 87 Sqn Exeter
Mid-air collision during routine patrol. Bailed out but believed to have hit tailplane as ripcord was not pulled

F/O M. Jebb British, Died of injuries,
15 Sep, S.E.London
Hurricane, 504 Sqn Hendon
Pilot crashed at Dartford after combat with enemy aircraft. Hospitalised but died of injuries 19th September

F/O A.J.O. Jeffery British, Killed,
25 Jul, Dover
Spitfire, 64 Sqn Kenley
Aircraft last seen crashing into the Channel. Pilot's body subsequently washed up on the Dutch coast

Sgt G.W. Jeffries British, Killed,
18 Sep, Chatham
Hurricane, 46 Sqn Stapleford
Aircraft shot down by enemy aircraft. Pilot bailed out but parachute failed to open

P/O D.N.O. Jenkins British, Killed,
30 Aug, Redhill
Hurricane, 253 Sqn Kenley
Pilot bailed out when aircraft hit by gunfire from Bf 109. Pilot machine-gunned during descent & killed

Sgt. J.I. Johnson British, Killed,
30 Aug, Bishopsbourne
Spitfire, 222 Sqn Hornchurch
Aircraft shot down by Bf 109. Crashed and burnt out

P/O J.T. Johnston Canadian, Killed,
15 Aug, Dymchurch
Hurricane, 151 Sqn North Weald
Aircraft shot down into the Channel by Bf

109. Pilot was dead when picked up by rescue boat

P/O J.S.B. Jones British, Killed,
11 Aug, South of Isle of Wight
Spitfire, 152 Sqn Warmwell
Aircraft shot down by Bf 109 in mid Channel. Pilot recovered and buried at Le Havre (France)

P/O A.R.I.G. Jottard Belgian, Listed as missing, 27 Oct, Isle of Wight
Hurricane, 145 Sqn Tangmere
Shot down by Bf 109 five miles south east of the Isle of Wight

Sgt L. Jowitt British, Missing believed drowned, 12 Jul, Off Felixstowe
Hurricane, 85 Sqn Martlesham Heath
Aircraft hit by gunfire from He 111 from 11/KG53 off Felixstowe and crashed into sea. Pilot's body not found

F/O Lord R.U.P Kay-Shuttleworth
British, Listed as missing,
8 Aug, South of Isle / Wight
Hurricane, 145 Sqn Westhampnett
Aircraft failed to return after combat over convoy CW9 in the Channel

P/O P.F. Kennard-Davis British, Died of injuries, 10 Aug, Dover
Spitfire, 64 Sqn Kenley
Aircraft hit by enemy gunfire. Pilot bailed out but sustained serious burns and died of injuries

F/Lt J.C.Kennedy Australian, Killed,
13 Jul, Southdown (Sussex)
Hurricane, 238 Sqn Middle Wallop
Aircraft crash landed on returning to base after taking gunfire from a Dornier17

Sgt M. Keymer British, Killed,
22 Aug, Dover
Spitfire, 65 Sqn Hornchurch
Aircraft shot down by Bf 109 into Channel. Body recovered and buried at Bazinghem (France)

P/O P.J.C .King British, Killed,
5 Sep, Rochester
Spitfire, 66 Sqn Kenley
Shot down by Bf 109s. Pilot bailed out but parachute failed to open

P/O M.A. King British, Killed,
16 Aug, Southampton
Hurricane, 249 Sqn Boscombe Down
Aircraft shot down by Bf 110. Pilot bailed out but parachute collapsed on descent

S/L E.B. King British, killed,
30 Aug, Strood
Hurricane, 151 Sqn Stapleford
Aircraft crashed and exploded during routine patrol. No known cause

Sgt T.B. Kirk British, Killed,
20 Oct, Coxheath
Spitfire, 72 Sqn Croydon
Shot down in combat with enemy fighters over Maidstone. Died of wounds 22nd July 1941

Sgt D.I. Kirton British, Killed,
8 Aug, Manston
Spitfire, 65 Sqn Hornchurch
Aircraft hit by gunfire from Bf 109 and crashed in flames near airfield

P/O W. Krepski Polish, Listed as missing,
7 Sep, Flamborough
Spitfire, 54 Sqn Catterick
Believed to have crashed into sea during

operational flight

Sub/Lt J.H.Kestin British, Missing,
1 Aug, Hastings
Hurricane, 145 Sqn Westhampnett
Aircraft shot down by gunfire and crashed into Channel

Sgt J Kwiecinski Polish, Listed as missing,
12 Aug, South of Isle of Wight
Hurricane, 145 Sqn Westhampnett
Aircraft failed to return to base

Sgt J. Landsdell British, Killed,
17 Sep, Beltring
Hurricane, 607 Sqn Tangmere
Aircraft shot down during combat with Bf 109. Pilot failed to bail out

P/O G.A. Langley British, Killed,
15 Sep, Thurrock
Spitfire, 41 Sqn Hornchurch
Aircraft crashed into building after being shot down by Bf 109s

P/O J.E.P. Laricheliere Canadian, Listed as missing, 16 Aug, Portland
Hurricane, 213 Sqn Exeter
Failed to return after combat over Portland

P/O A.F. Laws British, Killed,
30 Sep, Patrol
Spitfire, 64 Sqn Kenley
Collided with another Spitfire during a patrol

P/O J.G.Lecky British, Killed,
11 Oct, Maidstone
Spitfire, 41 Sqn Hornchurch
Shot down in combat with Bf 109s, crashed at Preston Hall, Maidstone, pilot bailed out but presumed parachute failed

F/O R.H.A. Lee British, Killed,

18 Aug, Over East Coast
Hurricane, 85 Sqn Martlesham
Took return fire while engaging three Bf 109s

P/O J.D. Lenahan British, Killed,
9 Sep, Mayfield
Hurricane, 607 Sqn Tangmere
Aircraft shot down by Bf 109 during attack on Dornier17. Crashed at Cranbrook

P/O P. Litchfield British, Killed,
18 Jul, Off Calais
Spitfire, 610 Sqn Biggin Hill
Aircraft shot down by Bf 109 over Channel. Pilot's body never recovered

Sgt R. Little British, Listed as missing,
28 Sep, Isle of Wight
Hurricane, 238 Sqn Middle Wallop
Shot down into sea during combat with Bf 109s.

Sgt P.D. Lloyd British, Killed,
15 Oct, Over Channel
Spitfire, 41 Sqn Hornchurch
Shot down in a surprise attack and crashed in the Channel

S/L T.G. Lovell-Gregg New Zealander, Killed, 15 Aug, Portland
Hurricane, 87 Sqn Exeter
Aircraft damaged by enemy gunfire. Crashed attempting to reach Warmwell Airfield

F/Lt R.E. Lovett British, Killed,
7 Sep, Billericay
Hurricane, 73 Sqn Debden
Aircraft shot down by enemy aircraft during combat

F/O K. Lukaszewicz Polish, Listed as

missing, 12 Aug, Off Ramsgate
Hurricane, 501 Sqn Gravesend
Aircraft shot down over the Channel after combat with Bf 109s

F/O D.C. McCaw British, Killed,
8 Aug, Off Isle of Wight
Hurricane, 238 Sqn Middle Wallop
Aircraft shot down while engaging enemy over convoy CW9, crashed into the sea

F/Lt H.K. MacDonald British, Killed,
28 Sep, Gilligham
Spitfire, 603 Sqn Hornchurch
Shot down by a Bf 109 of JG 26

P/O D.K. MacDonald British, Listed as missing, 28 Aug, Dover
Spitfire, 603 Sqn Hornchurch
Aircraft failed to return to base. Possibly shot down into sea

P/O J. Macinski Polish, Listed as missing,
4 Sep, 5 miles East of Folkestone
Hurricane, 111 Sqn Croydon
Shot down by Bf 109. Pilot bailed out but body was never found. (The above is as recorded, but aircraft excavated at West Stourmouth is believed to be Hurricane Z2309)

P/O G.H. Maffett British, Killed,
31 Aug, Clacton
Hurricane, 257 Sqn Debden
Aircraft engaged in combat and shot down by Bf 110. Crashed at Walton-on-the-Naze

Sgt A D W Main British, Killed,
16 Jul, Church Fenton
Hurricane, 249 Sqn Church Fenton
Engine cut out during take off from base airfield

P/O E.E. Males British, Killed,
27 Sep, Sevenoaks
Spitfire, 72 Sqn Croydon
Bailed out of Spitfire after having been shot down by Bf 109 but was killed

P/O K. Manger British, Listed as missing,
11 Aug, East Coast
Hurricane, 17 Sqn Debden
Aircraft crashed into sea after combat with Bf 110 off the Suffolk coast

Sgt. E. Manton British, Killed,
28 Aug, Hurst Green
Spitfire, 610 Sqn Biggin Hill
Aircraft shot down during combat with Bf 109s over Hurst Green and crashed. NB: RAF Casualty Records state that Sgt E.Manton was killed on August 28, 1940 which is incorrect 610 Operations Record Book confirms action on August 29

P/O R.A. Marchand British, killed,
15 Sep, Maidstone
Hurricane, 73 Sqn Debden
Aircraft crashed into farm at Teynham after being shot down by Bf 109s

Sgt F. Marek Czech, Killed,
14 Sep, Orsett
Spitfire, 19 Sqn Duxford
Aircraft crashed during routine patrol. Possibly due to oxygen failure

Sgt H.J. Marsh British, Listed as missing,
13 Aug, Portland
Hurricane, 238 Sqn Middle Wallop
Believed shot down by Bf 109. Failed to return to base

P/O J.R. Mather British, Killed,
27 Oct, Hildenborough
Spitfire, 66 Sqn Gravesend

Crashed and burned at Half Moon Lane, Hildenborough. Cause unknown but possibly anoxia

F/O H.K.F. Matthews British, Killed,
7 Oct, Over Kent
Spitfire, 603 Sqn Hornchurch
Shot down by Bf 109s of JG 26

Sgt L.D. May British, Listed as missing,
25 Oct, Exmouth
Hurricane, 601 Sqn Exeter
Mid-air collision with Sgt F. Mills-Smith.
Crashed in sea off Exmouth

F/O G.F. McAvity Canadian, Killed,
19 Oct, Exercise
Hurricane, 3 Sqn Castletown
Crashed while attempting slow roll during AA co-operation exercise

P/O J. McGibbon British, Killed,
29 Sep, Practice
Hurricane, 615 Sqn Prestwick
During a routine practice flight, dived into ground from 7,000ft, cause unknown

Sgt P.R.C. McIntosh British, Killed,
12 Oct, Over Channel
Hurricane, 605 Sqn Croydon
Shot down in action against Bf 109s.
Crashed by Littlestone Golf Course

P/O J.W. McKenzie British, Listed as missing, 11 Aug, Margate
Hurricane, 111 Sqn Croydon
Aircraft shot down by Bf 109 over the Thames Estuary, crashed into sea

Sgt A.L. McNay British, Listed as missing,
5 Sep, Burnham
Hurricane, 73 Sqn Debden
Shot down by enemy aircraft and crashed at North Fambridge

P/O J.R.B.Meaker British, Killed,
27 Sep, Over Sussex
Hurricane, 249 Sqn North Weald
Bailed out after attacking a Ju 88 but struck the tailplane of his Hurricane and died

Sgt C.V. Meeson British, Killed,
20 Sep, Amesbury
Hurricane, 56 Sqn Boscombe Down
Aircraft crashed during formation flying practice

P/O R.F.G.Miller British, Killed,
27 Sep, Kingcome
Spitfire, 609 Sqn Warmwell
Spitfire collided with a Bf 110 of ZG 26 near Kingcome in Dorset

P/O W.H. Millington Australian, Listed as missing, 30 Oct, Over Channel
Hurricane, 249 Sqn North Weald
Failed to return from action with enemy fighters over the Channel

Sgt F. Mills-Smith British, Listed as missing, 25 Oct, Exmouth
Hurricane, 601 Sqn Exeter
Mid-air collision with Sgt L.D. May

F/O L.R.G. Mitchell British, Listed as missing, 7 Sep, Thames Estuary
Hurricane, 257 Sqn Debden
Last seen in combat. Believed to have crashed into the sea

P/O G.T.M. Mitchell British, Killed,
11 Jul, Off Portland
Spitfire, 609 Sqn Warmwell
Aircraft lost at sea after being shot down in combat by Bf 109 over Channel off

Portland while protecting convoy. Pilot's body was washed ashore at Newport I.O.W

F/O G.E. Moberley British, Killed, 26 Aug, Dover
Spitfire, 616 Sqn Kenley
Aircraft shot down over Channel by Bf 109. Pilot did not bail out

P/O C.R. Montgomery British, Killed,
14 Aug, Dover
Hurricane, 615 Sqn Kenley
Aircraft failed to return to base. Believed shot down over Channel

Sgt H.F. Montgomery British, Killed,
14 Aug, Beachy Head
Hurricane, 43 Sqn Tangmere
Aircraft last seen in combat with He111.
Failed to return to base

P/O H.W. Moody British, Listed as missing, 7 Sep, Biggin Hill
Spitfire, 602 Sqn Westhampnett
Aircraft failed to return to base after combat operation

Sgt J.P. Morrison British, Killed,
22 Oct, Dungeness
Hurricane, 46 Sqn Stapleford
Shot down in combat with enemy fighters. Crashed near Newchurch Church

Sub/Lt W.J.M. Moss British, Listed as missing, 27 Aug, Over Channel
Hurricane, 213 Sqn Exeter
Believed lost control of his aircraft during patrol and crashed into sea

P/O M.R. Mudie British, Died of injuries,
14 Jul, Dover
Hurricane, 615 Sqn Kenley
Aircraft crashed into sea. Pilot bailed out

badly injured, and was rescued by the Navy but died the next day

P/O I.J. Muirhead British, Killed,
15 Oct, Maidstone
Hurricane, 605 Sqn Croydon
Shot down in combat with Bf 109s.
Possibly bailed out too low, crashed at Spekes Bottom, Darland near Gillingham

Sgt W.J. Neville British, Listed as missing,
11 Aug, Calais
Spitfire, 610 Sqn Biggin Hill
Aircraft shot down while on patrol over the French coast

Sgt. D. Noble British, Killed,
30 Aug, Nr Bognor
Hurricane, 43 Sqn Tangmere
Aircraft shot down by Bf 109 in combat over Sussex coast. Crashed near Brighton, East Sussex

Sgt P.P. Norris British, Killed,
13 Aug, Portland
Hurricane, 213 Sqn Exeter
Aircraft shot down off Portland and crashed into the sea. Body subsequently washed ashore in France

S/L J.S. O'Brien British, Killed,
7 Sep, St Mary Cray
Spitfire, 234 Sqn Middle Wallop
Aircraft shot down by enemy aircraft and crashed near Biggin Hill

P/O J.R.S. Oelofse South African, Killed,
8 Aug, Sth of Isle of Wight
Hurricane, 43 Sqn Tangmere
Aircraft hit by enemy gunfire and crashed into the sea

Sgt. T.G. Oldfield British, Killed,

27 Sep, Dartford
Spitfire, 92 Sqn Biggin Hill
Shot down by Bf 109

F/O D.H. O'Neill British, Killed,
11 Oct, Ash
Spitfire, 41 Sqn Hornchurch
Mid-air collision during battle climb to engage Bf 109s, crashed near Crooked Billet, Ash, pilot bailed out but parachute failed

P/O A. Ostowicz Polish, Killed
11 Aug, Swanage
Hurricane, 145 Sqn Westhampnett
(Aircraft crashed on Isle of Wight) Aircraft shot down by Bf 109s off Swanage coast. Pilot not seen to bail out

F/Lt W.Pankratz Polish, Listed as missing,
12 Aug, South of Isle of Wight
Hurricane, 145 Sqn Westhampnett
Shot down over Channel during combat with Ju 88s and Bf 109s

Sgt K.B. Parker British, Killed,
15 Oct, Thames Estuary
Spitfire, 92 Sqn Biggin Hill
Shot down in combat with Bf 109s. Reputedly crashed in sea off Hoo Marina

Sgt C.Parkinson British, Killed,
20 Jul, Off Swanage
Hurricane, 238 Sqn Middle Wallop
Pilot bailed out after being shot down by Bf 109. Rescued by ship but died of injuries 21st July

P/O S.B. Parnall British, Killed,
9 Sep, Mayfield
Hurricane, 607 Sqn Tangmere
Aircraft shot down during combat with Do 17s and Bf 109s. Crashed at Cranbrook

F/Lt D.G. Parnall British, Killed,
18 Sep, Gravesend
Hurricane, 249 Sqn North Weald
Aircraft crashed and burnt out after combat with enemy aircraft

F/O L.W. Pasziewicz Polish, Killed,
27 Sep, Kent
Hurricane, 303 Sqn Northolt
Shot down over Kent

F/O J.A. Paterson New Zealander, Killed,
27 Sep, Sevenoaks
Spitfire, 92 Sqn Biggin Hill
Shot down in combat with enemy aircraft over Sevenoaks, crashed and burned at Sparepenny Lane, Farningham

Midshipman P.J. Patterson British, Listed as missing,
20 Aug, Off Winterton (East Coast)
Hurricane, 242 Sqn Coltishall
Aircraft crashed into sea during combat

F/O A.J.S. Pattinson British, Killed,
12 Oct, Hawkinge
Spitfire, 92 Sqn Biggin Hill
Shot down by Bf 109 in combat over Hawkinge, crashed and burned out in Bartholomews Wood, Postling Wents

Sgt K.C. Pattison British, Killed,
13 Oct, Kidderminster
Spitfire, 611 Sqn Ternhill
Became lost on return from sortie, crashed at Crooksey Green, near Kidderminster, critically injured and died 13th October 1940

P/O W.B. Pattullo British, Killed,
26 Oct, Romford
Hurricane, 46 Sqn Stapleford

Crashed into house following routine patrol, cause unknown. Died in hospital the next day

Sub/Lt F.D Paul British, Died of injuries, 30 Jul, East of Folkestone
Spitfire, 64 Sqn Kenley
Shot down by Bf 109 and picked up by Germans but died of wounds 30th July

Sgt W.A. Peacock British, Listed as missing, 11 Sep, Thames Estuary
Hurricane, 46 Sqn Stapleford
Aircraft failed to return after combat. Presumed crashed into the sea

Sgt G.W. Pearson British, Killed, 6 Sep, Ashford
Hurricane, 501 Sqn Gravesend
Aircraft shot down in combat and crashed at Hothfield

Sgt I. Pearson British, Killed, 16 Oct, Gateshead
Spitfire, 65 Sqn Turnhouse
Killed following flying accident

P/O A.P. Pease British, Killed, 15 Sep, Kingswood Kent
Spitfire, 603 Sqn Hornchurch
Aircraft shot down by unknown enemy aircraft. Pilot did not bail out

F/O C.D.Peel British, Listed as missing, 17 Jul, Unknown Location
Spitfire, 603 Sqn Hornchurch
Aircraft failed to return from an operational flight

F/O G.C.B. Peters British, Killed, 29 Sep, Over Irish Sea
Hurricane, 79 Sqn Pembrey
Shot down during combat with a He 111

over the Irish Sea

P/O O.J. Peterson Canadian, Killed, 27 Sep, Hever
Hurricane, 1 RCAF Sqn Northolt
During combat with Ju 88s and Bf 110s was shot down and killed

P/O J.A.L.Phillipart Belgian, Killed, 25 Aug, Portland
Hurricane, 213 Sqn Exeter
Aircraft shot down by Bf 109 over Channel. Body washed ashore two days later

F/Sgt N.T Phillips British, Killed, 8 Aug, Manston
Spitfire, 65 Sqn Hornchurch
Shot down by Bf 109 and crashed in flames

P/O S. Piatkowski Polish, Killed, 25 Oct, Carew Cheriton
Hurricane, 79 Sqn Pembrey
Crashed after routine patrol over Linney Head, cause unknown

Sgt L. Pidd British, Killed, 15 Sep, Kenley
Hurricane, 238 Sqn Middle Wallop
Pilot bailed out after being shot down by enemy aircraft but was dead on landing

F/O O.St J. Pigg British, Killed, 1 Sep, Pluckley
Spitfire, 72 Sqn Croydon
Pilot failed to bail out after his aircraft was shot down during combat with Bf 109s

S/L P.C. Pinkham British, Killed, 5 Sep, Birling (Kent)
Spitfire, 19 Sqn Duxford
Shot down by Bf 109 while in combat over Channel. Pilot went down with aircraft

F/O R.P. Plummer British, Died of injuries, 4 Sep, Hawkwell
Hurricane, 46 Sqn Stapleford
Shot down in flames by Bf 110. Pilot bailed out with serious burns. Died of injuries 14th September

P/O F.H. Posener South African, Listed as missing, 20 Jul, Swanage
Spitfire, 152 Sqn Warmwell
Aircraft lost at sea. Aircraft crashed into Channel after being hit by gunfire from Bf 109

P/O L. L. Pyman British, Killed, 16 Aug, Off Deal
Spitfire, 65 Sqn Hornchurch
Aircraft crashed into Channel during combat

P/O J.B. Ramsay British, Killed, 18 Aug, Unknown
Hurricane, 151 Sqn North Weald
Aircraft failed to return from patrol

Sgt J.W. Ramshaw British, Killed, 4 Sep, Yalding
Spitfire, 222 Sqn Hornchurch
Crashed after combat with Bf 109s. Pilot was dead on arrival at West Kent Hospital

F/O M. Ravenhill British, Killed, 30 Sep, Igtham
Hurricane, 229 Sqn Northolt
Shot down in combat with a Bf 109 over Igtham, Kent

Sgt L.A.E. Reddington British, Killed, 30 Sep, Portland
Spitfire, 152 Sqn Warmwell
Shot down during combat

P/O H.W. Reilley Canadian, Killed,

17 Oct, Westerham
Spitfire, 66 Sqn Gravesend
Shot down in combat, crashed and burned at Crockham Hill, Sevenoaks

F/Lt R.C. Reynell Australian, Killed,
7 Sep, Blackheath
Hurricane, 43 Sqn Tangmere
Pilot bailed out after being shot down by Bf 109. Died on landing

F/Lt W.H. Rhodes-Moorehouse British,
Killed, 6 Sep, Tunbridge Wells
Hurricane, 601 Sqn Tangmere
Crashed at Southborough following combat with Bf 109s

F/O A.L. Ricalton British, Killed,
17 Oct, Maidstone
Spitfire, 74 Sqn Biggin Hill
Shot down in combat with Bf 109s over Maidstone, crashed near Hollingbourne

Sgt. M. Ridley British, Killed,
26 Aug, Dover
Spitfire, 616 Sqn Kenley
Aircraft hit by gunfire from Bf 109 over Kent coast. Crashed near town

F/Lt R.F. Rimmet British, Killed,
27 Sep, Burwash
Hurricane, 229 Sqn Northolt
Shot down by a Bf 109

Sgt R.D. Ritchie British, Killed,
9 Aug, Dunbar Coast (Scotland)
Hurricane, 605 Sqn Drem
Aircraft crashed into sea after developing serious glycol leak. Pilot's body recovered by boat

P/O A.T. Rose-Price British, Listed as missing, 2 Sep, Dungeness

Hurricane, 501 Sqn Gravesend
Aircraft failed to return to base after combat

P/O M. Rozwadwski Polish, Listed as missing, 15 Aug, Dover
Hurricane, 151 Sqn North Weald
Aircraft failed to return to base after combat over the Channel

F/Lt F.W. Rushmer British, Killed,
5 Sep, Weald of Kent
Spitfire, 603 Sqn Hornchurch
Shot down in a fierce dogfight with a Bf 109

P/O W.M.C. Samolinski Polish, Killed,
26 Sep, Over Channel
Hurricane, 253 Sqn Kenley
Shot down and killed

F/O D.J. Sanders British, Killed,
7 Sep, Catterick
Spitfire, 54 Sqn Catterick
Crashed during low altitude training practice flight

S/L H.C. Sawyer British, Killed,
2 Aug, Rochford Airfield
Spitfire, 65 Sqn Hornchurch
Burnt out. Aircraft crashed on take off during night patrol and exploded in flames

F/O L.H. Schwind British, Killed,
7 Sep, Gatwick
Hurricane, 213 Sqn Tangmere
Shot down by a Bf 110

P/O K.M. Sclanders Canadian, Killed,
9 Sep, Thames Haven
Hurricane, 242 Sqn Coltishall
Aircraft shot down in combat with Dornier Do 17s and Bf 110s. Crashed at Caterham, Surrey

F/O W.J.M. Scott British, Killed,
8 Sep, Dover
Spitfire, 41 Sqn Hornchurch
Possibly shot down by Bf 109. Crashed in flames

Sgt J.A. Scott British, Killed,
27 Oct, Maidstone
Spitfire, 74 Sqn Biggin Hill
Shot down in combat with Bf 109s. Crashed and exploded at Dundas Farm, Elmstead

Sgt. E. Scott British, Killed,
27 Sep, Unknown
Spitfire, 222 Sqn Hornchurch
Failed to return in his Spitfire

P/O L.A. Sears British, Listed as missing,
8 Aug, South of Isle of Wight
Hurricane, 145 Sqn Westhampnett
Last seen in combat with Bf 109s, failed to return to base. Assumed crashed in Channel

Sgt M.M. Shanahan British, Listed as missing, 16 Aug, Harwich
Hurricane, 1 Sqn Northolt
Aircraft last seen in combat with enemy fighters over the North Sea

P/O R.H. Shaw British, Listed as missing,
3 Sep, Chart Sutton
Hurricane, 1 Sqn Northolt
Crashed from unknown circumstances. Pilot killed in aircraft

Sgt F.E.R. Shepherd British, Killed,
11 Sep, Croydon
Spitfire, 611 Sqn Digby
Aircraft caught fire during combat. Pilot bailed out but died of injuries. Aircraft

crashed into houses

P/O D.C.Shepley British, Listed as missing, 12 Aug, South of Isle of Wight
Spitfire, 152 Sqn Warmwell
Aircraft last seen in combat with Ju 88. Failed to return to base

Sgt E.E. Shepperd British, Killed, 18 Oct, Tadnoll Mill
Spitfire, 152 Sqn Warmwell
Crashed at Tadnoll Mill, Dorchester. Exact circumstances not known

Sgt F.A. Sibley British, Listed as missing, 1 Oct, Poole Harbour
Hurricane, 238 Sqn Middle Wallop
Failed to return from combat with enemy fighters

Sgt W.G. Silver British, Killed, 25 Sep, Portsmouth
Spitfire, 152 Sqn Warmwell
Shot down off Portsmouth

Sgt R.B. Sim British, Listed as missing, 11 Aug, Margate
Hurricane, 111 Sqn Croydon
Aircraft failed to return after combat with Bf 109s escorting bombers, presumed crashed into sea

F/O G.M. Simpson New Zealander, Listed as missing, 26 Oct, French Coast
Hurricane, 229 Sqn Northolt
Shot down by Bf 109s whilst attacking He 59, crashed into the sea

Sgt A. Siudak Polish, Killed, 6 Oct, Northolt Airfield
Hurricane, 303 Sqn Northolt
Hurricane bombed on the ground by lone raider

P/O D.N.E. Smith British, Killed, 11 Aug, East Coast
Spitfire, 74 Sqn Hornchurch
(Crashed into sea) Aircraft crashed into sea off Harwich after combat with Bf 110

P/O D.S. Smith British, Killed, 27 Sep, Faversham
Spitfire, 616 Sqn Coltishall
Shot down by Bf 109 on 27th September, died of wounds on 28th September

S/L A.T. Smith British, Killed, 25 Jul, Hawkinge Airfield
Spitfire, 610 Sqn Biggin Hill
Aircraft crashed and burnt out after stalling on landing. Previously been in combat with Bf 109

S/Lt F.A. Smith British, Listed as missing, 8 Aug, South of Isle of Wight
Hurricane, 145 Sqn Westhampnett
Aircraft shot down over the Channel while attacking Ju 87s. Possibly hit by gunfire from escort Bf 109

Sgt A.D. Smith British, Died of injuries, 6 Sep, Ashford
Spitfire, 66 Sqn Kenley
Pilot bailed out with serious injuries after combat with enemy aircraft. Died of injuries 6th September

Sgt K.B. Smith British, Listed as missing, 8 Aug, St Catherines Point
Hurricane, 257 Sqn Northolt
Aircraft failed to return to base after action over the Channel protecting convoy CW9

F/O R. Smither Canadian, Killed, 15 Sep, Tunbridge Wells
Hurricane, 1 RCAF Sqn Northolt

Aircraft shot down by Bf 109. Pilot failed to bail out

P/O J.L. Smithers British, Killed, 11 Aug, Portland
Hurricane, 601 Sqn Tangmere
Crashed into sea. Aircraft shot down by unknown enemy aircraft. Pilot's body recovered and buried at St Marie Le Havre, France

P/O N.D. Solomon British, Killed, 18 Aug, Dover
Hurricane, 17 Sqn
Aircraft took fatal fire from Bf 109 attack while patrolling Dover area

Sgt M.H. Sprague British, Killed, 11 Sep, Selsey Bill
Spitfire, 602 Sqn Westhampnett
Aircraft attacked by Bf 110s over Channel. Pilot's body washed ashore at Brighton on October 10th

F/O P.C.B. St John British, Killed, 22 Oct, South Nutfield
Spitfire, 74 Sqn Biggin Hill
Shot down in combat with Bf 109s. Crashed at South Nutfield, Surrey

Sgt D.O. Stanley New Zealander, Killed, 26 Oct, Take-off
Hurricane, 151 Sqn Digby
Crashed and burst into flames on take-off from Coleby Grange on night-flying practice. Died from injuries the next day

S/L H.M. Starr British, Killed, 31 Aug, Grove Ferry
Hurricane, 253 Sqn Kenley
Aircraft shot down by Bf 109s. Pilot crash landed but died beside aircraft at Eastry brickworks

F/O M.J. Steborowski Polish, Killed,
11 Aug, Portland
Hurricane, 238 Sqn Middle Wallop
Crashed into sea. Aircraft shot down by
unknown enemy aircraft over Channel

P/O J. Sterbacek Czech, Listed as
missing, 31 Aug, Thames Estuary
Hurricane, 310 Sqn Duxford
Aircraft shot down by Bf 109 while
attacking a Do 215 bomber

F/Lt G.E.B. Stoney British, Killed,
18 Aug, Thames Estuary
Hurricane, 501 Sqn Gravesend
Aircraft took fatal fire from Bf 109 during
combat

Sgt D.R. Stoodley British, Killed,
24 Oct, Landing
Hurricane, 43 Sqn Usworth
Accident at base while attempting to land
cross-wind, stalled at 250ft

Sgt S.G.Stuckey British, Listed as missing,
12 Aug, Off Bognor
Hurricane, 213 Sqn Exeter
Shot down over Channel by Bf 109s

P/O J.A.P. Studd British, Killed,
19 Aug, Off Orfordness
Spitfire, 66 Sqn Coltishall
Aircraft hit by gunfire from He 111. Pilot
bailed out. Although rescued, did not
regain consciousness

P/O I.W. Sutherland British, N/A,
4 Aug,
Spitfire, 19 Sqn Duxford

P/O N. Sutton British, Killed,
5 Oct, Take-off
Spitfire, 72 Sqn Croydon

Killed in a mid-air collision shortly after
take-off. Crashed and burned

F/Sgt C. Sydney British, Killed,
27 Sep, Kingston
Spitfire, 92 Sqn Biggin Hill
Shot down and killed over Kingston in
Surrey

P/O E.J.H. Sylvester British, Listed as
missing, 20 Jul, Lyme Bay
Hurricane, 501 Sqn Middle Wallop
Aircraft damaged by Bf 109 off Cherbourg
and crashed while approaching coast

F/Sgt J.H. Tanner British, Killed,
11 Aug, Calais
Spitfire, 610 Sqn Biggin Hill
Failed to return to base. Aircraft shot down
off the French coast. Pilot recovered &
buried at Calais, (France)

Sgt L.V. Toogood British, Killed,
27 Oct, Edmondsley
Hurricane, 43 Sqn Usworth
Crashed vertically from height during high-
altitude aerobatics. Cause unknown, but
suspected oxygen failure

F/O J. Topolnicki Polish, Killed,
21 Sep, Exeter
Hurricane, 601 Sqn Exeter
Killed in a flying accident.

F/O A.A.G. Trueman Canadian, Killed,
4 Sep, Banstead
Hurricane, 253 Sqn Kenley
Aircraft shot down during combat action
over Kenley aerodrome

F/Lt D.E Turner British, Listed as missing,
8 Aug, South of Isle of Wight
Hurricane, 238 Sqn Middle Wallop

Aircraft presumed shot down while
engaging enemy over convoy CW9. Failed
to return to base

Sgt T.R. Tweed British, Killed,
15 Sep, Boscombe Down
Hurricane, 56 Sqn Boscombe Down
Pilot failed to come out of spin during
dogfight practice

P/O A.E.A van den Hove d'Ertsenrijck
Belgian, Killed, 11 Sep, Ashford
Hurricane, 501 Sqn Kenley
Aircraft exploded in mid-air after hit by
gunfire from Bf 109

Sgt F.F. Vinyard British, Killed,
6 Oct, Flamborough Head
Spitfire, 64 Sqn Kenley
Crashed into sea while on patrol off
Flamborough Head, Yorkshire. Cause
unknown

F/Lt R. Voase-Jeff British, Killed,
11 Aug, Portland Bill
Hurricane, 87 Sqn Exeter
Aircraft last seen in combat over the
Channel, failed to return to base

Sgt J.V. Wadham British, Killed,
12 Oct, Hastings
Hurricane, 145 Sqn Tangmere
Shot down by Bf 109s, crashed
Coursehorn Farm, Chittenden, near
Cranbrook

P/O E.C.J. Wakeham British, Listed as
missing, 8 Aug, Off Isle of Wight
Hurricane, 145 Sqn Westhampnett
Last seen in combat with Ju 87s and Bf
110s. Aircraft failed to return to base

Sgt. S.R.E Wakeling British, Killed,

25 Aug, Portland
Hurricane, 87 Sqn Exeter
Aircraft shot down by Bf 109 and burst into flames. Crashed near Dorchester

F/Lt S.C. Walch Australian, Listed as missing, 11 Aug, Weymouth
Hurricane, 238 Sqn Middle Wallop
Aircraft shot down in combat over Channel East of Weymouth

Sgt P.K. Walley British, Killed,
18 Aug, Morden Park
Hurricane, 615 Sqn Kenley
Aircraft took fatal fire from Bf 109 during combat

Sgt J.P. Walsh British, Killed,
4 Aug, Kirton in Lindsey
Spitfire, 616 Sqn Leconfield
Aircraft spun out of control at 5,000ft during combat practice

P/O S. Wapniarek Polish, Killed,
18 Oct, Thames Ditton
Hurricane, 302 Sqn Northolt
Crashed attempting forced landing at Nutwood Farm, Thames Ditton on return from patrol in bad weather

Sgt R.A. Ward British, Killed,
8 Oct, Borstal
Spitfire, 66 Sqn Gravesend
Shot down in combat with Bf 109s over Kent

F/Lt W.H.C. Warner British, Listed as missing, 16 Aug, Dungeness
Spitfire, 610 Sqn Biggin Hill
Last seen in combat with Bf 109 over Channel. Aircraft failed to return

Sgt S. Warren British, Listed as missing, 9 Oct, Over The Wash

Hurricane, 1 Sqn Wittering
Failed to return from section cloud formation flight

F/O R.M. Waterston British, Killed,
23 Aug, Sth. East London
Spitfire, 603 Sqn Hornchurch
Aircraft shot down by Bf 109 and broke up mid-air before crashing in Woolwich

Sgt P.I. Watson-Parker British, Killed,
13 Jul, Tatsfield (Biggin Hill)
Spitfire, 610 Sqn Biggin Hill
Aircraft crashed in unknown circumstances

F/Lt B.H. Way British, Missing believed drowned, 25 Jul, Off Dover
Spitfire, 54 Sqn Rochford
Aircraft shot down by Bf 109 and crashed into the Channel

F/Lt P.S. Weaver British, Listed as missing, 31 Aug, Colchester
Hurricane, 56 Sqn North Weald
Aircraft crashed into Blackwater River after being hit by Bf 109 gunfire

F/Lt J.T Webster British, Killed,
5 Sep, Thames Estuary
Spitfire, 41 Sqn Hornchurch (Manston)
Collided with Spitfire P9428. Pilot bailed out but killed. Aircraft crashed at Laindon (Essex)

P/O F.K. Webster British, Killed,
26 Aug, Folkestone
Spitfire, 610 Sqn Biggin Hill
Aircraft badly damaged by Bf 109. Crashed attempting to land at Hawkinge Airfield

F/O K.V. Wendel New Zealander, Died of injuries, 7 Sep, Thames Estuary
Hurricane, 504 Sqn Hendon

Aircraft shot down over Estuary. Crash landed in flames at Faversham

Sgt. T.E. Westmoreland British, Listed as missing, 25 Aug, Canterbury
Spitfire, 616 Sqn Kenley
Aircraft failed to return to base

Sgt B.E.P. Whall British, Killed,
7 Oct, Lullington
Spitfire, 602 Sqn Westhampnett
Died of his wounds when crash landed Spitfire after combat with Ju 88s

P/O H.L. Whitbread British, Killed,
20 Sep, Rochester
Spitfire, 222 Sqn Hornchurch
Aircraft shot down by Bf 109s and crashed at Pond Cottage. Pilot thrown clear but already dead

Sgt J.J. Whitfield British, Listed as missing, 13 Oct, Calais
Hurricane, 56 Sqn North Weald
Aircraft hit by gunfire from Bf 109 over Channel. Crashed into sea. Pilot's body not recovered

F/Lt R.D.G. Wight British, Killed,
11 Aug, Off Portland
Hurricane, 213 Sqn Exeter
Aircraft shot down in combat with enemy aircraft. Pilot believed to be recovered and buried at Cayeux sur Mer (France)

F/O E.J. Wilcox British, Killed,
31 Aug, Staplehurst
Spitfire, 72 Sqn Biggin Hill
Aircraft shot down by enemy aircraft over Dungeness

P/O T.S. Wildblood British, Listed as missing, 25 Aug, Portland

Spitfire, 152 Sqn Warmwell
Aircraft shot down by Bf 109s over Channel
and crashed into sea

Sgt G.N. Wilkes British, Listed as missing,
12 Aug, Off Bognor
Hurricane, 213 Sqn Exeter
Aircraft last seen in combat with Bf 109s.
Failed to return to base

S/L R.L. Wilkinson British, Killed,
16 Aug, Off Deal
Spitfire, 266 Sqn Hornchurch
Aircraft believed to have collided with Bf
109 over Channel

F/Sgt E.E. Williams British, Listed as
missing, 15 Oct, Thames Estuary
Hurricane, 46 Sqn Stapleford
Shot down in combat with Bf 109s,
crashed in Gravesend

P/O D.G. Williams British, Killed,
10 Oct, Tangmere
Spitfire, 92 Sqn Biggin Hill
Killed in mid-air collision during attack on
Do 17. Crashed east of Brighton

P/O W.S. Williams New Zealander, Killed,
21 Oct, Take-off
Spitfire, 266 Sqn Wittering
Landed at Stradishall to refuel but crashed
on take-off, cause unknown

S/L C.W. Williams British, Listed as
missing, 25 Aug, Portland
Hurricane, 17 Sqn Tangmere
Aircraft broke in two after combat with Bf
110 & crashed into the sea

P/O R.R. Wilson Canadian, Listed as
missing, 11 Aug, Margate
Hurricane, 111 Sqn Croydon

Crashed into sea. Aircraft last seen
attacking Bf 109 escorts over the Thames
Estuary

P/O D.C. Winter British, Killed,
5 Sep, Eltham
Spitfire, 72 Sqn Croydon
Aircraft shot down by Bf 109. Pilot tried to
bail out at too low altitude

F/Lt L.C. Withall Australian, Listed as
missing, 12 Aug, South of Isle of Wight
Spitfire, 152 Sqn Warmwell
Aircraft shot down by return gunfire from
Ju 88, believed to have crashed into the
sea

Sgt A. Wojcicki Polish, Listed as missing,
11 Sep, Selsey Bill
Hurricane, 213 Sqn Tangmere
Aircraft shot down over Channel during
combat with Bf 110s. Pilot's body never
recovered

Sgt S. Wojtowicz Polish, Killed,
11 Sep, South London
Hurricane, 303 Sqn Northolt
Aircraft crashed and burnt out at
Westerham after being shot down by Bf
109s

F/O P.P. Woods-Scawen British, Killed,
1 Sep, Kenley
Hurricane, 85 Sqn Croydon
Aircraft shot down by Bf 109. Pilot bailed
out but parachute failed to open

P/O C.A. Woods-Scawen British, Killed,
2 Sep, Ivychurch (Kent)
Hurricane, 43 Sqn Tangmere
Aircraft caught fire after combat with Bf
109. Pilot bailed out too low

Sgt J. Wright British, Died of injuries,
6 Sep, Biggin Hill
Hurricane, 79 Sqn Biggin Hill
Shot down by Bf 110 over base. Pilot crash
landed aircraft at Surbiton. Died of injuries
5th September

P/O J.H.R. Young British, Listed as
missing, 28 Jul, Ramsgate
Spitfire, 74 Sqn Hornchurch.
Aircraft crashed in Channel off Ramsgate

Sgt J.S. Zaluski Polish, Killed,
17 Oct, Colliers End
Hurricane, 302 Sqn Northolt
Overturned while attempting forced landing

P/O P. Zenker Polish, Listed as missing,
24 Aug, North West of Dover
Hurricane, 501 Sqn Gravesend
Aircraft failed to return to base after
combat with Dornier Do 17s and Bf 109s

P/O A. Zukowski Polish, Killed,
18 Oct, Detling
Hurricane, 302 Sqn Northolt
Ran out of fuel having lost bearings in
deteriorating weather conditions

Twin and Three-Seat Aircraft

P/O C.J. Arthur British, Listed as missing,
27 Aug, Off Norwegian Coast
Blenheim, 248 Squadron Sumburg
With Sgt. E.A. Ringwood British
And Sgt. R.C.R. Cox British
Aircraft crashed into the sea. Reasons
unknown

F/L R.C.V. Ash British, Killed,
28 Aug, Faversham
Defiant, 264 Squadron Hornchurch

Aircraft shot down by Bf 109 and crashed in flames

Sgt. B. Baker British, Listed as missing, 26 Aug, Off Herne Bay
Defiant, 264 Squadron Hornchurch
Crashed into Thames Estuary after hit by gunfire from Bf 109. Pilot safe

P/O R.V. Baron British, Killed, 12 Oct, Night Patrol
Blenheim, 219 Squadron Redhill
Unexpected engine vibration during routine night patrol. High speed stall and crash at Ewhurst, crew bailed out but P/O Baron's parachute failed

Sgt C.S.F Beer British, N/A, 10 Sep, N/A
Blenheim, 235 Squadron Bircham Newton
P/O C.C. Bennett Australian, Listed as missing, 1 Oct, Norwegian Coast
Blenheim, 248 Squadron Sumburgh
With Sgt G.B. Brash British
And Sgt G.S. Clarke British
Failed to return from a sortie off the Norwegian Coast

F/Lt C.H. Bull British, Killed, 8 Aug, Blenheim, 25 Squadron North Weald

P/O C.F. Cardnell British, Killed, 8 Aug, Peterborough
Blenheim, 23 Squadron Henlow
And Sgt C. Stephens British
Killed whilst on night patrol

Sgt R. Copcutt British, Listed as missing, 20 Oct, Coast of Norway
Blenheim, 248 Squadron Sumburgh
Shot down in attack on enemy aircraft. Three remaining crew were captured

S/L J.A. Davies British, Killed, 6 Oct, Blenheim, 604 Squadron. Middle Wallop

F/Lt I.D.G.Donald British, Killed, 19 Jul, Dover
Defiant, 141 Squadron Hawkinge
With P/O A.C.Hamilton British
Aircraft shot down by Bf 109 and crashed into street in Dover

S/L P.E.Drew British, Killed, 1 Aug, Querqueville (France)
Blenheim IV, 236 Squadron Thorney Island
And F/O B.Nokes-Cooper British
Aircraft shot down on bomber escort by ground fire

Sgt J.L. Feather British, Killed, 18 Sep, Blenheim, 235 Squadron Bircham Newton

P/O S.R. Gane British, Listed as missing, 20 Oct, Coast of Norway
Blenheim, 248 Squadron. Sumburgh
With P/O M.D. Green British
And Sgt N.J. Stocks British
Failed to return from reconnaissance sortie over Norwegian Coast

Sgt W.J. Garfield British, Listed as missing, 13 Sep, Norwegian Coast
Blenheim, 248 Squadron. Sumburgh
With Sgt A. Kay British
And Sgt B.W. Mesner British
Aircraft failed to return from reconnaissance over Norwegian coast

P/O H.I. Goodall British, Killed, 10 Oct, Marlow
Defiant, 264 Squadron. Luton
With Sgt R.B.M Young New Zealander
Crashed at Marlow, exact cause unknown but likely to be due to enemy action

F/O D.N. Grice British, Killed, 8 Aug, Ramsgate
Blenheim, 600 Squadron Manston
With Sgt F.J. Keast British
And AC1 J.B.W. Warren British
Aircraft damaged in action. Pilot avoided town and crashed into the sea

Sgt. C.Haigh British, Killed, 25 Aug, Exeter
Blenheim, 604 Squadron. Middle Wallop
With Sgt. J.G.B.Fletcher British
And LAC A.L. Austin (died next day) British
Aircraft crashed during night operation. Reason unknown

P/O R.H. Haviland South African, Killed, 28 Aug, Aberdeen
Blenheim, 248 Squadron
Killed in an accident while a passenger in Magister R1832

P/O C.A. Hobson British, Killed, 3 Oct, Patrol
Blenheim, 600 Squadron Hornchurch
With Sgt D.E. Hughes New Zealander
And AC2 C.F. Cooper British
Incurred engine failure during a night patrol in poor weather and crashed into trees

P/O D.W. Hogg British, Killed, 3 Sep, North Weald
Blenheim, 25 Squadron North Weald
Aircraft wrongly identified as a Bf 110 and shot down by a Hurricane. Sgt E.Powell bailed out unhurt

P/O R.A.Howley Canadian, Listed as missing, 19 Jul, Off Dover
Defiant, 141 Squadron Hawkinge
With Sgt A.G.Curley British
Aircraft lost at sea. Aircraft crashed into

Channel after being shot down by Bf 109

S/L P.A.Hunter British, Listed as missing, 24 Aug, Off Ramsgate
Defiant, 264 Squadron Hornchurch
With P/O F.H.King British
Aircraft last seen chasing a Junkers Ju 88 out to sea after an attack on Manston

P/O P.R.S. Hurst British, Killed, 23 Oct, Kirkby Malzeard
Blenheim, 600 Squadron Hornchurch
Crashed into hillside during practice flight through cloud

P/O J. T.Jones British, Listed as missing, 24 Aug, Off Ramsgate
Defiant, 264 Squadron Hornchurch
And P/O W.A. Ponting British
Aircraft last seen in combat with Junkers Ju 88s & Bf 109s over the Channel

Sgt L.R. Karasek British, Killed, 25 Sep, Broughton
Blenheim, 23 Squadron. Ford
With P/O E. Orgias New Zealander
And AC2 R.I. Payne British
Aircraft stalled and crashed while landing

P/O J.R.Kemp New Zealander, Listed as missing, 19 Jul, Off Dover
Defiant, 141 Squadron Hawkinge
With Sgt R.Crombie British
Aircraft crashed into Channel after being shot down by Bf 109

P/O P.L. Kenner British, Killed, 28 Aug, Thanet (Kent)
Defiant, 264 Squadron Hornchurch
And P/O C.E. Johnson British
Aircraft shot down by Bf 109 during combat

P/O R.Kidsun New Zealander, Listed as missing, 19 Jul, Off Dover
Defiant, 141 Squadron Hawkinge
With Sgt F.P.J.Atkins British
Aircraft crashed into Channel after being shot down by Bf 109

P/O J.C. Kirkpatrick Belgian, Listed as missing, 9 Oct, Over Channel
Blenheim, 235 Squadron. Thorney Island
With P/O R.C. Thomas British
And Sgt G.E. Keel British
Missing following combat with enemy aircraft

F/Lt H.M.S. Lambert British, Killed, 15 Sep, N/A
Beaufighter, 25 Squadron Martlesham Heath
With P/O M.J. Miley British
And Sgt J.P. Wyate British

Sgt E.E.Lockton British, Listed as missing, 20 Jul, Off Cherbourg
Blenheim, 236 Squadron Thorney Island
With Sgt H.Corcoran British
Aircaft shot down by Bf 109 during escort mission. Crashed into the Channel

Sgt W.H. Machin British, Died of wounds, 24 Aug, Manston
Defiant, 264 Squadron Hornchurch
Aircraft shot down by Bf 109 over base. Pilot escaped with slight injuries

Sgt. W. Maxwell British, Listed as missing, 26 Aug, Off Herne Bay
Defiant, 264 Squadron Hornchurch
Aircraft crashed into Thames Estuary after being hit by gunfire from Bf 109. Pilot safe

P/O B.M. McDonough Australian, Killed, 1

Aug, Querqueville (France)
Blenheim, 236 Squadron Thorney Island
And Sgt F.A.P. Head British
Aircraft shot down during bomber escort by ground fire

F/O D.H.C. O'Malley British, Killed, 4 Sep, Kirton-in-Lindsey
Defiant, 264 Squadron. Kirton in Lindsey
With Sgt L.A.W.Rasmussen New Zealander
Aircraft crashed during night landing practice

P/O R.L. Patterson British, Certified as missing, 18 Jul, Off Essex coast
Blenheim, 235 Squadron Bircham Newton
With Sgt R.Y. Tucker British
And Sgt L.H.M. Reece British
Aircraft failed to return from operational flight

P/O J.S. Priestley New Zealander, Killed, 30 Aug, Bircham Newton
Blenheim, 235 Squadron Bircham Newton
With Sgt E. A. Graves British
Killed in crash after take-off to practice circuits. Aircraft spun into ground killing both crew

P/O R.A.Rhodes British, Listed as missing, 25 Aug, Wainfleet
Blenheim, 29 Squadron Digby
With Sgt. N.Jacobson British
And Sgt R.J. Gouldstone British
Believed shot down and crashed into sea during night combat

Sgt. C.J. Richardson British, Listed as missing, 31 Jul, N/A
Blenheim, 29 Squadron Wellingore

P/O R.H. Rigby British, Killed,
18 Jul, Le Havre
Blenheim, 236 Squadron Thorney Island
With Sgt D.D. Mackinnon British
Aircraft shot down by Bf 109 during photo-reconnaissance mission over France

Sgt J.H. Round British, Missing in action,
18 Aug, Off the Norwegian Coast
Blenheim, 248 Squadron. Sumburgh
With Sgt W.H. Want British
And Sgt M.P.Digby-Worsley British
Aircraft failed to return from reconnaissance mission over Southern Norway

Sgt A.F.C. Saunders British, Killed,
7 Sep, Rainham
Blenheim, 600 Squadron Hornchurch
With Sgt J.W.Davies British
Aircraft crashed due to engine failure during landing approach

F/O I.G.Shaw British, Listed as missing,
24 Aug, Off Manston
Defiant, 264 Squadron Hornchurch
With Sgt A.Berry British
Aircraft believed to have been shot down by Bf 109 over the Channel after raid on Manston

Sgt. G.E. Shepperd British, Killed,
30 Sep, Patrol
Blenheim, 219 Squadron Redhill
With Sgt. C. Goodwin British
And AC2 J.P. McCaul British
Aircraft crashed during routine night patrol, exact cause unknown

P/O N.B. Shorrocks British, Listed as missing, 11 Sep, Channel Area
Blenheim, 235 Squadron. Thorney Island

With Fl/Lt F.W. Flood Australian
And Sgt B.R. Sharp British
Aircraft failed to return from bomber escort mission to Calais

P/O D.M.Slatter British, Listed as missing,
19 Jul, Off Dover
Defiant, 141 Squadron Hawkinge
Aircraft crashed into Channel after being shot down by Bf 109. Pilot wounded

Sgt R.E. Stevens British, Killed,
19 Oct, Point of Aire
Blenheim, 29 Squadron. Digby
With Sgt O.K. Sly British
And AC2 A. Jackson British
Shot down in error by Hurricanes of 312 Squadron

P/O C.R.D. Thomas British, Killed,
18 Jul, Le Havre
Blenheim, 236 Squadron Thorney Island
With Sgt H.D.B. Elsdon British
Aircraft shot down during photo-reconnaissance mission over France

Sgt J.B. Thompson British, Killed,
31 Jul, N/A
Blenheim, 25 Squadron Martlesham Heath

Sgt E. Waite British, Listed as missing,
31 Jul, N/A
Blenheim, 29 Squadron Wellingore

P/O D. Whitley British, Killed, 28 Aug,
North of Ashford
Defiant, 264 Squadron Hornchurch
And Sgt. R.C. Turner British
Aircraft shot down by Bf 109 during combat

P/O P.C. Wickings-Smith British, Listed as missing, 11 Sep, Channel Area

Blenheim, 235 Squadron Thorney Island
With P/O A.W.V. Green British
And Sgt R.D.H. Watts British
Aircraft believed to have been shot down by Bf 109 during bomber escort mission to Calais

Sgt J.F.Wise British, Listed as missing,
19 Jul, Off Dover
Defiant, 141 Squadron Hawkinge
Aircraft sustained damage from Bf 109.
Sgt Wise bailed out over Channel. Pilot managed to get the aircraft back to base

P/O D.N. Woodger British, Listed as missing, 24 Aug, West of Selsey
Blenheim, 235 Squadron Thorney Island
With Sgt D.L. Wright Killed British
Aircraft mistakenly shot down by Hurricanes of 1 RCAF and crashed into Bracklesham Bay

F/O H.J. Woodward British, Killed,
30 Oct, South Bersted
Blenheim, 23 Squadron Ford
With P/O A.A. Atkinson British
And Sgt H.T. Perry British
Crashed having suffered R/T failure during deteriorating weather conditions following night patrol

P/O K.W. Worsdell British, Killed,
30 Oct, Balcombe Place
Beaufighter, 219 Squadron Redhill
With Sgt E.C. Gardiner British
Hit trees trying to locate base in bad visibility. Crashed and exploded south of Balcombe Place

Roll of Honour

The official list of aircrew who fought in an operational unit under the direction of RAF Fighter Command between July 10th and October 30th 1940

Name	Nationality	Squadron	Status
Baker Pilot Officer H C	British	421 Flt	
Baker Sergeant A C	British	610	
Baker Pilot Officer H C	British	41	
Baker Sergeant R D	British	56	KIA*
Baker Pilot Officer S	British	54-66	KIA
Baker Sergeant B	British	264	KIA*
Baker Sergeant E D	British	145	KIA*
Baker Pilot Officer C C M	British	23	
Bakiaer Sergeant L V	British	236	
Ball Flight Lieut G E	British	242	K
Bamberger Sergeant C S	British	610-41	
Bandinel Pilot Officer J J F	British	3	KIA
Banham Flight Lieutenant A	British	264-229	
Banister Sergeant T H	British	219	
Banks Sergeant W H	British	245-32-504	
Bann Sergeant E S	British	238	KIA*
Baraldi Pilot Officer F H R	British	609	
Baranski Flight Lieut W	Polish	607	
Barber Pilot Officer R H	British	46	
Barclay Pilot Officer R G A	British	249	KIA
Barker Sergeant J K	British	152	KIA*
Barker Pilot Officer G L	British	600	KIA
Barker Sergeant F J	British	264	
Barnard Sergeant E C	British	600	
Barnes Pilot Officer W	British	405	
Barnes Sergeant L D	British	257,615,607	
Barnes Flying Officer J G C	British	600	
Barnett Squad Ldr R E	British	234	
Baron Pilot Officer R V	British	219	KIA*
Barraclough Sergeant S M	British	92	
Barraclough Sergeant R G V	British	266	
Barran Flight Lieut. P H	British	609	KIA*
Barrett Sergeant W E	British	25	
Barron Sergeant N P G	British	236	
Barrow Sergeant H I R	British	607-43-213	KIA
Barry Flying Officer N J M	Sth. Afr	3-501	KIA*
Barthropp Flying Officer P	British	602	
Bartlett Sergeant L H	British	17	
Bartley Pilot Officer A C	British	92	
Barton Pilot Officer A R H	British	32-253	KIA
Barton Flt Lt. R A	British	249	
Bartos Pilot Officer J	Czech	312	KIA
Barwell Pilot Officer E G	British	264-242	
Bary Pilot Officer R E	British	229	KIA
Bashford Sergeant H	British	248	
Bassett Flying Officer F B	British	222	KIA
Batcheloe Pilot Officer G H	British	54	KIA
Batt Sergeant L G	British	238	
Baxter Sergeant S	British	222	KIA*
Bayles Flying Officer I N	British	152	
Bayley Sergeant E A	British	32-249	KIA*
Bayliss Pilot Officer D	British	604	
Bayliss Sergeant E J	British	248	KIA
Bayly Sergeant J	N.Zealander	111	
Bayne Flight Lieut A W A	British	17	
Bayne Squad Ldr D W	British	257	
Baynham Pilot Officer G T	British	234-152	
Bazin Flight Lieut J M	British	607	
Bazley Flight Lieut S H	British	206	KIA
Beake Pilot Officer P H	Canadian	64	
Beamish Wing Com F V	Irish	151-249-56	KIA
Beamish Sergeant R	British	601	
Beamont Flying Officer R P	British	87	
Beard Sergeant J M B	British	249	
Beardmore Pilot Officer E	Canadian	1(401)	
Beardsley Pilot Officer R A	British	610-41	
Beatty Sergeant M A	British	266	
Beaumont Pilot Officer W	British	152	KIA*
Beaumont Flight Lieut S G	British	609	
Beazley Pilot Officer H J S	British	249	
Beda Sergeant A	Polish	302	
Bee Sergeant E H	British	29	
Beechey Sergeant A F	British	141	
Beer Sergeant C S F	British	235	KIA*
Begg(FAA) Sub Lieut G W	British	151	KIA
Belc Sergeant M	Polish	303	KIA
Balchem Squad Ldr L G	British	264	KIA
Beley Pilot Officer W G	Canadian	151	KIA*
Bell Flying Officer C A	British	29	
Bell Sergeant C H	British	234	KIA
Bell Flying Officer J S	British	616	KIA*
Bell Sergeant D	British	23	KIA
Bell Sergeant R	British	219	
Bell-Slater Flying Officer D	British	253	
Bell-Walker Sergeant H J	British	72	
Benn Sergeant G W	British	219	
Bennett Pilot Officer C C	Australian	248	KIA*
Bennett Sergeant H E	British	43	KIA
Bennette Flying Officer G R	British	17	KIA
Bennions Pilot Officer G H	British	41	
Bennison Sergeant A A	N.Zealander	25	
Benson Pilot Officer N J V	British	603	KIA*
Benson Pilot Officer J G	British	141	
Bent Sergeant B	British	25	
Benzie Pilot Officer J	Canadian	242	KIA*
Beresford Flight Lieut H R A	British	257	KIA*
Bergman Pilot Officer V	Czech	310	
Berkley Sergeant T C E	British	85	KIA
Bernard Sergeant F A	Czech	238-601	
Bernas Pilot Officer B	Polish	302	
Berridge Sergeant H W	British	219	DOI
Berry Flight Sergeant F G	British	1	KIA*
Berry Pilot Officer R	British	603	
Berry Sergeant A	British	264	KIA*
Berwick Sergeant R C	British	25	KIA
Beveridge Sergeant C	British	219	
Beytagh Squad Ldr M L	British	73	DOI
Bickerdyke Pilot Officer J L	N.Zealander	85	KIA*
Bicknell Sergeant	British	23	
Bicknell Squad Ldr L C	British	23	
Bidgood Pilot Officer E G	British	253	KIA
Bidgood Sergeant I K	British	213	KIA
Biggar Squad Ldr A J	British	111	
Bignall Sergeant J	British	25	KIA
Binham Sergeant A E	British	64	
Birch(FAA) Lieutenant R A	British	804	KIA
Bird-Wilson Pilot Officer H	British	17	
Birkett Pilot Officer T	British	219	KIA
Birrell(FAA) Midshipman M	British	804-79	
Bisdee Pilot Officer J D	British	609	

Name	Nationality	Squadron	Status
Bisgood Pilot Officer D L	British	3	KIA
Bitmead Squad Ldr E R	British	266-310-253	DOI
Black Sergeant A	British	54	KIA
Black Sergeant H E	British	46-257-32	KIA*
Blackadder Flight Lieut W F	British	607	
Blackwood Sqdn Ldr G D M	British	310-213	DOI
Blair Pilot Officer C E	British	600	KIA
Blair Pilot Officer K H	British	151	DOI
Blaize Warrant Officer P	Fr. French	111	
Blake(FAA) Sub Lieut A G	British	19	KIA*
Blake Squad Ldr M V	N.Zealander	238-231	
Bland Pilot Officer J W	British	601-501	KIA*
Blane Sergeant W H	British	604	
Blatchford Flying Officer H	Canadian	17-257	KIA
Blayney Pilot Officer A J	British	609	
Blenkharn Sergeant F	British	25	
Bloomeley Pilot Officer D H	British	151	
Bloor Sergeant E	British	46	KIA
Blow Sergeant K L O	British	235	KIA
Boddington Sergeant M C B	British	234	
Bodie Pilot Officer C A W	British	66	KIA
Boitel-Gill Flight Lieut B P A	British	152	KIA
Bolton Sergeant H A	British	79	KIA*
Bomford Sergeant	British	601	
Bon-Seigneur Pilot Officer C A	Canadian	257	KIA*
Boot Pilot Officer P V	British	1	
Booth Sergeant J J	British	23-600	
Booth Sergeant G B	British	85	KIA*
Boret Pilot Officer R J	British	41	KIA
Borowski Flying Officer J	Polish	302	KIA*
Boswell Sergeant R A	British	19	
Boulding Flying Officer R J E	British	74	
Boulter Flying Officer J C	British	603	KIA
Boulton Flying Officer J E	British	603-310	KIA*
Bouquillard Adjutant H	Fr. French	615-249	KIA
Bowen Pilot Officer F D	British	264	KIA
Bowen Pilot Officer N G	British	266	KIA*
Bowen Flight Lieut C E	British	607	KIA*
Bowen-Morris Sergeant H	British	92	
Bowerman Sergeant D R	British	222	
Bowman Sergeant L D	British	141	
Bowring Flying Officer B H	British	111-600	
Boyd Flight Lieut R F	British	602	
Boyd Flight Lieut A H McN	British	145-600	
Bowyer Flying Officer W S	British	257	KIA
Boyle Sergeant C	British	236	
Boyle Flying Officer J G	Canadian	41	KIA*
Bracton Sergeant	British	602	
Braham Squad Ldr J R D	British	29	
Bramah(FAA) Sub Lieut H G K	British	213	
Branch Flying Officer G R	British	145	KIA*
Brash Sergeant G B	British	248	KIA*
Breeze Sergeant R A	British	222	KIA
Brejcha Sergeant V	Czech	43	KIA
Brennan Sergeant J S	N.Zealander	23	
Brett Flying Officer P N	British	17	
Brewster Pilot Officer J	British	615-616	KIA
Briere Pilot Officer Y J	Fr. French	257	KIA
Briese Flying Officer	Canadian	1(401)	
Briggs Pilot Officer M F	British	234	KIA
Briggs Sergeant D R	British	236	KIA
Bright Flying Officer V M	British	299	KIA
Brimble Sergeant G W	British	242	KIA
Brimble Sergeant J J	British	73	KIA*
Brinsden Flight Lieut F N	N.Zealander	19	
Britton Pilot Officer H W A	British	17	KIA*
Britton Flying Officer A W N	British	263	KIA*
Broadhurst Squadron Ldr H	British	1	
Broadhurst Pilot Officer J W	British	222	KIA*
Brooker Flying Officer R E P	British	56	KIA
Brookman Sergeant R W A	N.Zealander	253	
Broom Sergeant P W	British	25	
Brothers Flight Lt P M	British	32-257	
Brown Sergeant C B	British	245	
Brown Flight Lieut G A	British	253	
Brown Flight Sergeant F S	British	79	DOI
Brown Flying Officer D P	Canadian	1(401)	
Brown Pilot Officer M K	Canadian	242	KIA
Brown Flight Lieut M H	Canadian	1	KIA
Brown Pilot Officer B W	British	610-72	
Brown Pilot Officer M P	British	611-41	
Brown Pilot Officer R C	British	229	
Brown Pilot Officer R J W	British	111	
Brown Pilot Officer A W	British	25	
Brown Sergeant J W	British	600	KIA
Brown Sergeant C W D	British	236	KIA
Brown Sergeant R S	British	604	
Brown Sergeant P G F	British	234	KIA
Brown Flying Officer D M	British	1	
Browne Sergeant C	British	219	
Browne Pilot Officer D O M	British	1	KIA*
Bruce Flight Lieut D C	British	111	KIA*
Brumby Sergeant N	British	615-607	KIA*
Brunner Pilot Officer G C	British	43	
Bryant-Fenn Pilot Officer L T	British	79	
Bryne Sergeant E L	British	FIU	
Bryson Pilot Officer J S	Canadian	92	KIA*
Brzezina Flight Lieut S	Polish	74	KIA
Brzozowski Sergeant M	Polish	303	KIA*
Buchanan Pilot Officer J	British	29	KIA
Buchanan Pilot Officer J R	British	609	KIA*
Buchin Pilot Officer M S H C	Belgian	213	KIA*
Buck Sergeant J A	British	43	KIA*
Bucknole Sergeant J S	British	54	KIA
Budd Flight Lieut G O	British	604	
Budzinski Sergeant J	Polish	605-145	
Bull Pilot Officer J C	British	600	
Bull Flight Lieut C H	British	25	KIA
Bulmer(FAA) Sub Lt G G R	British	32	KIA*
Bumstead Sergeant R F	British	111	
Bunch Sergeant D C	British	219	
Bunch(FAA) Sub Lt. S H	British	804	KIA
Bungey Flying Officer R W	Australian	145	
Burda Pilot Officer F	Czech	310	
Burdekin Sergeant A G	British	600	
Burgess Sergeant J H H	British	222	
Burgoyne Pilot Officer E	British	19	KIA*
Burley Sergeant P S	British	600	
Burnard Flight Sergeant F P	British	74-616	
Burnell-Phillips Sgt. P A	British	607	KIA

Name	Rank	Nationality	Squadron	Status
Burnett Flying Officer N W		British	266-46	KIA
Burns Sergeant W R		N.Zealander	236	
Burns Sergeant O V		British	235	
Burt Sergeant A D		British	611-603	
Burtenshaw Sergeant A A		British	54	KIA
Burton Flight Sergeant C G		British	23	
Burton Squad Ldr H F		British	66	
Burton Flight Lieut H		British	242	
Burton Flying Officer P R F		Sth. Afr	249	KIA*
Burton Pilot Officer L G		N.Zealander	236	KIA
Burton Sergeant L		British	248	
Bush Pilot Officer C R		N.Zealander	242	
Bush Sergeant B M		British	504	
Bushell Sergeant G D		British	213	KIA
Butterfield Sergeant S L		British	213	KIA*
Butterick Sergeant A F		British	3-232	KIA
Butterworth Sergeant K		British	23	
Byng-Hall Pilot Officer P		British	29	DOI
Cain Sergeant A R		British	235	KIA
Caister Pilot Officer J R		British	603	
Calderhead Pilot Officer G D		British	54	KIA
Calderwood Sergeant T M		British	85	
Cale Pilot Officer F W		Australian	266	KIA*
Calthorpe Sergeant		British	25	
Cambell Sergeant D C O		British	66	
Cambridge Flight Lieut. W P		British	253	KIA*
Cameron Sergeant N		British	1-17	
Cameron Flight Sergeant M		British	66	
Cameron Sergeant J D		British	604	KIA
Campbell Pilot Officer A R M		Canadian	54	
Campbell Sergeant A		N.Zealander	264	
Campbell Flight Lieut. A M		British	29	
Campbell Sergeant D B		N.Zealander	23	
Campbell Pilot Officer G L		British	236	KIA
Campbell Pilot Officer K C		British	43	KIA*
Campbell Pilot Officer N N		Canadian	242	KIA*
Campbell-Colquhoun Flight Lieut E		British	264-66	
Candy Pilot Officer R J		British	25	
Canham Sergeant A W		British	600	
Cannon Sergeant B		British	604	
Capel Sergeant B		British	23	
Capon Pilot Officer C F A		British	257	KIA
Capstick Pilot Officer H		Jamaican	236	DOI
Carbury Flying Officer B J G		N.Zealander	603	
Cardell Pilot Officer P M		British	603	KIA*
Cardnell Pilot Officer C F		British	23	KIA*
Carey Flight Lieut F R		British	43	
Carlin Pilot Officer S		British	264	KIA
Carnaby Flying Officer W F		British	264-85	KIA
Carnall Sergeant R		British	111	
Carpenter(FAA) Sub Lieut. J C		British	229-46	KIA*
Carpenter Pilot Officer J M V		British	222	
Carr Flying Officer W J		British	235	KIA
Carr-Lewty Sergeant R A		British	41	
Carrier Pilot Officer J C		Canadian	219	
Carswell Flying Officer M K		N.Zealander	43	
Carter Pilot Officer V A		British	607	
Carter Sergeant L R		British	610-41	KIA
Carter Pilot Officer C A W		British	611	
Carter Pilot Officer P E G		British	73-302	KIA*
Carthew Pilot Officer G C T		Canadian	253-145	
Carver(FAA) Lieut. R H P		British	804	
Carver Pilot Officer K M		British	229	
Carver Flying Officer J C		British	87	KIA
Case Pilot Officer R		British	64-72	KIA*
Cassidy Flying Officer E		British	25	
Casson Pilot Officer L H		British	616-615	
Castle Sergeant C E P		British	219	KIA
Cawse Pilot Officer F N		British	238	KIA*
Cave Pilot Officer J G		British	600	
Cebrzynski Flying Officer A		Polish	303	KIA*
Chabepa Sergeant F		Czech	312	
Chadwick Sergeant D F		British	64	
Chaffe Pilot Officer R L		British	245-43	KIA
Chalder Pilot Officer H H		British	266-41	KIA*
Chalupa Pilot Officer S J		Polish	310	KIA*
Chamberlain Pilot Officer J T R		British	235	
Chamberlain Wg Cmdr G P		British	FIU	
Chandler Sergeant H H		British	610	
Chapman Sergeant V R		British	246	
Chappell Pilot Officer A K		British	236	
Chappell Pilot Officer C G		British	65	
Chapple Sergeant D W E		British	236	KIA
Chard Sergeant W T		British	141	
Charles Flying Officer E F J		Canadian	54	
Charnock Sergeant G		British	25	
Charnock Sergeant H W		British	64-19	
Chater Flight Lieut G F		Sth. Afr	3	
Cheetham Sergeant J B		British	23	KIA
Chelmecki Pilot Officer M		Polish	257-17-6	
Chesters Pilot Officer P		British	74	KIA
Chetham Pilot Officer C A G		British	1	KIA
Chevrier Pilot Officer J A		Canadian	1	
Chew Sergeant C A		British	17	KIA
Chignell Squad Ldr R A		British	145	KIA
Chilton(FAA) Sub Lieut. P S C		British	804	
Chipping Sergeant D J		British	222	
Chisholm Pilot Officer R E		British	604	
Chlopik Flight Lieut. T P		Polish	302	KIA*
Chomley Pilot Officer J A G		British	257	KIA*
Choran Flight Sergeant		French	64	
Christie Sergeant J McBean		British	152	KIA*
Christie Flight Lieut. G P		British	66-242	KIA
Christmas Pilot Officer B E		British	1(401)	
Chrystall Sergeant C		British	235	
Churches Pilot Officer E W G		British	74	KIA
Churchill Squad Ldr W M		British	605	KIA
Cizek Pilot Officer E		Czech	1	KIA
Clackson Flight Lieut. D L		British	600	
Clandillon Flying Officer J A		British	219	KIA
Clark Pilot Officer H D		British	213	
Clark Sergeant W T M		British	219	
Clark Pilot Officer C A G		Sth. Afr	FIU	KIA
Clark Sergeant G P		British	604	
Clarke Squad Ldr D de B		British	600	
Clarke Sergeant H R		British	610	
Clarke Squad Ldr R N		British	235	KIA
Clarke Pilot Officer A W		British	504	KIA*
Clarke Sergeant G S		British	248	KIA*

128

Name	Nationality	Sqn	Status
Clarke Pilot Officer R W	British	79	KIA
Clarke Sergeant G T	British	151	KIA
Cleaver Flying Officer G N S	British	601	
Clenshaw Sergeant I C C	British	253	KIA*
Clerke Flight Lieut. R F H	British	79	
Clift Flying Officer D G	British	79	
Clifton Pilot Officer J K G	British	253	KIA*
Clouston Squad Ldr A E	N.Zealander	219	
Couston Flight Lieut. W G	N.Zealander	19	
Clowes Pilot Officer A V	British	1	DOI
Clyde Flying Officer W C	British	601	
Coates(FAA) Lieutenant J P	British	804	KIA
Cobden Pilot Officer D G	N.Zealander	74	KIA*
Cochrane Pilot Officer A C	Canadian	257	KIA
Cock Pilot Officer J R	Australian	87	
Cockburn(FAA) Lieut Cmdr J C	British	804	
Cockburn(FAA) Sub Lieut. R C	British	808	
Coggins Pilot Officer J	British	235	KIA
Coghlan Flying Officer J H	British	56	KIA
Coke Flying Officer (Hon) D A	British	257	KIA
Cole Sergeant C F J	British	236	
Coleman Pilot Officer E J	British	54	KIA
Colebrook Pilot Officer	British	54	
Collard Flying Officer P	British	615	KIA*
Collett Sergeant G R	British	54	KIA*
Collingbridge Pilot Officer L W	British	66	
Collins Squadron Ldr A R	British	72	
Collyns Pilot Officer B G	N.Zealander	238	KIA
Comely Pilot Officer P W	British	87	KIA*
Comerford Flight Lt. H A G	British	312	
Compton Sergeant J W	British	25	
Connell Pilot Officer W C	British	32	
Connor Flying Officer F H P	British	234	
Connors Flight Lieut. S D P	British	111	KIA*
Considine Pilot Officer B B	Irish	238	
Constantine Pilot Off'ic A N	Australian	141	KIA
Cook Sergeant A W	British	604	
Cook Sergeant H	British	66-266	
Cook Sergeant R V	British	219	
Cooke Pilot Officer C A	British	66	
Cooke Sergeant H R	British	23	
Coombes Sergeant E	British	219	KIA
Coombs Sergeant R J	British	600	
Cooney Flight Sergeant C J	British	56	KIA*
Coope Squad Ldr W E	British	17	KIA
Cooper Sergeant C F	British	600	KIA*
Cooper Sergeant T A	British	266	
Cooper Sergeant S F	British	253	
Cooper Sergeant D C	British	235	
Cooper Sergeant J E	British	610	KIA
Cooper Sergeant R N	British	610	KIA
Cooper-Key Pilot Officer A M	British	46	KIA*
Cooper-Slipper Pilot Officer T P	British	605	
Coote Sergeant L E M	British	600	KIA
Copcutt Sergeant R	British	248	KIA*
Copeland Sergeant P	British	616-66	KIA
Copeland Sergeant N D	British	235	
Copeman Pilot Officer J H H	British	111	KIA*
Corbett Flight Lieut V B	Canadian	1(401)	
Corbett Pilot Officer G H	Canadian	66	KIA*
Corbin Sergeant W J	British	610-66	
Corcoran Sergeant H	British	236	KIA*
Cordell Sergeant H A	British	64	
Corfe Sergeant D F	British	73-66-610	KIA
Cork(FAA) Sub Lieut. R J	British	242	KIA
Corkett Pilot Officer A H	British	253	
Corner Pilot Officer M C	British	264	DOI
Cory Pilot Officer G W	British	41	
Cory Pilot Officer	British	25	
Cosby Sergeant E T	British	3-615	
Cosby Flight Lieut I H	British	610-72	
Cotes-Preedy Pilot Officer D V C	British	236	
Cottam Sergeant G	British	25	
Cottam Pilot Officer H W	British	213	KIA
Courtis Sergeant J B	N.Zealander	111	
Courtney Flying Officer R N H	British	151	
Coussens Sergeant H W	British	601	
Couzens Pilot Officer G W	British	54	
Coverley Flying Officer W H	British	602	KIA*
Covington Pilot Officer A R	British	238	
Coward Flight Lieut J B	British	19	
Cowen Sergeant W	British	25	
Cowley Sergeant J	British	87	
Cowsill Sergeant J R	British	56	KIA*
Cox Sergeant D G S R	British	19	
Cox Pilot Officer G J	British	152	
Cox Pilot Officer K H	British	610	KIA*
Cox Flying Officer P A N	British	501	KIA*
Cox Sergeant R C R	British	248	KIA*
Cox Sergeant	British	421 Flt	
Cox Sergeant G P	British	236	
Cox Sergeant W E	British	264	KIA
Coxon Sergeant J H	British	141	KIA
Crabtree Sergeant D B	British	501	KIA
Craig Sergeant J T	British	111	KIA
Craig Flying Officer G D	British	607	
Cranwell Sergeant E W	British	610	
Crawford Pilot Officer H H	N.Zealander	235	KIA
Cresty Sergeant K G	British	219	KIA
Creswell Sergeant D G	British	141	KIA
Crew Pilot Officer E D	British	604	
Crise Sergeant J L	British	43	KIA
Crockett Pilot Officer R F	British	236	KIA
Crofts Flying Officer P G	British	615-605	KIA*
Croker Sergeant E E	N.Zealander	111	
Crombie Sergeant R	British	141	KIA*
Crook Pilot Officer D M	British	609	KIA
Crook Sergeant V W	N.Zealander	264	
Crook Sergeant H K	British	219	
Croskell Sergeant M E	British	213	
Crossey Pilot Officer J T	British	249	
Crossley Flight Lieut. M N	British	32	
Crossman Sergeant R	British	25	KIA
Crossman Pilot Officer J D	Australian	46	KIA*
Crowley Pilot Officer H R	British	219-600	
Crowley-Milling Pilot Officer D W	British	242	
Cruikshanks Pilot Off'c I J A	British	66	KIA*
Cruttenden Pilot Officer J	British	43	KIA*
Cryderman Pilot Officer L E	Canadian	242	
Crystall Sergeant C	British	235	

Name	Nationality	Squadron	Status
Cuddie Pilot Officer W A	British	141	KIA
Cukr Sergeant Vaclav Eric	Czech	253	
Cullen Sergeant R W	British	23	
Culmer Sergeant J D	British	25	
Culverwell Sergeant J H	British	87	KIA*
Cumbers Sergeant A B	British	141	
Cunningham Flight Lieut J L G	British	603	KIA*
Cunningham Flight Lieut. W	British	19	
Cunningham Flight Lieut. J	British	604	
Cunningham Sergeant J	British	29	
Cunnington Sergeant W G	British	607	KIA
Cupitt Sergeant T	British	29	
Curchin Pilot Officer J	British	609	KIA
Curley Sergeant A G	British	141	KIA*
Currant Pilot Officer C F	British	605	
Curtis Sergeant F W	British	25	
Cutts Flying Officer J W	British	222	KIA*
Czajkowskiai Pilot Officer F	Polish	151	KIA
Czerniak Pilot Officer J M	Polish	302	KIA
Czernin Fling Officer Count M B	British	17	DOI
Czerny Flight Lieut H	Polish	302	
Czerwinski Flying Officer T	Polish	302	KIA
Czternastek Pilot Officer	Polish	32	
Dafforn Flying Officer R C	British	501	KIA
Dalton Sergeant R W	British	604	
Dalton-Morgan Flight Lieut. T F	British	43	
Daly Sergeant J J	British	141	
Dann Sergeant J E	British	23	
Dannatt Sergeant A G	British	29	
D'Arcy-Irvine Flying Officer B W J	British	257	KIA*
Dargie Sergeant A M S	British	23	KIA
Darley Squadron Leader H S	British	609	
Darling Sergeant A S	British	611-603	KIA
Darling Sergeant E V	British	41	KIA
Darwin Pilot Officer C W W	British	87	KIA
Daszewski Pilot Officer J	Polish	303	
Davey Pilot Officer B	British	257-32	KIA
Davey Pilot Officer J A J	British	1	KIA*
David Pilot Officer W D	British	87-213	
Davidson Sergeant H J	British	249	KIA
Davies Pilot Officer R B	British	29	
Davies Pilot Officer A E	British	222	KIA*
Davies Pilot Officer C G A	British	222	
Davies Sergeant M P	British	1-213	KIA
Davies Flight Lieut J A	British	604	KIA
Davies Flying Officer P F M	British	56	
Davies Sergeant L	British	151	
Davies-Cooke Pilot Officer P J	British	72-610	KIA*
Davis Sergeant	British	222	KIA
Davis Flight Lieut C R	American	601	KIA*
Davis Flying Officer C T	British	238	KIA
Davis Sergeant W L	British	249	
Davis Sergeant J N	British	600	
Davis Sergeant J	British	54	
Davis Sergeant P E	British	236	
Davis Sergeant A S	British	235	
Davison Pilot Officer	British	235	
Davy Pilot Officer T D H	British	72-266	KIA
Daw Pilot Officer V G	British	32	KIA
Dawbarn Pilot Officer P L	British	17	
Dawick Sergeant K	N.Zealander	111	
Dawson Sergeant T	British	235	
Dawson-Paul(FAA) Sub Lieut F	British	64	KIA*
Day Pilot Officer R L F	British	141	KIA
Day Sergeant F S	British	248	KIA
Deacon Sergeant A H	British	85-111	
Deacon-Elliott Pilot Officer R	British	72	
Deansley Flight Lieut. E C	British	152	
Debenham Pilot Officer K B L	British	151	KIA
Debree Pilot Officer	British	264	
Dee Sergeant O J	British	235	KIA
Deere Flight Lieut A L	N.Zealander	54	
De Grunne Pilot Officer R C C	Belgian	32	KIA
De Jace Pilot Officer L J	Belgian	236	KIA
De La Boucher War't Of F H	Fr. French	85	KIA
De La Perrele Pilot Officer V B	N.Zealander	245	
Deller Sergeant A L M	British	43	
De Mancha Pilot Officer R A	British	43	KIA*
Demetriadi Flying Officer R S	British	601	KIA*
Demoulin Sergeant R J G	Belgian	236	
De Mozay 2nd Lieut J E	French	1	
Denby Pilot Officer G A	British	600	KIA
Denchfield Sergeant H D	British	610	
Denholm Squad Ldr G L	British	603	
Denison Flight Lieut R W	British	236	KIA
Denton Sergeant D A	British	236	KIA
Derbyshire Pilot Officer J M	British	236	
Dermott Pilot Officer	British	600	
De Scitivaux Cpt. C J M P	French	245	
Desloges Flying Officer	Canadian	1(401)	
De Spirlet Pilot Officer V X E	Belgian	87	KIA
Deuntzer Sergeant D C	British	247	
Devitt Squad Ldr P K	British	152	
Dewar Wing Com J S	British	87-213	KIA*
Dewar Pilot Officer J M F	British	229	KIA
Dewey Pilot Officer R B	British	611-603	KIA*
Dewhurst Flying Officer K S	British	234	
Dexter Pilot Officer P G	British	603-54	KIA
Dibnah Pilot Officer R H	Canadian	1-242	
Dickie Pilot Officer W G	British	601	KIA*
Dickinson Sergeant J H	British	253	KIA*
Dieu Pilot Officer G E F	Belgian	236	
Difford Flying Officer I B	Sth. Afr	607	KIA*
Digby-Worsley Sgt M P	British	248	KIA*
Ditzel Sergeant J W	British	25	
Dixon Sergeant F J P	British	501	KIA*
Dixon Pilot Officer J A	British	1	
Dixon Sergeant C A W	British	601	
Dixon Sergeant G	British	FIU	
Dixon Sergeant L	British	600	
Dodd Pilot Officer J D	British	248	KIA
Dodge Sergeant C W	British	219	
Doe Pilot Officer R F T	British	234-238	
Dolezal Pilot Officer F	Czech	19	
Domagala Sergeant M	Polish	238	
Don Pilot Officer R S	British	501	KIA
Donahue Pilot Officer A G	American	64	KIA
Donald Flight Lieut I D G	British	141	KIA*
Donaldson Squad. Ldr E M	British	151	

Name	Nationality	Squadron	Status
Dossett Sergeant W S	British	29	
Doughty Pilot Officer N A R	British	247	
Douglas Pilot Officer W A	British	610	
Doulton Pilot Officer M D	British	601	KIA*
Douthwaite Pilot Officer B	British	72	
Doutrepont Pilot Officer G L J	Belgian	229	KIA*
Dowding Pilot Officer (Hon) D H T	British	74	
Down Pilot Officer P D M	British	56	
Draby Sergeant	British	25	
Drake Pilot Officer G J	Sth. Afr	607	KIA*
Drake Flying Officer B	British	213-1	
Draper Pilot Officer B V	British	74	KIA
Draper Flying Officer G G F	British	41-610	
Draper Flying Officer R A	British	232	
Dredge Sergeant A S	British	253	KIA
Drever Flying Officer N G	British	610	
Drew Squad Ldr P E	British	236	KIA*
Drobinski Pilot Officer B H	Polish	65	
Drummond Flying Officer J F	British	46-92	KIA*
Duart Pilot Officer J H	British	219	
Dubber(FAA) Pilot Officer R E	British	808	DOI
Duckenfield Pilot Officer B L	British	501	
Duda Pilot Officer J	Czech	312	
Duff Pilot Officer S S	British	23	
Duke-Woolley Flight Lieut R M B D	British	253-23	
Dulwich Sergeant W H	British	235	KIA
Duncan Sergeant	British	29	
Dundas Pilot Officer J C	British	609	KIA
Dundas Flying Officer H S L	British	616	
Dunlop-Urie Flight Lieut J	British	602	
Dunmore Sergeant J T	British	22	KIA
Dunn Sergeant I L	British	235	
Dunning-White Flying Officer P W	British	145	
Dunscombe Sergeant R D	British	213-312	KIA
Dunworth Squad Ldr T P R	British	66-54	
Dupee Sergeant O A	British	219	
Durrant Sergeant C R	N.Zealander	23	KIA
Duryasz Flight Lieut M	Polish	213	
Duszynski Sergeant S	Polish	238	KIA*
Dutton Squad Ldr R G	British	145	
Dutton Sergeant G W	British	604	
Du Vivier Pilot Officer R A L	Belgian	229	KIA
Dvorak Sergeant A	Czech	310	KIA
Dye Sergeant B E	British	219	KIA
Dyer Sergeant	N.Zealander	600	
Dygryn Sergeant J	Czech	1	
Dyke Sergeant L A	British	64	KIA*
Dymond Sergeant W L	British	111	KIA*
Eade Sergeant A W	British	266-602	
Earp Sergeant R L	British	46	
Easton Sergeant D A	British	248	
Eckford Flight Lieut. A F	British	23-253-242	
Edge Flight Lieut G R	British	253-605	
Edge Flying Officer A R	British	609	
Edgley Sergeant A	British	601-253	
Edgworthy Sergeant G H	British	46	KIA*
Edmiston Pilot Officer G A F	British	151	
Edmond Pilot Officer N D	Canadian	615	KIA*
Edmunds Pilot Officer E R	N.Zealander	245-615	
Edridge Pilot Officer H P M	British	222	KIA*
Edsall Pilot Officer E F	British	54-222	DOI
Edwards Flying Officer R L	Canadian	1401)	KIA*
Edwards Pilot Officer H D	Canadian	92	KIA*
Edwards Sergeant F	British	29	
Edwards Sergeant	British	204	
Edwards Pilot Officer K C	British	600	
Edwards Sergeant H H	British	248	
Edwards Pilot Officer I N	British	234	
Edwards Flight Lieut R S J	Irish	56	
Edwards Sergeant	British	247	
Edworthy Sergeant G H	British	46	KIA*
Edy Pilot Officer A L	British	602	KIA
Egan Sergeant E J	British	600-501	KIA*
Eiby Pilot Officer W T	N.Zealander	245	
Ekins Sergeant V H	British	111-501	
Elcombe Sergeant D W	British	602	KIA*
Eley Sergeant F W	British	74	KIA*
Elger Pilot Officer F R C	Canadian	248	
Eliot Pilot Officer H W	British	73	KIA
Elkington Pilot Officer J F D	British	1	
Ellacombe Pilot Officer J L W	British	151	
Ellery Pilot Officer C C	British	264	
Elliott Flying Officer G J	Canadian	607	
Ellis Sergeant R V	British	73	
Ellis Flight Lieut J	British	610	
Ellis Sergeant J H M	British	85	KIA*
Ellis Sergeant W T	British	92	
Ellis Flying Officer G E	British	64	
Elsdon Flying Officer T A F	British	72	
Elsdon Sergeant H D B	British	236	KIA*
Else Sergeant P	British	610	
Emeny Sergeant C	N.Zealander	264	
Emmett Flying Officer W A C	British	25	KIA*
Emmett Sergeant G	British	236	
English Pilot Officer C E	British	85-605	KIA*
Ensor Flying Officer P S B	British	23	KIA
Etherington Sergeant W J	British	17	
Evans Pilot Officer H A C	British	236	
Evans Sergeant W R	British	85-249	
Evans Pilot Officer D	British	607-615	KIA
Evans Sergeant C R	British	235	KIA
Evans Sergeant G J	British	604	
Everitt Sergeant G C	British	29	KIA
Everitt Sergeant A D	British	235	
Eyles Sergeant P R	British	92	KIA*
Eyre Flying Officer A	British	615	KIA
Fajtl Flight Lieut. F	Czech	17-17	
Falkowskj Flying Officer J P	Polish	32	
Farley Flight Lieut	British	151-46	
Farmer Flight Lieut J N W	British	302	
Farnes Sergeant P C P	British	501	
Farnes Pilot Officer E	British	141	
Farquhar Wing Com A D	British	257	
Farrow Sergeant J R	British	1-229	KIA*
Farthing Sergeant J	British	235	
Fawcett Sergeant D R	British	29	KIA
Fayolle Warrant Officer F E	Fr. French	85	KIA
Feary Sergeant A N	British	609	KIA*

Name	Nationality	Squadron	Status
Feather Sergeant J L	British	235	KIA*
Fechtner Pilot Officer E	Czech	310	KIA*
Fejfar Flying Officer S	Czech	310	KIA
Fenmore Sergeant S A	British	245-501	KIA*
Fenn Sergeant C F	British	248	
Fenton Squad Ldr H A	British	238	
Fenton Sergeant	British	604	
Fenton Pilot Officer J O	British	235	KIA
Fenwick Pilot Officer C R	British	601	
Fenwick Flying Officer	British	601	
Ferdinand Pilot Officer R F	British	263	KIA
Ferguson Sergeant E H	British	141	KIA
Ferguson Flying Officer P J	British	602	
Feric Pilot Officer M	Polish	303	
Ferriss Flight Lieut H M	British	111	KIA*
Fildes Sergeant F	British	25	
Finch Flying Officer T R H	British	151	
Finlay Squad Ldr D O	British	41-54	
Finnie Pilot Officer A	British	54	KIA*
Finnis Flight Lieut. J F F	British	1-229	
Finucane Pilot Officer B E	Irish	65	KIA
Fisher Pilot Officer A G A	British	111	
Fisher Pilot Officer G	British	602	
Fisher Flying Officer B M	British	111	KIA*
Fiske Pilot Officer W M L	American	601	KIA*
Fitzgerald Flight Lieut. T B	N.Zealander	141	
Fizell Sergeant J F	British	29	
Fleming Pilot Officer J	British	605	
Fleming Pilot Officer R D S	British	249	KIA*
Fletcher Sergeant J G B	British	604	KIA*
Fletcher Flight Lieut. A W	Canadian	235	
Fletcher Sergeant	British	3	
Fletcher Sergeant W T	N.Zealander	23	
Flinders Pilot Officer J L	British	32	
Flood Flight Lieut F W	Australian	235	KIA*
Flower Sergeant H L	British	248	
Foglar Sergeant V	Czech	245	
Fott Pilot Officer E A	Czech	310	
Fokes Sergeant R H	British	92	KIA
Folliard Sergeant J H	British	604	
Fopp Sergeant D	British	17	
Forbes Squad Ldr A S	British	303-66	
Ford Sergeant R C	British	41	
Ford Sergeant E G	British	3-232	KIA
Forde Flying Officer D N	British	145-605	
Forrest Sergeant D H	British	66	
Forrester Pilot Officer G M	British	605	KIA*
Forshaw Flying Officer T H T	British	609	
Forster Flying Officer A D	British	151-607	
Forsyth Sergeant C L M	N.Zealander	23	KIA
Forward Sergeant R V	British	257	
Foster Pilot Officer R W	British	605	
Fotheringham Sergeant	British	3	
Fowler Sergeant R J	British	247	
Fowler Flying Officer A L	British	248	KIA
Fox Sergeant P H	British	56	
Fox Sergeant L	British	29	
Foxley-Norris Flying Officer C N	British	3	
Fox-Male Pilot Officer D H	British	152	
Francis Pilot Officer C D	British	253	KIA*
Francis Sergeant D N	British	257	
Francis Sergeant C W	British	74	
Francis Sergeant J	British	23	
Francis Sergeant	British	3	
Francis Pilot Officer N I C	British	247	KIA
Franklin Flying Officer W D K	British	74	
Franklin Pilot Officer W H	British	65	KIA
Frantisek Sergeant J	Czech	303	KIA*
Fraser Sergeant R H B	British	257	KIA*
Freeborn Flight Lieut. J C	British	74	
Freeman Sergeant R R	British	29	
Freer Sergeant P F	British	29	KIA
Freese Sergeant L E	British	611-74	KIA
French Sergeant T L	British	29	KIA
Frey Flight Lieut J A	Polish	607	
Friend Sergeant J R	British	25	KIA
Friendship Pilot Officer A H B	British	3	
Fripp Sergeant J H	British	248	
Frisby Pilot Officer E M	British	504	KIA
Frith Sergeant E T G	British	611-92	KIA*
Frizell Pilot Officer C G	Canadian	257	
Frost Pilot Officer J L	British	600	
Fulford Sergeant D	British	64	KIA
Fulford Sergeant	British	19	
Fumerton Pilot Officer R C	Canadian	32	
Furneaux Sergeant R H	British	3-73	
Furst Sergeant B	Czech	310-605	
Gabszewicz Flying Officer A	Polish	607	
Gadd Sergeant Pilot J	British	611	
Gage Pilot Officer D H	British	602	KIA
Gallus Sergeant	British	3	
Gamblen Flying Officer D R	British	41	KIA*
Gane Pilot Officer S R	British	248	KIA*
Gant Sergeant E	British	236	
Gardiner Flying Officer F T	British	610	KIA
Gardiner Sergeant G C	British	219	KIA*
Gardiner Sergeant W M	British	3	
Gardner Sergeant B G D	British	610	KIA
Gardner Pilot Officer P M	British	32	
Gardner(FAA) Sub Lieut. R E	British	242	
Gardner Pilot Officer J R	British	141	
Garfield Sergeant W J	British	248	KIA*
Garrard Pilot Officer A H H	British	248	KIA
Garside Sergeant G	British	236	
Garton Sergeant G W	British	73	
Garvey Sergeant L A	British	41	KIA*
Garvin Squad Ldr G D	British	264	
Gash Sergeant F	British	264	
Gaskell Pilot Officer R S	British	264	
Gaunce Flight Lieut L M	Canadian	615	KIA
Gaunt Pilot Officer G N	British	609	KIA*
Gaunt Sergeant W D	British	23	
Gavan Sergeant A	British	54	
Gawith Pilot Officer A A	N.Zealander	23	
Gayner Flying Officer J R H	British	615	
Gear Sergeant A W	British	32	
Geddes Pilot Officer K I	British	604	
Gee Sergeant V D	British	219	KIA
Genney Pilot Officer T	British	604	KIA

Name	Nationality	Squadron	Status
Gent Sergeant R J K	British	501-32	KIA
Gibbins Sergeant D G	British	54-222	
Gibbons Sergeant C M	British	236	
Gibson Flight Lieut. J A A	British	501	
Giddings Flight Lieut H S	British	615-111	KIA
Gil Pilot Officer J	Polish	229-43	
Gilbert Pilot Officer E G	British	64	
Gilbert(FAA) Midship' P R J	British	111	
Gilbert Pilot Officer H T	British	601	KIA
Gilders Sergeant J S	British	72	KIA
Gill Sergeant J V	British	23	KIA
Gillam Flight Lieut D E	British	312-616	
Gillam Sergeant E	British	248	KIA
Gillan Flying Officer J	British	601	KIA*
Gillen Flying Officer T W	British	247	
Gillespie Pilot Officer J L	British	23	KIA
Gillies Sergeant	British	421 Flt	
Gillies Flight Sergeant J	British	602	KIA
Gillies Flight Lieut K M	British	66	KIA*
Gillman Pilot Officer K R	British	32	KIA*
Gilroy Pilot Officer G K	British	603	
Gilyeat Sergeant H R	British	29	
Girdwood Sergeant A G	British	257	KIA*
Glaser Pilot Officer E D	British	65	
Gleave Squad Ldr T P	British	253	
Gledhill Sergeant G	British	238	KIA*
Gleed Flight Lieut I R	British	87	KIA
Glegg Pilot Officer A J	British	600	
Glendenning Sergeant J N	British	54-74	KIA
Glew Sergeant N	British	72	KIA
Glowacki Sergeant W J	Polish	605-145	KIA*
Glowacki Sergeant A	Polish	501	KIA*
Glyde Flying Officer R L	Australian	87	KIA*
Gmur Sergeant F	Polish	151	KIA*
Gnys Pilot Officer W	Polish	302	
Goddard Flight Lieut H G	British	219	
Goddard Pilot Officer W B	British	235	KIA
Godden Squad Ldr S F	British	3	
Goldsmith Flying Officer C W	Sth. Afr	54-603	KIA*
Goldsmith Sergeant J E	British	236	KIA

Name	Nationality	Squadron	Status
Gonay Pilot Officer H A C	Belgian	235	KIA
Goodall Pilot Officer H I	British	264	KIA*
Gooderham Sergeant A T	British	46	
Gooderham Sergeant A J	British	25	KIA
Goodman Sergeant G	British	85	
Goodman Pilot Officer G E	Palestinian	1	KIA
Goodman Sergeant M V	British	604	
Goodwin Pilot Officer H	British	609	KIA*
Goodwin Sergeant C	British	219	KIA*
Goodwin Sergeant S A	British	266	
Goodwin Sergeant R D	British	64	
Gordon Squad Ldr J A G	Canadian	151	KIA
Gordon Pilot Officer W H G	British	234	KIA*
Gordon Sergeant S	British	235	KIA
Gore Flight Lieut W E	British	607	KIA*
Gorrie Pilot Officer D G	British	43	KIA
Gorzula Pilot Officer M	Polish	607	
Gosling Pilot Officer R C	British	266	
Goth Pilot Officer V	Czech	501-310	KIA*
Gothorpe Sergeant	British	25	
Gould Pilot Officer D L	British	601-607	
Gould Flying Officer C L	British	607-32	KIA
Gould Sergeant G L	British	235	
Gouldstone Sergeant R J	British	29	KIA*
Gout Pilot Officer G K	British	234	KIA*
Gowers Pilot Officer A V	British	85	KIA
Gracie Flight Lieut E J	British	56	KIA
Graham Flight Lieut E	British	72	
Graham Pilot Officer L W	Sth. Afr	56	
Graham Sergeant J	British	236	KIA
Graham Pilot Officer K A G	British	600	KIA
Grandy Squad Ldr J	British	249	
Grant Sergeant E J F	British	600	KIA
Grant Pilot Officer S B	British	65	
Grant Sergeant	N.Zealander	151	
Grant(FAA) Sub Lieut. M D	British	804	
Grassick Pilot Officer R D	Canadian	242	
Graves Sergeant	British	235	
Graves Pilot Officer R C	British	253	
Gray Flying Officer A P	British	615	

Name	Nationality	Squadron	Status
Gray Pilot Officer C F	British	54	
Gary Pilot Officer C K	British	43	
Gray Pilot Officer D McT	British	610	KIA
Gray Sergeant M	British	72	KIA*
Gray Sergeant E W	British	85	KIA
Gray Pilot Officer T	British	64	
Grayson Flight Sergeant C	British	213	KIA
Green Flight Lieut C P	British	421 Flt	
Green Sergeant S J	British	501	
Greene Pilot Officer M D	British	248	KIA*
Green Pilot Officer W V	British	235	KIA*
Green Sergeant H E	British	141	
Green Sergeant G G	British	236	
Green Sergeant F W W	British	600	
Greenwood Pilot Officer J D B	British	253	
Greenshields(FAA)			
Sub Lieut H la Fore	British	266	KIA*
Gregory Pilot Officer F S	British	65	KIA*
Gregory Sergeant A E	British	219	
Gregory Sergeant A H	British	111	KIA
Gregory Sergeant W J	British	29	
Grellis Pilot Officer H E	British	23	DOI
Gretton Sergeant R H	British	266-222	
Gribble Pilot Officer D G	British	54	KIA*
Grice Pilot Officer D H	British	32	
Grice Pilot Officer D H	British	600	KIA*
Gridley Sergeant R V	British	235	KIA
Grier Pilot Officer T	British	601	KIA
Griffen Sergeant J J	British	73	KIA
Griffiths Sergeant G	British	17-601	
Griffiths Sergeant	British	32	
Grogan Pilot Officer G J	Irish	23	
Groszewski Flying Officer	Polish	43	
Grove Sergeant H C	British	501-213	KIA
Grubb Sergeant D G	British	219	
Grubb Sergeant H F	British	219	
Gruszka Flying Officer F	Polish	65	KIA*
Grzeszczak Flying Officer B	Polish	303	
Guerin Adjutant C	Fr. French	232	KIA
Guest Pilot Officer T F	British	56	

Name	Nationality	Squadron	Status
Gundry Pilot Officer K C	British	257	KIA
Gunn Pilot Officer H R	British	74	KIA*
Gunning Pilot Officer P S	British	46	KIA*
Gunter Pilot Officer E M	British	43-501	KIA*
Gurteen Pilot Officer J V	British	504	KIA*
Guthrie(FAA) Sub Lieut. G C M	British	808	
Guthrie Sergeant N H	British	604	
Guy(FAA) Midshipman P	British	808	KIA
Guy Sergeant L N	British	601	KIA*
Guymer Sergeant E N L	British	238	
Hackwood Pilot Officer G H	British	264	KIA
Haig Pilot Officer J G E	British	603	
Haigh Sergeant C	British	604	KIA*
Haine Pilot Officer R C	British	600	
Haines Flying Officer L A	British	19	KIA
Haire Sergeant J K	British	145	KIA
Hairs Pilot Officer P R	British	501	
Hall Pilot Officer R M D	British	152	
Hall Flight Lieut N M	British	257	KIA*
Hall Pilot Officer R C	British	219	
Hall Sergeant	British	235	
Hall Sergeant	British	29	
Hall Pilot Officer W C	British	248	KIA
Hallam Flying Officer I L McG	British	222	KIA
Halliwell Pilot Officer A B	British	141	
Hallowes Sergeant H J L	British	43	
Halton Sergeant D W	British	615	KIA*
Hamale Sergeant R E de J'a	Belgian	46	KIA
Hamar Pilot Officer J R	British	151	KIA*
Hamblin Wing Com	British	17	
Hamer Sergeant	British	141	
Hamill Pilot Officer J W	N.Zealander	299	KIA
Hamilton Flight Lieut. H R	Canadian	85	KIA*
Hamilton Sergeant J S	British	248	KIA
Hamilton Sergeant C B	British	219	KIA
Hamilton Pilot Officer A L	Australian	248	
Hamilton Pilot Officer A C	British	141	KIA*
Hamilton Pilot Officer C E	British	234	KIA
Hamlyn Sergeant R F	British	610	
Hammerton Sergeant J	British	615	KIA
Hammerton Sergeant J	British	3	KIA
Hammond Pilot Officer D J	British	253-245	
Hampshire Sergeant C W	British	85-111-249	
Hanbury Pilot Officer B A	British	1	
Hanbury Pilot Officer O V	British	602	KIA
Hancock Pilot Officer N P W	British	1	
Hancock Pilot Officer N E	British	152-65	
Hancock Pilot Officer E L	British	609	
Hannon Pilot Officer G H	British	236	
Hanson Flying Officer D H W	British	17	KIA*
Hanus Pilot Officer J	Czech	310	
Hanzlicek Sergeant O	Czech	312	KIA*
Hardacre Flying Officer J R	British	504	KIA*
Hardcastle Sergeant J	British	219	KIA
Hardie Sergeant	British	232	
Harding Sergeant N D	British	29	
Harding Flying Officer N M	British	23	KIA
Hardman Pilot Officer H G	British	111	
Hardwick Sergeant W R H	British	600	
Hardy Pilot Officer R	British	234	
Hardy Sergeant O A	British	264	
Hare Sergeant M	British	245	
Hargreaves Pilot Officer F N	British	92	KIA*
Harket Sergeant A S	British	234	
Harkness Squad Ldr H	Irish	257	
Harnett Flying Officer T P	Canadian	219	
Harper Flight Lieut W J	British	17	
Harris Pilot Officer P A	British	3	KIA
Harrison Sergeant A R J	British	219	
Harrison Pilot Officer J H	British	145	KIA*
Harrison Pilot Officer D S	British	238	KIA*
Harrold Pilot Officer F C	British	151-501	KIA*
Hart Flying Officer J S	Canadian	602-54	
Hart Pilot Officer K G	British	65	KIA
Hart Pilot Officer N	Canadian	242	KIA
Hartas Pilot Officer P McD	British	603-421 Flt	KIA
Harvey Sergeant L W	British	54	
Hastings Pilot Officer D	British	74	KIA*
Hatton Sergeant	British	604	
Havercroft Sergeant R E	British	92	
Haviland Pilot Officer J K	American	151	
Haviland Pilot Officer R H	Sth. Afr	248	KIA
Haw Sergeant C	British	504	
Hawke Sergeant P S	British	64	
Hawke Sergeant S N	British	604	KIA
Hawkings Sergeant R P	British	601	KIA*
Hawley Sergeant F B	British	266	KIA*
Haworth Flying Officer J F J	British	43	KIA*
Hay Flying Officer I B D E	Sth. Afr	611	
Hay(FAA) Lieutenant R C	British	808	
Hayden Sergeant L H	British	264	
Hayes Squad Ldr	British	242	
Hayes Flying Officer T N	British	600	
Haylock Sergeant R A	British	236	
Hayson Flight Lieut G D L	British	79	
Hayter Flying Officer J C F	N.Zealander	605-615	
Haywood Sergeant D	British	504	
Haywood Sergeant D	British	151	
Head Sergeant F A P	British	236	KIA*
Head Sergeant G M	British	219	KIA
Heal Pilot Officer P W D	British	604	
Healy Sergeant T W R	British	41-611	KIA
Heath Flying Officer B	British	611	
Hebron Pilot Officer G S	British	235	
Hedges Pilot Officer A L	British	245-257	
Heimes Sergeant L	British	235	
Helcke Sergeant D A	British	504	KIA*
Hellyer Flight Lieut R O	British	616	
Hemingway Pilot Officer J A	Irish	85	
Hemptinne Pilot Officer B M de	Belgian	145	KIA
Henderson Pilot Officer J A McD	British	257	
Hendry Pilot Officer D O	British	219	
Henn Sergeant W B	British	501	
Henneberg Flying Officer Z	Polish	303	
Henson Sergeant B	British	32-257	KIA
Henstock Flight Lieut. L F	British	64	
Heron Pilot Officer H M T	British	266-66	
Herrick Pilot Officer M J	British	25	KIA*
Herrick Pilot Officer B H	N.Zealander	236	KIA

Name	Rank	Nationality	Squadron	Status
Heslop Sergeant V W	British	56	
Hess Pilot Officer A	Czech	310	
Hetherington Sergeant E L	British	601	KIA
Hewett Sergeant G A	British	607	
Hewitt Pilot Officer D A	Canadian	501	KIA*
Hewlett Sergeant C R	British	65	KIA
Heycock Squad Ldr G F W	British	23	
Heywood Pilot Officer N B	British	32-607-257	KIA*
Heyworth Squad Ldr J H	British	79	
Hick Sergeant D T	British	32	
Higgins Sergeant W B	British	253-32	KIA*
Higginson Flight Sgt. F W	British	56	
Higgs Flying Officer T P K	British	111	K*
Hight Pilot Officer C H	N.Zealander	234	KIA*
Hiles Pilot Officer A H	British	236	KIA
Hilken Sergeant C G	British	74	
Hill Pilot Officer H P	British	92	KIA*
Hill Squad Ldr J H	British	222	
Hill Pilot Officer S J	British	609	KIA
Hill Pilot Officer M R	Sth. Afr	266	KIA
Hill Sergeant C R	N.Zealander	141	
Hill Pilot Officer A E	British	248	KIA
Hill Sergeant A M	British	25	
Hill Sergeant G	British	65	
Hill Pilot Officer G E	British	245	KIA
Hillary Pilot Officer R H	British	603	KIA
Hillcoat Flight Lieut. H B L	British	1	KIA*
Hillock Pilot Officer F W	Canadian	1(401)	
Hillman Sergeant R W	British	235	KIA
Hillwood Sergeant P	British	56	
Himr Pilot Officer J J	Czech	56	KIA
Hindrup Sergeant F G	N.Zealander	600	
Hine Sergeant	British	65	
Hird Sergeant L	British	604	KIA
Hithersay Sergeant A J B	British	141	
Hlavac Sergeant J	Czech	56	KIA*
Hlobil Pilot Officer A	Czech	312	
Hoare-Scott Pilot Officer J H	British	601	KIA
Hobbis Pilot Officer D O	British	219	KIA
Hobbs Sergeant S J	British	235	KIA
Hobbs Pilot Officer J B	British	3	KIA
Hobbs Sergeant W H	British	25	
Hobson Pilot Officer C A	British	600	KIA*
Hobson Squad Ldr W F C	British	601	
Hobson Flight Lieut. D B	British	64	
Hoods Sergeant W H	British	25	
Hodge Sergeant J S A	British	141	KIA
Hodgkinson Pilot Officer A J	British	219	KIA
Hodgson Pilot Officer W T	N.Zealander	85	KIA
Hodson Sergeant C G	British	229-1	
Hogan Squad Ldr H A V	British	501	
Hogg Flying Officer E S	British	152	
Hogg Sergeant R D	British	17-257-56	KIA*
Hogg Pilot Officer R M	British	152	KIA*
Hogg Pilot Officer D W	British	25	KIA*
Hogg Sergeant J H	British	141	KIA
Hogg Sergeant R V	British	616	KIA
Holden Flight Lieut E	British	501	KIA
Holden Pilot Officer K	British	616	
Holder Sergeant R	N.Zealander	151	KIA*
Holder Pilot Officer G A	British	151	KIA
Holderness Flight Lieut. J B	S. Rhodesian	1-229	
Holland Squad Ldr A L	British	501-65	
Holland Pilot Officer D F	British	72	KIA*
Holland Sergeant K C	Australian	152	KIA*
Holland Pilot Officer R H	British	92	KIA
Holland Sergeant R M	British	600	
Hollis Sergeant E J	British	25	
Holloway Sergeant S V	British	25	
Hollowell Sergeant K B	British	25	
Holmes Pilot Officer F H	British	152	KIA*
Holmes Sergeant R T	British	504	
Holmes Pilot Officer G H	British	600	KIA
Holmes Sergeant G	British	25	
Holmes Sergeant E L	British	248	KIA
Holroyd Sergeant W B	British	501-151	
Holton Sergeant A G V	British	141	
Homer Flying Officer M G	British	242-1	KIA*
HOne Pilot Officer D H	British	615	
Honor Flying Officer D S G	British	145	
Hood Squad Ldr H R L	British	41	KIA*
Hook Sergeant A	British	248	KIA
Hookway Pilot Officer D N	British	234	
Hooper Flying Officer B G	British	25	
Hope Flying Officer R	British	605	KIA*
Hope Flight Lieut. Sir A P	British	601	
Hopewell Sergeant J	British	616-66	KIA
Hopgood Sergeant	British	64	
Hopkin Pilot Officer W P	British	54-602	
Hopton Sergeant B W	British	73	KIA
Hornby Sergeant W H	British	234	
Horner Sergeant F G	British	610	
Horrox Flying Officer J M	British	151	KIA
Horsky Sergeant V	Czech	238	KIA*
Horton Flying Officer P W	N.Zealander	234	KIA
Hough Pilot Officer H B L	British	600	KIA
Houghton Pilot Officer C G	British	141	
Houghton Sergeant O V	British	501	KIA*
Howard Pilot Officer J	British	74-54	KIA
Howard Sergeant	British	235	
Howard-Williams Pilot Officer P I	British	19	
Howarth Sergeant E F	British	501	KIA
Howe Pilot Officer B	British	25	KIA
Howe Pilot Officer D C	British	235	
Howell Flight Lieut F J	British	609	KIA
Howell Sergeant F	British	87	
Howes Pilot Officer P	British	54-603	KIA*
Howes Sergeant H N	British	85-605	KIA
Howitt Pilot Officer G L	British	615-245	
Howitt Sergeant I E	British	41	
Howley Pilot Officer R A	Canadian	141	KIA*
Hoyle Sergeant H N	British	257	
Hoyle Sergeant G V	British	232	KIA
Hradil Pilot Officer F	Czech	19-310	KIA
Hruby Pilot Officer O	Czech	111	
Hubacek Sergeant J	Czech	310	
Hubbard Flying Officer T E	British	601	
Hubbard Sergeant B F R	British	235	KIA
Huckin Sergeant P E	British	600	
Hughes Flight Lieut. J McM	British	25	KIA

Name	Nationality	Squadron	KIA
Hughes Flight Lieut. D P	British	238	KIA*
Hughes Pilot Officer F D	British	264	
Hughes Flight Lieut. P C	Australian	234	KIA*
Hughes Sergeant D E	N.Zealander	600	KIA*
Hughes Flight Sergeant W R	British	23	
Hughes Pilot Officer D L	British	141	
Hughes Sergeant A J	British	245	
Hughes-Rees Sergeant J	British	609	KIA
Hugo Pilot Officer P H	Sth. Afr	615	
Hulbert Sergeant F H R	British	601	
Hulbert Sergeant D J	British	257-501	
Hull Flight Lieut C B	Sth. Afr	263-43	KIA*
Humpherson Flying Officer J B W	British	32-607	KIA
Humphrey Pilot Officer A H	British	266	
Humphreys Pilot Officer J S	N.Zealander	605	
Humphreys Pilot Officer P C	British	32	
Humphreys Pilot Officer J D	British	29	KIA
Humphreys Flying Officer P H	British	152	KIA
Hunt Sergeant D A C	British	66	
Hunt Pilot Officer D W	British	257	
Hunt Pilot Officer H N	British	504	KIA
Hunter Flight Lieut.	British	600	
Hunter Squad Ldr P A	British	264	KIA*
Hunter Sergeant	British	604	KIA
Hunter Sergeant D J	British	29	
Hunter Pilot Officer A S	British	604	KIA
Hunter-Tod Flight Lieut	British	23	
Hurry Sergeant C A L	British	43-46	
Hurst Pilot Officer P R S	British	600	KIA*
Hutchinson Sergeant I	British	222	
Hutchinson(FAA) Sub Lieut D A	British	804	KIA
Hutley Pilot Officer R R	British	32-213	KIA*
Hutton Sergeant R S	British	85	KIA
Hybler Pilot Officer J	Czech	310	
Hyde Sergeant R J	British	66	
Hyde Pilot Officer J W	British	229	
Hyde Flying Officer	Canadian	1(401)	
Ievers Flight Lieut N L	Irish	312	
Igglesden Flying Officer C P	British	234	
Imray Sergeant H S	British	600	
Ingle Flying Officer A	British	605	
Ingle-Finch Pilot Officer M R	British	607-151-56	
Innes Sergeant R A	British	253	
Inness Pilot Officer R F	British	152	
Inniss Flying Officer A R de H	British	236	
Irving Flight Lieut M M	British	607	KIA*
Isherwood Sergeant D W	British	29	
Isaac Sergeant L R	British	64	KIA*
Iveson Sergeant T C	British	616	
Ivey Sergeant R	British	248	
Jack Flying Officer D M	British	602	
Jackson Sergeant P F	British	604	KIA
Jackson Sergeant A	British	29	KIA*
Jackson Pilot Officer P A C	British	236	
Jacobs Pilot Officer H	British	219-600	
Jacobson Sergeant N	British	29	KIA*
James Sergeant R H	British	29	
James Sergeant R S S	British	248	KIA
Jameson Squad Ldr P G	British	266	
Janicki Pilot Officer Z	Polish	32	
Jankiewicz Flying Officer J S	Polish	601	KIA
Janough Pilot Officer S	Czech	310	
Januszewicz Pilot Officer W	Polish	303	KIA*
Jarrett Sergeant G W J	British	501-245	KIA
Jaske Pilot Officer J A	Czech	312	
Jastrzevski Flight Lieut F	Polish	302	KIA*
Javaux Pilot Officer L L G	Belgian	235	KIA
Jay Pilot Officer D T	British	87	KIA*
Jebb Flying Officer M	British	504	KIA*
Jeff Flight Lieut R V	British	87	KIA*
Jeffcoat Pilot Officer H J	British	236	KIA
Jefferies Pilot Officer C G St D	British	3-232	
Jefferies Flight Lieut. J	British	310	
Jefferson Sergeant G	British	43	
Jefferson Pilot Officer S F	British	248	
Jeffery Flying Officer A J O	British	64	KIA*
Jeffery-Cridge Sergeant H R	British	236	
Jefferys Sergeant G W	British	46-43	KIA*
Jeka Sergeant J	Polish	238	
Jenkins Pilot Officer D N O	British	253	KIA*
Jennings Sergeant B J	British	213	
Jeram(FAA) Sub Lieut. D N	British	213	
Jereczek Pilot Officer E W	Polish	229-43	
Jessop Sergeant E R	British	253-111-43-257	KIA
Jicha Pilot Officer V	Czech	1	KIA
Jiroudex Flight Sergeant M	Czech	310	
Johns Sergeant G B	British	229	
Johnson Pilot Officer A E	British	46	KIA
Johnson Pilot Officer J E	British	616	
Johnson Sergeant J I	British	222	KIA*
Johnson Pilot Officer C E	British	264	KIA*
Johnson Sergeant W J	British	145	
Johnson Sergeant R B	British	222	
Johnson Sergeant G B	N.Zealander	23	
Johnson Pilot Officer S F	British	600	KIA
Johnson Sergeant R A	British	43	
Johnson Sergeant C A	British	25	
Johnson Sergeant A E	British	23	KIA
Johnson Sergeant R K H	British	235	KIA
Johnston Pilot Officer J T	Canadian	151	KIA*
Johnstone Squad Ldr A V R	British	602	
Joll Pilot Officer I K S	British	604	
Jones Pilot Officer W R	British	266	
Jones Flying Officer D A E	British	3-501	
Jones Sergeant H D B	British	504	KIA
Jones Pilot Officer C A T	British	611	
Jones Pilot Officer J S B	British	152	KIA*
Jones Pilot Officer R E	British	605	
Jones Pilot Officer R L	British	64-19	
Jones Sergeant E	British	29	KIA
Jones Pilot Officer J T	British	264	KIA*
Jones Flying Officer	British	616	
Jottard Pilot Officer A R I	Belgian	145	KIA*
Joubert Pilot Officer C C O	British	56	
Jowitt Sergeant L	British	85	KIA*
Juleff Pilot Officer JR	British	600	
Kahn Pilot Officer A H E	British	248	KIA

Name	Nationality	Squadron	Status
Kane Pilot Officer T M	British	234	
Kania Flight Sergeant J	Polish	303	
Karasek Sergeant L R	British	23	KIA*
Karubin Sergeant S	Polish	303	KIA
Karwoski Pilot Officer W E	Polish	302	
Kaucky Sergeant J	Czech	310	
Kawalecki Pilot Officer T W	Polish	151	
Kay Pilot Officer D H S	British	264	KIA
Kay Pilot Officer J K	British	111-257	
Kay Sergeant A	British	248	KIA*
Kayll Squad Ldr J R	British	615	
Keard Pilot Officer J A	British	235	KIA
Kearsey Pilot Officer P J	British	607-213	KIA
Kearsey Sergeant A W	British	152	
Keast Sergeant F J	British	600	KIA*
Keatings Sergeant J	British	219	
Kee Sergeant E H C	British	253	KIA
Keel Sergeant G E	British	235	KIA*
Keeler Sergeant R R G	British	236	
Keighley Pilot Officer G	British	610	
Kellett Squad Ldr R G	British	303-249	
Kellett Flying Officer M	British	111	
Kellit Sergeant W H	British	236	
Kellow Flying Officer R W	British	213	
Kells Pilot Officer L G H	British	29	DOI
Kelly Flight Lieut D P D G	British	74	
Kelsey Sergeant E N	British	611	KIA
Kemp Pilot Officer J R	N.Zealander	141	KIA*
Kemp Pilot Officer N L D	British	242	
Kemp Pilot Officer J L	British	54	
Kendal Pilot Officer J B	British	66	KIA
Kennard Pilot Officer H C	British	66	
Kennard-Davis Pilot Officer P F	British	64	KIA*
Kennedy Sergeant R W	British	604	KIA
Kennedy Flight Lieut. J C	Australian	238	KIA*
Kenner Pilot Officer P L	British	264	KIA*
Kennett Pilot Officer P	British	3	KIA
Kensall Sergeant G	British	25	KIA
Kent Flight Lieut J A	Canadian	303	
Kent Pilot Officer R D	British	235	
Keough Pilot Officer V C	American	609	KIA
Keprt Sergeant J	Czech	312	
Ker-Ramsay Flight Lieut. R G	British	25-FIU	
Kershaw Pilot Officer A	British	1	KIA
Kerwin Flying Officer B V	Canadian	1(401)	DOI
Kestin(FAA) Sub Lieut. J H	British	145	KIA*
Kestler Sergeant O	Czech	111	KIA
Keymer Sergeant M	British	65	KIA*
Keynes Sergeant J D	British	236	KIA
Kidsun Pilot Officer R	N.Zealander	141	KIA*
Killick Sergeant P	British	245	
Killingback Sergeant F W G	British	249	
Kilmartin Flight Lieut. J I	Irish	43	
Kilner Sergeant J R	British	65	
Kinder Pilot Officer M C	British	607	
Kinder Pilot Officer D S	British	73	
Kindersley(FAA) Lieut. A T J	British	808	KIA
King Squad Ldr E B	British	249-151	KIA*
King Flying Officer P J C	British	66	KIA*
King Pilot Officer F H	British	264	KIA*
King Pilot Officer R	British	238	
King Flying Officer L F D	British	64	KIA
King Pilot Officer M A	British	249	KIA*
King Pilot Officer W L	British	236	KIA
Kingaby Sergeant D E	British	266-92	
Kingcombe Flight Lieut C B F	British	92	
Kings Pilot Officer R A	British	238	
Kirk Sergeant T B	British	74	KIA*
Kirkpatrick Pilot Officer J C	Belgian	235	KIA*
Kirkwood Pilot Officer M T	British	610	KIA
Kirton Sergeant D I	British	65	KIA*
Kital Sergeant S	Polish	253	
Kitson Pilot Officer T R	British	245	KIA
Klelzkowski Pilot Officer S	Polish	302	
Klein Sergeant Z	Polish	234-152	KIA
Klozinski Sergeant W	Polish	54	
Knight Flight Lieut. R A L	British	23	KIA
Knocker Pilot Officer W R A	British	264	
Komaroff Sergeant L A	British	141	DOI
Kominex Flight Sergeant J	Czech	310	
Konrad Sergeant	Polish	111-253	
Kopecky Sergeant V A	Czech	236	
Kopriva Sergeant J	Czech	310	
Korber Sergeant	Czech	32	
Kordula Pilot Officer F	Czech	17-1	
Kosarz Sergeant	Polish	302	KIA
Kosinski Flight Lieut	Polish	32	
Koukal Sergeant F	Czech	310	KIA
Kowalski Flying Officer J	Polish	302	
Kowalski Sergeant J	Polish	303	
Kozlowski Pilot Officer F	Polish	501	
Kramer Pilot Officer M	British	600	KIA
Krasnodebski Squad Ldr Z	Polish	303	
Kratkoruky Sergeant B	Czech	1	KIA
Kredba Flight Lieut M	Czech	310	KIA
Krepski Pilot Officer W	Polish	54	KIA*
Krol Pilot Officer W	Polish	302	
Kucera Sergeant J V	Czech	111-238	
Kucera Sergeant J	Czech	245	KIA
Kumiega Pilot Officer L	British	17	
Kustrzynski Flying Officer Z	Polish	607	
Kuttlewascher Sergeant .K M	Czech	1	D
Kwiecinski Sergeant J	British	145	KIA*
Lacey Sergeant J H	British	501	
Lacey Sergeant E R	British	219	
Lackie Sergeant W L	British	141	
Lafont Adjutant Henrie G	Fr. French	615	
Laguna Flight Lieut	Polish	302	
Laing Flying Officer A J A	British	64	
Laing Sergeant A	British	151	
Lake Flying Officer D M	British	219	KIA
Lamb Pilot Officer R L	British	600	
Lamb Sergeant A	British	25	
Lamb(FAA) Sub Lieut. R R	British	804	KIA
Lamb Flying Officer P G	British	610	
Lamb Pilot Officer O E	N.Zealander	151	KIA
Lambert Flight Lieut. H M S	British	25	KIA*
Lambie Pilot Officer W G M	British	219	KIA
Lammer Pilot Officer A	British	141	

Name	Nationality	Squadron	Fate
Landels Pilot Officer L N	British	32-615	KIA
Landsdell Sergeant J	British	607	KIA*
Lane Flight Lieut B J E	British	19	KIA
Lane Pilot Officer R	British	43	KIA
Langdon Pilot Officer	British	43	
Langham-Hobart Plt Of N G	British	73	
Langley Sergeant L	British	23	DOI
Langley Pilot Officer G A	British	41	KIA*
Lanning Pilot Officer F C A	British	141	
Lapka Pilot Officer S	Polish	302	
Lapkowski Pilot Officer W	Polish	203	
Larbalestier Pilot Officer B D	British	600	
Laricheliere Pilot Off'c J E P	Canadian	213	KIA*
Latta Pilot Officer J B	Canadian	242	KIA
Laughlin Flying Officer J H	British	235	
Lauder Sergeant A J	British	264	
Laurance Pilot Officer	British	234	
Laurance Sergeant G	British	141	KIA
Law Pilot Officer K S	British	605	
Lawford Sergeant D N	British	247	
Lawler Sergeant E S	British	604	
Lawrence Sergeant N A	British	54	DOI
Lawrence Pilot Officer K A	British	242-603-234-421 Flt	
Lawrence Sergeant	British	235	
Laws Sergeant G G S	British	501-151	KIA
Laws Pilot Officer A F	British	64	KIA*
Lawson Pilot Officer W J	British	19	KIA
Lawson Pilot Officer R C	British	601	KIA
Lawson-Brown Pilot Officer	British	64	DOI
Lawton Flying Officer P C F	British	604	
Laycock Pilot Officer H K	British	79	KIA
Laycock Flying Officer	British	87	
Lazoryk Flight Lieut W	Polish	607	
Leary Pilot Officer D C	British	17	KIA
Leathart Squad Ldr J A	British	54	
Leatham Pilot Officer E G C	British	248	
Leather Flight Lieut. W J	British	611	
Le Cheminant Sergeant J	British	616	
Leckrone Pilot Officer P H	American	616	KIA
Lecky Pilot Officer J G	British	610-41	KIA*
Le Conte Sergeant E F	British	FIU	
Ledger Sergeant L	British	236	
Le Dong Sergeant T	British	219	KIA
Lee Pilot Officer N T	British	501	
Lee Sergeant M A W	British	72	KIA
Lee Sergeant M A	British	421 Flt	
Lee Flying Officer R H A	British	85	KIA*
Lees Squad Ldr R B	British	72	
Lees Pilot Officer A F Y	British	236	
Le Fevre Pilot Officer P W	British	46	KIA
Legg Pilot Officer R J	British	601	
Leggett Pilot Officer P G	British	245	
Leigh Squad Ldr R H A	British	66	
Leigh Sergeant A C	British	64-72	
Le Jeune Sergeant O G	Belgian	235	KIA
Lenahan Pilot Officer J P	British	607	KIA*
Leng Sergeant M E	British	73	
Lennard(FAA) Midshipman P L	British	501	KIA
Lenton Pilot Officer E C	British	56	
Le Rougetel Flying Officer S P	British	600	
Le Roy Du Vivier Pilot Officer D A	Belgian	43	
Lerway Sergeant F T	British	236	
Leslie Sergeant G M	British	219	KIA
Leverson Sergeant S A	British	611	KIA
Lewis Pilot Officer A G	Sth. Afr	85-249	
Lewis Sergeant W G	British	25	KIA
Lewis Sergeant C S	British	600	
Lewis Pilot Officer R G	Canadian	1(401)	KIA
Leyland Sergeant R H	British	FIU	
Lille Sergeant	British	264	
Lilley Sergeant R	British	29	KIA
Limpenny Sergeant E R	British	64	
Lindsay Pilot Officer A I	British	72	KIA
Lindsay Pilot Officer P C	British	601	KIA*
Lines Flying Officer A P	British	17	
Lingard Pilot Officer J G	British	25	
Linney Pilot Officer A S	British	229	
Lipscombe Sergeant A J	British	600	KIA
Lister Squad Ldr R C F	British	92-41	
Litchfield Pilot Officer P	British	610	KIA*
Litson Sergeant F W R	British	141	
Little Flying Officer B W	British	609	
Little Pilot Officer A G	British	235	
Little Sergeant R	British	238	KIA*
Little Flying Officer T B	Canadian	1(401)	KIA
Little Squad Ldr J H	British	219	KIA
Little Squad Ldr	British	600	
Llewellyn Sergeant R T	British	213	
Llewellyn Flying Officer	British	29	
Lloyd Sergeant D E	British	19-64	
Lloyd Sergeant P D	British	41	KIA*
Lloyd Pilot Officer J P	British	72-64	
Lloyd Sergeant	British	29	
Lockhart Pilot Officer J	British	85-213	KIA
Lochman Flying Officer P W	Canadian	1(401)	KIA
Lock Pilot Officer E S	British	41	KIA
Lockton Sergeant E E	British	236	KIA*
Lockwood Sergeant J C	British	54	KIA
Lofts Pilot Officer K T	British	615-249	KIA
Logan Pilot Officer C	British	266	KIA
Logie Pilot Officer O A	British	29	
Lokuciewski Pilot Officer W	Polish	303	
Long Sergeant	British	236	
Lonsdale Sergeant R V H	British	242-501	
Lonsdale Pilot Officer J	British	3	KIA
Looker Pilot Officer D J	British	615	
Loudon Flight Lieut. M J	British	141	
Lovell Pilot Officer A D J	British	41	KIA
Lovell-Gregg Squad Ldr T G	N.Zealander	87	KIA*
Loverseed Sergeant J E	British	501	
Lovett Flight Lieut R E	British	73	KIA*
Lowe Sergeant J	British	236	
Loweth Pilot Officer P A	British	249	
Lowther Sergeant W	British	219	
Loxton Squad Ldr W W	British	25	
Lucas Pilot Officer R M M D	British	141	
Lucas Sergeant S E	British	32-257	
Lukaszewicz Flying Officer K	Polish	501	KIA*
Lumsden Pilot Officer D T M	British	236	
Lumsden Sergeant J C	British	248	

Name	Nationality	Squadron(s)	Status
Lund Pilot Officer J W	British	611-92	KIA
Lusk Pilot Officer H S	N.Zealander	25	
Lusty Pilot Officer K R	British	25	
Lyall Flight Lieut A McL	British	25	
Lyall Pilot Officer A	British	602	KIA
Lynch Sergeant J	British	25	KIA
Lyons Pilot Officer E B	British	65	
Lysek Sergeant A	Polish	302	
MacArthur Flying Off'c M R	British	236	
McCaw Flying Officer D C	British	238	KIA*
MacConochie Sgt. S R D	British	235	
MacDonald Sergeant A S	British	601	
MacDonald Pilot Officer D K	British	603	KIA*
MacDonald Flight Lieut. H K	British	503	KIA*
MacDonell Squad Ldr A R D	British	64	
MacDougal Sergeant C W	British	111	KIA
MacDougall Pilot Officer L N	British	141	
MacDougall Squad Ldr R I G	British	17	
Macejowski Sergeant M K	Polish	111-249	
MacFie Pilot Officer C H	British	616-611	
MacGregor Sergeant A N	British	19	
Machacek Pilot Officer J	Czech	145	DOI
Machin Sergeant W H	British	264	KIA*
Macinski Pilot Officer J	Polish	111	KIA*
MacKay Pilot Officer	British	234	
MacKenzie Pilot Officer	British	43	
MacKenzie Pilot Officer D C	N.Zealander	56	KIA
MacKenzie Pilot Officer K W	British	501	
MacKenzie Pilot Officer J N	N.Zealander	41	
MacKinnon(FAA) Lieut. A McL	British	804	
MacKinnon Sergeant D D	British	236	KIA*
MacLachlan Squad Ldr A H	British	92	
MacLachlan Flying Officer J A F	British	73-145	KIA
MacLachlan Squad Ldr J R	British	46	
MacLaren Pilot Officer A C	British	604	
MacLean Pilot Officer C H	British	602	
MacLeod Sergeant G S M	British	235	KIA
MacNamara Flying Officer B R	British	603	
MacPhail Pilot Officer F J	British	603	DOI
MacRae Sergeant I N	British	FIU	
MacRory Sergeant H L	British	23	KIA
Madle Pilot Officer S J	British	615-605	
Maffett Pilot Officer G H	British	257	KIA*
Maggs Pilot Officer M H	British	264	
Maguire Squad Ldr H J	British	229	
Mahoney(FAA) Petty Officer T J	British	804	
Main Sergeant A D W	British	249	KIA*
Main Sergeant H R	British	25	KIA
Maitland-Walker Plt. Of W H	British	65	
Makins Sergeant	British	247	
Malan Flight Lieut A G	Sth. Afr	74	
Malengreau Pilot Officer F F G	Belgian	87	
Males Pilot Officer E E	British	72	KIA*
Malinowski Sergeant B	Polish	302	
Malinski Pilot Officer J L	Polish	302	
Mallett Sergeant R S	British	29	KIA
Maly Pilot Officer J M	Czech	310	DOI
Mamedoff Pilot Officer A	American	609	DOI
Manger Flying Officer K	British	17	KIA*
Mann Pilot Officer H J	British	1	
Mann Sergeant J	British	92-64	
Mansel-Lewis Pilot Officer J	British	92	
Mansfield Sergeant M J	Czech	111	
Mansfield Sergeant B M	British	236	KIA
Mansfield Sergeant D E	British	236	
Manton Squad Ldr G A L	British	56	
Manton Sergeant E	British	610	KIA*
Marchand Pilot Officer R A	British	73	KIA*
Marek Sergeant F	Czech	310-19	KIA*
Markiewicz Sergeant A L	Polish	302	
Marland Sergeant R G	British	222	KIA
Marples Pilot Officer R	British	616	KIA
Marrs Pilot Officer E S	British	152	KIA
Marsh Sergeant	British	152	
Marsh Sergeant W C	British	236	
Marsh(FAA) Lieutenant A E	British	804	
Marsh Sergeant H J	British	238	KIA*
Marshall Sergeant A E	British	73	DOI
Marshall Pilot Officer J E	British	85	KIA
Marshall Sergeant T R	British	219	KIA
Marshall Sergeant T B	British	235	
Marshall Pilot Officer J V	British	232	
Marsland Pilot Officer G	British	245-253	
Marston Flying Officer K J	British	56	KIA
Martel Pilot Officer B	Polish	603-54	
Martin Flying Officer J C	N.Zealander	257	KIA
Martin Pilot Officer A W	British	235	
Martin Sergeant	British	264	
Martin(FAA) Sub Lieut. R M S	British	808	KIA
Maslen Sergeant T A	British	235	KIA
Mason Sergeant W	British	235	KIA
Massey Sergeant K	British	248	
Mather Pilot Officer J R	British	66	KIA*
Mathers Sergeant J W	British	29-23	
Matheson Flight Lieut. G C	British	222	KIA
Matthews Sergeant H G	British	236	
Matthews Pilot Officer K L	British	23	
Matthews Pilot Officer H K F	British	54-603	KIA*
Matthews Flying Officer P G H	British	1	
Matthews Sergeant I W	British	64	DOI
Maxwell Pilot Officer M C	British	56	
Maxwell Sergeant W	British	264	KIA*
Maxwell Pilot Officer D A	British	611-603	KIA
Maxwell Squad Ldr H L	British	600	
Mayers Pilot Officer H C	British	601	KIA
Mayhew Pilot Officer P F	British	79	KIA
Mayne Warrant Officer E	British	74	
McAdam Sergeant W D	British	23	KIA
McAdam Sergeant J	British	41	KIA
McAllister Sergeant P J	British	29-23	
McArthur Flight Lieut. J H G	British	609-238	
McCall Pilot Officer S V	British	607	
McCann Sergeant T A	British	601	DOI
McCarthy Sergeant T F	British	235	KIA
McCarthy Sergeant J P	British	235	
McCaul Sergeant J P	British	219	KIA*
McChesney Sergeant R I	N.Zealander	236	KIA
McClintock Pilot Officer J A P	British	615	KIA
McComb Squad Ldr J E	British	611	

Name	Nationality	Squadron(s)	Status
McConnell Sergeant J	British	145	
McConnell Pilot Officer W W	Irish	607-245-249	
McCormack Sergeant J B	British	25	KIA
McDermott Sergeant J	N.Zealander	23	
McDonough Pilot Officer B M	Australian	236	KIA*
McDougall Pilot Officer R	British	3-232	
McDowall Sergeant A	British	602	
McFadden Pilot Officer A	British	73	
McGaw Pilot Officer C A	British	73-66	KIA
McGibbon Pilot Officer J	British	615	KIA*
McGlashan Pilot Officer K B	British	245	
McGowan Flying Officer R A	British	46	
McGowan Pilot Officer H W	British	92	
McGrath Pilot Officer J K	British	601	
McGregor Flight Lieut G R	Canadian	1(401)	
McGregor Pilot Officer P R	British	46	
McGregor Squad Ldr H D	British	213	
McGregor Pilot Officer A J	British	504	
McGugan Sergeant R	British	141	
McHardy Pilot Officer E H	N.Zealander	248	
McHardy Pilot Officer D B H	British	229	
McInnes Pilot Officer A	British	601-238	
McIntosh Sergeant R P C	British	151-605	KIA*
McIntyre Pilot Officer A G	British	111	
McKay Sergeant D A S	British	501-421 Flt	
McKellar Flight Lieut. A A	British	605	KIA
McKenzie Pilot Officer J W	British	111	KIA*
McKie Sergeant E J	British	248	
McKnight Pilot Officer W L	Canadian	242	KIA
McLaughlin Sergeant J W	British	238	
McLure Pilot Officer A C R	British	87	KIA
McMahon Sergeant	British	235	
McMullen Flying Officer D A P	British	222-54	
McNab Squad Ldr E A	Canadian	1(401)-111	
McNair Sergeant R J	British	249-3	
McNay Sergeant A	British	73	KIA*
McPhee Sergeant J	British	249-151	
McPherson Flight Sgt. R R	British	65	KIA
Meaker Pilot Officer J R B	British	249	KIA*
Meares Squad Ldr	British	54	
Measures Flight Lieut. W E G	British	74-238	
Medworth Sergeant J	British	25	
Meeson Sergeant C V	British	56	KIA
Melville Pilot Officer J C	British	264	
Melville-Jackson Pilot Officer G H	British	236	
Mercer Sergeant	British	609	
Merchant Sergeant H J	British	1	
Meredith Sergeant A D	British	242-141	
Mermagen Squad Ldr H W	British	266-222	
Merrett Sergeant J C	British	235	
Merrick Pilot Officer C	British	610	
Merryweather Sergeant S W	British	229	KIA
Mesner Sergeant B W	British	248	KIA*
Metcalfe Sergeant A C	British	604	
Metham Sergeant J	British	253	KIA
Meyer Sergeant R H R	British	236	KIA
Michail Sergeant	British	501	
Michiels Sergeant A C A	Belgian	235	DOI
Middlemiss Sergeant W	British	235	
Middleton Pilot Officer	British	266	
Mierzwa Pilot Officer B	Polish	303	
Milburn Sergeant R A	British	601	
Mildren Pilot Officer P R	British	54-66	KIA
Mileham Pilot Officer D E	British	41	KIA
Miles Sergeant E E	British	236	
Miles Sergeant S F	British	23	
Miley Pilot Officer M J	British	25	KIA*
Millar Flying Officer W B N	Canadian	1(401)	
Millard Pilot Officer J G P	British	1	
Miller Flight Lieut A G	British	17-FIU	
Miller Pilot Officer R F G	British	609	KIA*
Miller Sergeant A J	British	23	
Miller Sergeant A C	British	604	
Miller Sergeant T H	British	25	KIA
Miller Flight Lieut R R	British	3	KIA
Millington Pilot Officer W H	Australian	79-249	KIA*
Millist Pilot Officer K M	British	73-615	KIA
Mills Squad Ldr R S	British	87	
Mills Sergeant J P	British	43-249	
Mills Sergeant J B	British	23	
Milne Pilot Officer J A	Canadian	605	
Milne Flying Officer R M	British	151	
Milnes Sergeant A H	British	32	
Mitchell Pilot Officer H	Canadian	87	
Mitchell Flying Officer R G	British	257	KIA*
Mitchell Flying Officer P H G	British	266	
Mitchell Squad Ldr H M	British	25	
Mitchell Sergeant G	British	23	
Mitchell Pilot Officer G T M	British	609	KIA*
Mitchell Sergeant R R	British	229	
Mitchell Sergeant H R	N.Zealander	3	
Mitchell Sergeant	British	65	
Moberley Flying Officer G E	British	616	KIA*
Molson Flying Officer R H de M	Canadian	1(401)	
Monk Pilot Officer E W J	British	25	KIA
Monk Sergeant D A	British	236	
Montagu Squad Ldr G W	British	236	KIA
Montague-Smith Flight Lieut A M	British	264	
Montbon Sergeant Zavier de	Free French	64	
Montgomery Sergeant H F	British	43	KIA*
Montgomery Pilot Officer C R	British	614	KIA*
Moody Pilot Officer H W	British	602	KIA*
Moody Sergeant D G	British	604	
Moore Sergeant A R	British	245-615-3	
Moore Pilot Officer W R	British	264	
Moore Sergeant P J	British	253	KIA
Moore Flying Officer W S	British	236	KIA
More Squad Ldr J W C	British	73	KIA
Morewood Flight Lieut. R E G	British	248	
Morfill Flight Sergeant P F	British	501	
Morgan Pilot Officer P J	British	238	
Morgan-Gray Pilot Officer H	British	46	KIA
Morris Pilot Officer E J	Sth. Afr	79	
Morris Pilot Officer G E	British	FIU	
Morris Pilot Officer J	British	248	
Morrison Sergeant N	British	54-74-72	KIA
Morrison Sergeant J P	British	46-43	KIA*
Morrough-Ryan Pilot Officer O B	British	41	KIA
Mortimer Pilot Officer P A	British	257	DOI
Morton Pilot Officer J S	British	603	

Name	Nationality	Squadron	Status
Moss(FAA) Sub Lieut. W J M	British	213	KIA*
Moss Sergeant R C	British	29	
Mott Sergeant W H	British	141	
Mottram Pilot Officer R	British	92	KIA
Mouchette Adjutant R	Free French	615	KIA
Mould Sergeant E A	British	74	KIA
Moulton Sergeant E W	British	600	
Mounsdon Pilot Officer M H	British	56	
Mount Flying Officer C J	British	602	
Mowat Flight Lieut N J	N.Zealander	245	
Mowat Sergeant R I	British	248	
Moynham Sergeant E F J	British	248	KIA
Mrazek Pilot Officer K	Czech	46	
Mudie Pilot Officer M R	British	615	KIA*
Mudry Sergeant M	Polish	79	
Muirhead Flight Lt. I J	British	605	KIA*
Mumler Wing Com M	Polish	302	
Mungo-Park Flying Officer J C	British	79-74	KIA
Munn Flight Sergeant W S	British	29	
Murch Flying Officer L C	British	253	DOI
Murland Sergeant W J	British	264	
Murray Sergeant J	British	610	
Murray Pilot Officer T B	British	616	
Murray Squad Ldr A D	British	73-501	
Murray Sergeant P H	British	23	KIA
Naish Sergeant K E	British	235	
Narucki Pilot Officer A R	Polish	607	
Naughtin Sergeant H T	British	235	KIA
Neer Sergeant	British	29	
Neil Pilot Officer T F	British	249	
Nelson Flying Officer W H	Canadian	74	
Nelson Flight Sergeant D	British	235	
Nelson-Edwards Pilot Officer G H	British	79	
Nenage Sergeant T N	British	29	KIA
Nesbitt Flying Officer A D	Canadian	1(401)	
Neville Sergeant W J	British	610	KIA*
Newbury Pilot Officer J C	British	609	
Newbury Pilot Officer M A	British	145	KIA
Newham Sergeant E A	British	235	
Newling Pilot Officer M A	British	145	DOI
Newport Sergeant D V	British	235	
Newton Sergeant H S	British	111	
Newton Sergeant E F	British	29	
Nicholas Flying Officer J B H	British	65	
Nicholls Sergeant T G F	British	23	KIA
Nicholls Sergeant D B F	British	151	
Nichols Sergeant D H	British	56	
Nicolson Flight Lieut. J B	British	249	KIA
Nicolson Sergeant B P	British	232	KIA
Niemiec Flying Officer P	Polish	17	
Nightingale Pilot Officer F G	British	219	KIA
Niven Pilot Officer H G	British	601-602	
Nixen Sergeant W	British	23	KIA
Noble Sergeant W J	British	54	
Noble Pilot Officer B R	British	79	
Noble Sergeant D	British	43	KIA*
Nokes-Cooper Flying Officer B	British	236	KIA*
Norfolk Pilot Officer N R	British	72	
Norris Flying Officer R W	Canadian	1(401)	
Norris Flight Lieut S C	British	610	
Norris Sergeant P P	British	213	KIA*
North Pilot Officer G	British	257	KIA
North Pilot Officer H R	British	43	
North-Bomford Sergenat D J	British	17	
Norwell Sergeant J K	British	54-41	
Norwood Pilot Officer R K C	British	65	
Nosowicz Pilot Officer Z	Polish	56	
Nowak Pilot Officer T	Polish	253	
Nowakiewicz SergeantE J A	Polish	302	
Nowell(FAA) Sub Lieut. W R	British	804	
Nowierski Pilot Officer T	Polish	609	
Nunn Pilot Officer S G	British	236	
Nute Sergeant R R J	British	23	KIA
Nutter Sergeant R C	British	257	
Oaks Sergeant T W	N.Zealander	235	
O'Brian Flying Officer P G StG	Canadian	247-152	
O'Brien Squad Ldr J S	British	92-234	KIA*
O'Brien Flight Lieut	British	247	
O'Bryne Sergeant P	British	73-501	
O'Connell Flying Officer A	British	264	
Obelofse Pilot Officer J R S	Sth. Afr	43	KIA*
Odbert Squad Ldr N C	British	64	
Offenberg Pilot Officer J H M	Belgian	145	KIA
Ogilvie Pilot Officer D B	British	601	
Ogilvie Flying Officer A K	Canadian	609	
Oldfield Sergeant T G	British	64-92	KIA*
O'Leary Sergeant A A	British	604	
Olensen Pilot Officer W P	British	607	KIA
Olenski Flying Officer Z	Polish	234-609	
Olewinski Sergeant B	Polish	111	KIA
Olive Flight Lieut. C G C	Australian	65	
Oliver Pilot Officer P	British	611	
Oliver Sergeant G C	British	23	KIA
Olver Pilot Officer	British	603	
O'Malley Flying Officer D H C	British	264	KIA*
O'Manney Sergeant R J	British	229	KIA
O'Meara Pilot Officer J J	British	421 Flt-64-72	
O'Neill Flying Officer D H	British	611-41	KIA*
O'Neill Flight Lieut J A	British	601-238	
Orchard Sergeant H C	British	65	KIA
Orgias Pilot Officer E	N.Zealander	23	KIA*
Ortmans Pilot Officer P M M	Belgian	229	KIA
Orzechowski Pilot Officer J	Polish	607	
Osmand Pilot Officer A I	British	3-213	
Ostowicz Pilot Officer A	Polish	145	KIA*
Ottewill Sergeant P G	British	43	
Overton Pilot Officer C N	British	43	
Owen Sergeant A E	British	600	
Owen Sergeant H	British	219	
Owen Sergeant W G	British	235	
Oxspring Flight Lieut. R W	British	66	
Page Pilot Officer A G	British	56	
Page Sergeant W T	British	1	KIA
Page Sergeant V O	British	610-601	
Page Sergeant A J	British	257	KIA
Page Flight Lieut C L	British	234	
Page Sergeant A D	British	111	KIA

Name	Nationality	Squadron	Status
Pledger Pilot Officer G F C	British	141	KIA
Plinderleith Sergeant R	British	73	
Plummer Flying Officer R P	British	46	KIA*
Plzak Sergeant S	Czech	310-19	KIA
Pocock Sergeant M H	British	72	
Pollard Pilot Officer P S C	British	611	KIA
Pollard Sergeant J K	British	232	KIA
Pond Flight Sergeant A H C	British	601	
Ponting Pilot Officer W A	British	264	KIA*
Pool Pilot Officer P D	British	266-72	
Poole Sergeant E R L	British	604	
Poplawski Pilot Officer J	Polish	111-229	
Porter Sergeant J A	British	615-19-242	
Porter Sergeant E F	British	141	KIA
Porter Sergeant O W	British	111	KIA
Posener Pilot Officer F H	Sth. Afr	152	KIA*
Poulton Pilot Officer H R C	British	64	
Pound Sergeant R R C	British	25	
Powell Flight Lt. R P R	British	111	
Powell Sergeant S W M	British	141	
Powell Pilot Officer R J	British	248	KIA
Powell Sergeant E	British	25	KIA
Powell-Shedden Flt. Lt. G	British	242	
Power Flight Lieutenant R M	Australian	236	
Prchal Sergeant E M	Czech	310	
Preater Sergeant S G	British	235	
Prevot Pilot Officer L O J	Belgian	235	
Priak Pilot Officer K	British	32-257	KIA
Price Pilot Officer A O	British	236	
Price Sergeant N A J	British	236	
Price Sergeant R B	British	245-222-73	KIA
Price Sergeant J	British	29	
Priestley Flying Officer	British	235	
Pritchard Flight Lt. C A	British	600	
Proctor Sergeant J	British	602	KIA
Proctor Pilot Officer J E	N.Zealander	32	
Prosser Sergeant P R	British	235	KIA
Proudman Sergeant D H	British	248	DOI
Prowse Pilot Officer H A R	British	256-603	
Ptacek Sergeant R	Czech	43	KIA
Puda Sergeant R	Czech	310-605	
Pudney(FAA) Sub Lt. G B	British	64	KIA
Pugh Sergeant J S	British	25	
Pugh Flight Lieutenant T P	British	263	KIA
Pushman Pilot Officer G R	Canadian	23	
Putt Flight Lieutenant A R	British	501	
Puxley Sergeant W G V	British	236	
Pye Sergeant J W	British	25	
Pyman Pilot Officer L L	British	65	KIA*
Pyne Sergeant C C	N.Zealander	219	
Quelch Sergeant B H	British	235	
Quill Flying Officer J K	British	65	
Quinn Sergeant J	British	236	
Rabagliati Flight Lt. A C	British	46	KIA
Rabone Pilot Officer P W	British	145	KIA
Rabone Flying Officer J H M	British	604	
Radomski Pilot Officer J	Polish	303	
Radwanski Pilot Officer G	Polish	151-56-607	
Rafter Pilot Officer R F	British	603	
Raine Sergeant W	British	610	KIA
Rains Sergeant D N	British	248	KIA
Ralls Sergeant L F	British	605	
Ramsay Sergeant N H D	British	610-222	
Ramsay Pilot Officer J B	British	151	KIA*
Ramsay Sergeant J S	British	235	KIA
Ramshaw Sergeant J W	British	222	KIA*
Rasmussen Sergeant L A W	N.Zealander	264	KIA*
Ravenhill Pilot Officer M	British	229	KIA*
Rawlence Pilot Officer A J	British	600	
Rawnsley Sergeant C F	British	604	
Ray Sergeant	British	56	
Raymond Flying Officer P	British	609	
Rayner Pilot Officer R M S	British	87	
Read Flying Officer W A A	British	603	
Ream Sergeant C A	British	235	
Reardon-Parker(FAA)S Lt. J	British	804	
Reddington Sergeant L A E	British	152	KIA*
Redfern Sergeant E A	British	232	KIA
Redman Pilot Officer J	British	257-245-43	KIA
Reece Sergeant L H M	British	235	KIA*
Reed Sergeant H	British	600	
Rees Pilot Officer B V	British	610	
Reid Pilot Officer R	British	46	KIA
Reilley Pilot Officer H W	Canadian	64-66	KIA*
Reilly Sergeant C C	N.Zealander	23	KIA
Renvoize Sergeant J V	British	247	
Reynell Flight Ltt R C	Australian	43	KIA*
Reyno Flight Lieutenant E M	Canadian	1(401)	
Rhodes Pilot Officer R A	British	29	KIA*
Rhodes-Moorehouse FO. W	British	601	KIA*
Ricalton Pilot Officer A L	British	74	KIA*
Rich Sergeant P G	British	25	
Richards(FAA) Sub Lt D H	British	111	DOI
Richards Sergeant W C	British	235	KIA
Richardson Sergeant E	British	242	
Richardson Squad Ldr W A	British	141	
Richardson Sergeant R W	British	610	
Richardson Sergeant	British	141	
Ricketts Sergeant H W	British	235	KIA
Ricketts Pilot Officer V A	British	248	KIA
Ricks Sergeant L P V J	Canadian	235	
Riddell-Hannam Sgt J D	British	236	
Riddle Flying Officer C J	British	601	
Riddle Flying Officer H J	British	601	
Ridley Sergeant M	British	616	KIA*
Rigby Pilot Officer R H	British	236	KIA*
Riley Flight Lieutenant W	British	302	KIA
Riley Pilot Officer F	British	236	KIA
Rimmet Flight Lt. R F	British	229	KIA*
Ringwood Sergeant E A	British	248	KIA*
Ripley Sergeant W G	British	604	DOI
Rippon Pilot Officer A J	British	601	KIA
Riseley Sergeant A H	British	600	
Ritcher Pilot Officer G L	British	234	
Ritchie Sergeant R D	British	605	KIA*
Ritchie Pilot Officer I S	British	603	
Ritchie Pilot Officer J R	British	111	
Ritchie Pilot Officer T G F	British	602	KIA

Name	Nationality	Squadron	Status
Ritchie Pilot Officer J H	British	141	
Ritchie Pilot Officer J R	British	600	
Roach Pilot Officer R J B	British	266	
Robb Pilot Officer R A L	British	236	
Robbins Pilot Officer R H	British	54-66	
Roberts Wing Cmdr D N	British	609-328	
Roberts Sergeant A J A	British	29	
Roberts Pilot Officer R	British	615-64	
Roberts Sergeant D F	British	25	KIA
Roberts Sergeant E C	British	23	
Roberts(FAA) Midsh'p G W	British	808	KIA
Robertson Sergeant F N	British	66	KIA
Robertson Sergeant	British	56	
Robertson Sergeant B L	British	54	KIA
Robinson Flight Lieut. A L	British	222	DOI
Robinson Sergeant D N	British	152	
Robinson Sergeant J	British	111	DOI
Robinson Pilot Officer J C E	British	1	KIA
Robinson Flight Lieut. M L	British	610-619-238-66	KIA
Robinson Pilot Officer G	British	264	
Robinson Squad Ldr M W S	British	73	
Robinson Flight Lieut. P B	British	601	
Robinson Sergeant P E M	British	56	KIA
Robinson Sergeant P T	British	257	
Robinson Squad Ldr M	British	616	
Robshaw Pilot Officer F A	British	229	
Robson Pilot Officer N C H	British	72	KIA
Roden Sergeant H A C	British	19	DOI
Roff Pilot Officer B J	British	25	KIA
Rogers Pilot Officer B A	British	242	KIA
Rogers Sergeant G W	British	234	KIA
Rogers Pilot Officer E B	British	501-615	
Rogowski Sergeant J	Polish	303-74	
Rohacek Pilot Officer R B	Czech	238-601	KIA
Rolls Sergeant W T E	British	72	
Roman Pilot Officer C L	Belgian	236	
Romanis Sergeant A L	British	25	KIA
Rook Flight Lieut A H	British	504	
Rook Pilot Officer M	British	504	
Roscoe Flying Officer G L	British	87	KIA
Rose Flying Officer J	British	32-3	
Rose Pilot Officer S N	British	602	
Rose Sergeant J S	British	23	KIA
Rose Pilot Officer E B M	British	234	KIA
Rose-Price Pilot Officer A T	British	501	KIA*
Rosier Squadron Leader F E	British	229	
Ross Pilot Officer J K	British	17	KIA
Ross Pilot Officer A R	British	25-610	KIA
Rothwell Pilot Officer J H	British	601-605-32	KIA
Round Sergeant J H	British	248	KIA*
Rourke Sergeant J	British	248	
Rouse Sergeant G W	British	236	
Rowden Pilot Officer J H	British	64-616	KIA
Rowell Sergeant P A	British	249	
Rowley Pilot Officer R M B	British	145	KIA
Royce Flying Officer M E A	British	504	
Royce Flying Officer W B	British	504	
Rozwadwski Pilot Officer M	Polish	151	KIA*
Rozycki Pilot Officer W	British	238	
Ruddock Sergeant W S	British	23	
Rudland Sergeant C P	British	263	
Rushmer Flight Lieut F W	British	603	KIA
Russell Flight Lieut H a'b	British	32	
Russell Flying Officer B D	Canadian	1(401)	
Russell Sergeant	N.Zealander	264	
Russell Pilot Officer G H	British	236	
Russell Sergeant A G	British	43	
Russell Pilot Officer	British	141	
Russell(FAA) Lieutenant. G F	British	804	KIA
Rust Sergeant C A	British	85-249	
Ruston Flight Lieut P	British	604	DOI
Rutter Pilot Officer R D	British	73	
Ryalls Pilot Officer D L	British	29-FIU	KIA
Ryder Flight Lieut E N	British	41	
Rypl Pilot Officer F	Czech	310	
Sadler Pilot Officer N A	British	235	KIA
Sadler Flight Sergeant H S	British	611	KIA
St Aubin Flying Officer E F	British	616	KIA
St John Pilot Officer P C B	British	74	KIA*
Salmon Flying Officer H N E	British	1-229	
Salway Sergeant E	British	141	KIA
Samolinski Pilot Officer W M C	Polish	253	KIA*
Sample Squad Ldr J	British	504	KIA
Sampson Sergeant A	British	23	
Sanders Pilot Officer J	British	92	
Sanders Flight Lieut. J G	British	615	
Sandifer Sergeant A K	British	604	
Sargent Sergeant R E B	British	219	
Sarre Sergeant A R	British	603	
Sasak Sergeant W	Polish	32	KIA
Satchell Squad Ldr W A J	British	302	
Saunders Pilot Officer C H	British	92	
Saunders Flight Lieut. G A W	British	65	
Savage Sergeant T W	British	64	KIA
Savill Sergeant J E	British	242-151	
Saville Sergeant	British	501	KIA
Saward Sergeant C J	British	615-501	
Sawice Flying Officer T	Polish	303	
Sawyer Squad Ldr H C	British	65	KIA*
Sayers Flight Sergeant J E	British	41	
Schollar Pilot Officer E C	British	248	
Schumer Pilot Officer F H	British	600	KIA
Schwind Flight Lieut LH	British	257-213	KIA*
Sclanders Pilot Officer K M	Canadian	242	KIA*
Scott Sergeant A E	British	73	KIA
Scott Sergeant G W	British	64-19	
Scott Sergeant	N.Zealander	246	
Scott Sergeant E	British	222	KIA*
Scott Sergeant J A	British	611-74	KIA*
Scott Flight Lieut D R	British	605	
Scott Pilot Officer A M W	British	3-607	KIA
Scott Pilot Officer D S	British	73	
Scott Flying Officer W J M	British	41	KIA*
Scott Flying Officer R H	British	604	
Scott Sergeant	British	422 Flt	
Scott-Malden Pilot Officer F D S	British	611-603	
Scrase Flying Officer G E T	British	600	KIA
Seabourne Sergeant E W	British	238	
Sears Pilot Officer L A	British	145	KIA*

Name	Nationality	Squadron	Status
Secretan Pilot Officer D	British	72-54	
Seda Sergeant K	Czech	310	
Sedoon Pilot Officer J W	British	601	KIA
Seghers Pilot Officer E G A	Belgian	46-32	KIA
Sellers Sergeant R F	British	45-111	
Selway Flying Officer J B	British	604	
Senior Sergeant J N	British	23	KIA
Senior Sergeant B	British	600	
Seredyn Sergeant A	Polish	32	
Service Sergeant A	British	29	KIA
Sewell Sergeant D A	British	17	KIA
Shanahan Sergeant M M	British	1	KIA*
Shand Pilot Officer	British	54	
Sharman Pilot Officer H R	British	248	
Sharp Pilot Officer L M	British	111	KIA
Sharp Sergeant B R	British	235	KIA*
Sharp Sergeant R J	British	236	
Sharply Sergeant H	British	234	KIA
Sharratt Sergeant W G	British	248	KIA
Shaw Pilot Officer R H	British	1	KIA*
Shaw Flying Officer I G	British	264	KIA*
Shaw(FAA) Petty Officer F J	British	804	KIA
Shead Sergeant H F W	British	257-32	
Sheard Sergeant H	British	236	KIA
Sheen Flying Officer D F B	Australian	72	
Shepherd Sergeant F W	British	264	KIA
Shepley Pilot Officer D C	British	152	KIA*
Sheppard Sergeant	British	236	
Sheppard Sergeant J B	British	234	KIA
Shepherd Sergeant G E	British	219	KIA*
Shepperd Sergeant E E	British	152	KIA*
Shepherd Sergeant F E R	British	611	KIA*
Sheridan Sergeant S	British	236	
Sherrington Pilot Officer T B A	British	92	
Shewel Sergeant	British	236	
Shipman Pilot Officer E A	British	41	
Shirley Sergeant S H J	British	604	KIA
Shorrocks Pilot Officer N B	British	235	KIA*
Shuttleworth Pilot Officer Lord R	British	145	KIA*
Sibley Sergeant F A	British	238	KIA*
Sika Sergeant J	Czech	43	
Silk Sergeant F H	British	111	
Silver Sergeant W G	British	152	KIA*
Silvestor Sergeant G F	British	229	
Sim Sergeant R B	British	111	KIA*
Simmons Pilot Officer V C	British	238	
Simpson Flying Officer G M	N.Zealander	229	KIA*
Simpson Flight Lieut. J W C	British	43	DOI
Simpson Pilot Officer P J	British	111-64	
Simpson Pilot Officer L W	British	141-264	
Sims Sergeant I R	British	248	KIA
Sims Pilot Officer J A	British	3-232	
Sinclair Flying Officer G L	British	310	
Sinclair Pilot Officer J	British	219	
Sing Flight Lieut J E J	British	213	
Siudak Sergeant A	Polish	302-303	KIA*
Sizer Pilot Officer W M	British	213	
Skalski Pilot Officer S	Polish	501-615	
Skillen Sergeant V H	British	29	KIA
Skinner Sergeant W M	British	74	
Skinner Flying Officer C D E	British	604	
Skinner Flight Lieut. S H	British	604	KIA
Skowron Sergeant H	Polish	303	KIA
Slade Sergeant J W	British	64	KIA
Slatter Pilot Officer D M	British	141	KIA*
Sleigh(FAA) Lieutenant J W	British	804	
Slouf Sergeant V	Czech	312	
Sly Sergeant O K	British	29	KIA*
Smallman Sergeant J	British	23	
Smart Pilot Officer T	British	65	KIA
Smith Sergeant A D	British	66	KIA*
Smith Pilot Officer D N E	British	74	KIA*
Smith Pilot Officer E	British	219	
Smith Pilot Officer D S	British	616	KIA*
Smith Squad Ldr A T	British	610	KIA*
Smith Pilot Officer E B B	British	610	
Smith Flight Lieut F M	British	72	
Smith Pilot Officer I S	N.Zealander	151	
Smith Pilot Officer J D	Canadian	73	KIA
Smith Flight Lieut R L	British	151	
Smith Sergeant K B	British	257	KIA*
Smith Pilot Officer R R	Canadian	229	
Smith Flight Lieut W A	British	229	
Smith Pilot Officer P R	British	25	KIA
Smith Flight Lieut. C D S	British	25	KIA
Smith Pilot Officer A W	British	141	KIA
Smith(FAA) Sub Lieut. F A	British	145	KIA*
Smith Pilot Officer A J	British	74	
Smith Sergeant R C	British	236	KIA
Smith Pilot Officer E L	British	604	
Smith Sergeant W B	British	602	
Smith Flying Officer E S	British	600	
Smith Sergeant L E	British	234-602	
Smith Sergeant St James	British	600	KIA
Smith Sergeant F	British	604	KIA
Smith Sergeant G E	British	254	
Smith Sergeant A	British	600	KIA
Smith Sergeant L	British	219	
Smith Sergeant P R	British	236	KIA
Smith Sergeant N H J	British	235	
Smith Sergeant E C	British	600	
Smith Flight Lieut W O L	British	263	KIA
Smither Flying Officer R	Canadian	1(401)	KIA*
Smithers Pilot Officer J L	British	601	KIA*
Smithson Sergeant R	British	249	KIA
Smyth Sergeant R H	British	111	
Smythe Sergeant G	British	56	
Smythe Pilot Officer R F	British	32	
Smythe Flying Officer D M A	British	264	
Snape Sergeant W G	British	25	KIA
Snell Pilot Officer V R	British	501-151	
Snowden Sergeant E G	British	213	KIA
Soars Sergeant H J	British	74	
Sobbey Sergeant E A	British	235	KIA
Soden Pilot Officer JF	British	266-603	KIA
Solak Pilot Officer J J	Polish	151-249	
Solomon Pilot Officer N D	British	17	KIA*
Sones Sergeant L C	British	605	
Southall Sergeant G	British	2	KIA
Southorn Sergeant G A	British	235	

Name	Nationality	Squadron	Status
Southwell Pilot Officer J S	British	245	KIA
Spears Sergeant	British	421 Flt	
Spears Sergeant A W P	British	222	
Speke Pilot Officer H	British	604	KIA
Spence Pilot Officer D J	N.Zealander	245	KIA
Spencer Squad Ldr D G J	British	266	
Spencer Sergeant G H	British	504	
Spiers Sergeant A H	British	236	
Spires Sergeant J H	British	235	
Sprague Sergeant M H	British	602	KIA*
Sprague Pilot Officer H A	Canadian	3	
Sprenger Flying Officer	Canadian	1(401)	
Spurdle Pilot Officer R L	N.Zealander	74	
Spyer Sergeant R A	British	607	KIA
Squier Sergeant J W C	British	64	
Stanger Sergeant N M	N.Zealander	235	
Stanley Pilot Officer D A	British	64	KIA
Stanley Sergeant D O	N.Zealander	151	KIA*
Stansfield Flying Officer W K	British	242-229	
Staples Sergeant R C J	British	72	
Staples Sergeant L	British	151	
Staples Pilot Officer M E	British	609	KIA
Stapleton Pilot Officer B G	Sth. Afr	603	
Starll Sergeant	British	601	
Starr Squad Ldr H M	British	245-253	KIA*
Stavert Pilot Officer C M	British	1-504	
Steadman Sergeant D J	British	245	
Steborowski Flying Officer M J	Polish	238	KIA*
Steele Sergeant R M	British	235	
Steere Flight Sergeant H	British	19	KIA
Steere Flight Sergeant J	British	72	
Stefan Sergeant J	Czech	1	
Stegman Pilot Officer S	Polish	111-229	
Stehlik Sergeant J	Czech	312	
Stein Pilot Officer D	British	263	KIA
Stenhouse Flying Officer J	British	43	
Stephen Pilot Officer H M	British	74	
Stephens Pilot Officer M M	British	232-3	
Stephens Sergeant C	British	23	KIA*
Stephenson Flight Lieut P J T	British	607	
Stephenson Flying Officer I R	British	264	KIA
Stephenson Pilot Officer S P	British	85	
Sterbacek Pilot Officer J	Czech	310	KIA
Stevens Sergeant G	British	213	
Stevens Pilot Officer L W	British	17	KIA
Stevens Pilot Officer RP	British	151	KIA
Stevens Pilot Officer E J	British	141	
Stevens Sergeant W R	British	23	
Stevens Sergeant R E	British	29	KIA*
Stevenson Pilot Officer P C F	British	74	KIA
Steward Sergeant G A	British	17	KIA
Stewart Sergeant C N D	British	604	KIA
Stewart Pilot Officer	N.Zealander	222-54	KIA
Stewart Pilot Officer D G A	British	615	KIA
Stewart Sergeant H G	British	236	
Stewart-Clarke Pilot Officer D	British	603	KIA
Stickney Flight Lieut. P A M	British	235	
Stillwell Sergeant R L	British	65	
Stock Sergeant E	British	604	
Stocks Sergeant N J	British	248	KIA*
Stockwell(FAA) Pilot Officer W E	British	804	
Stoddart Flight Lieut. K M	British	611	
Stokes Pilot Officer R W	British	264	KIA
Stokde Sergeant J	British	603	
Stokde Sergeant S	British	29	KIA
Stone Flight Lieut. C A C	British	249-254	
Stone Sergeant T F E	British	72	
Stones Pilot Officer D W A	British	79	
Stoney Flight Lieut G E B	British	501	KIA*
Stoodley Sergeant D R	British	43	KIA*
Storie Pilot Officer J M	British	607-615	
Storrar Sergeant	British	421 Flt	
Storrar Pilot Officer J E	British	145-73	
Storray Squad Ldr	British	501	
Storrie Pilot Officer A J	British	264	KIA
Straight Pilot Officer W W	British	601	
Strange Pilot Officer J T	N.Zealander	2353	
Streathfiend Squad Ldr V C	British	248	
Stretch Sergeant R R	British	235	
Strickland Pilot Officer C D	British	615	KIA
Strickland Pilot Officer J M	British	213	DOI
Strihauka Flight Sergeant J	Czech	310	
Stroud Sergeant G A	British	249	
Stuart Sergeant M	British	23	
Stuckey Sergeant S G	British	213	KIA*
Studd Pilot Officer J A P	British	66	KIA*
Sulman J E	British	607	KIA
Summers Sergeant R B G	British	219	
Sumner Sergeant F	British	23	KIA
Sumpter Sergeant C H S	British	604	
Surma Pilot Officer F	Polish	151-607-257	KIA
Sutcliffe Sergeant W A	British	610	KIA
Sutherland Pilot Officer I W	British	19	KIA*
Sutton Pilot Officer F C	British	264	
Sutton Pilot Officer F B	British	56	
Sutton Pilot Officer J R G	British	611	KIA
Sutton Pilot Officer N	British	72	KIA*
Sutton Sergeant H R	British	235	
Sutton Flying Officer K R	N.Zealander	264	
Sutton Pilot Officer N	British	611	
Swanwick Sergeant G W	British	54	
Swanwick Sergeant	British	141	
Switch Sergeant L	Polish	54	
Sword-Daniels Pilot Officer A T	British	25	
Sydney Flight Sergeant C	British	266-92	KIA*
Sykes(FAA) Sub Lieut. J H C	British	64	
Sykes Sergeant D B	British	145	
Sylvester Pilot Officer E J H	British	501	KIA*
Sylvester Sergeant	British	245	
Symonds Sergeant J E	British	236	
Szafranciec Sergeant W	Polish	151-56-607	KIA
Szaposznikow Flying Officer E	Polish	303	
Szczesny Pilot Officer H	Polish	74	
Szlagowski Sergeant J	Polish	234-152	
Szulkowski Pilot Officer W	Polish	65	KIA*
Tabor Sergeant	British	152	
Tabor Sergeant G	British	65	
Tait Flying Officer K W	British	87	
Talman Pilot Officer J M	British	213-145	KIA

Name	Rank	Nationality	Squadron	Status
Talman	Pilot Officer	British	151	
Tamblyn	Pilot Officer H N	Canadian	242-141	KIA
Tanner	Flight Sergeant J H	British	610	KIA*
Tate	Sergeant	British	604	
Tatnell	Sergeant R F	British	235	KIA
Taylor(FAA)	Petty Officer D E	British	808	
Taylor	Flying Officer D M	British	64	
Taylor	Pilot Officer R	British	235	DOI
Taylor	Sergeant K	British	29	
Taylor	Sergeant R N	British	601	KIA
Taylor	Sergeant R H W	British	604	KIA
Taylor	Sergeant G N	British	236	
Taylor	Sergeant G S	N.Zealander	3	
Taylor	Sergeant E F	British	29-600	KIA
Taylour (FAA)	Lieutenant. E W T	British	808	KIA
Tearle	Sergeant F J	British	600	
Temlett	Pilot Officer C B	British	3	KIA
Terry	Sergeant P A R R A	British	72-603	
Tew	Flight Sergeant P H	British	54	
Thatcher	Pilot Officer	British	32	
Theasby	Sergeant A J	British	25	KIA
Theilmann	Flight Sergeant J G	British	234	
Thomas	Sergeant	British	247	KIA
Thomas	Sergeant	British	236	
Thomas	Sergeant G S	British	604	
Thomas	Flying Officer E H	British	222-266	
Thomas	Flight Lieut F M	British	152	
Thomas	Pilot Officer S R	British	264	
Thomas	Flying Officer C R D	British	236	KIA*
Thomas	Pilot Officer R C	British	235	KIA*
Thompson	Flying Officer A R F	British	249	
Thompson	Flight Lieut. J A	British	302	
Thompson	Flying Officer R A	British	72	
Thompson	Squad Ldr J M	British	111	
Thompson	Pilot Officer P D	British	605-32	
Thompson	Flying Officer T R	British	213	
Thompson	Pilot Officer F N	British	248	
Thompson	Sergeant W W	British	234	
Thompson	Sergeant J B	British	25	KIA
Thompson	Sergeant J R	British	236	KIA
Thorn	Sergeant E R	British	264	KIA
Thorogood	Sergeant L A	British	87	
Thorpe	Sergeant	British	145	
Tidman	Pilot Officer A R	British	64	KIA
Till	Sergeant J	British	248	KIA
Tillard(FAA)	Lieutenant R C	British	808	KIA
Tillett	Pilot Officer J	British	238	KIA
Titley	Pilot Officer E G	British	609	KIA
Tobin	Pilot Officer E Q	American	609	KIA
Tomlinson	Pilot Officer P A	British	29	
Tongue	Pilot Officer R E	British	3-504	
Toogood	Sergeant L V	British	43	KIA*
Toombs	Sergeant J R	British	236-264	
Topham	Pilot Officer J G	British	219	
Topolnicki	Flying Officer J	Polish	601	KIA
Touch	Sergeant D F	British	235	KIA
Tower-Perkins	Pilot Officer W	British	238	
Townsend	Squad Ldr P W	British	85	
Townsend	Sergeant T W	British	600	
Tracey	Pilot Officer O V	British	79	KIA
Trevana	Flying Officer	Canadian	1(401)	
Trousdale	Pilot Officer R M	N.Zealander	266	KIA
Trueman	Flying Officer A A G	Canadian	253	KIA*
Truhlar	Sergeant F	Czech	312	
Trumble	Flight Lieut A J	British	264	
Truran	Pilot Officer A J J	British	615	
Tuck	Flight Lieut R R S	British	92-257	
Tucker	Flying Officer A B	British	151	
Tucker	Pilot Officer B E	British	266-66	
Tucker	Sergeant R Y	British	235	KIA
Tucker	Sergeant F D	British	236	
Turley-George	Pilot Officer D R	British	54	
Turnbull	Sergeant R N	British	25	
Turner	Flying Officer R S	Canadian	242	
Turner	Flight Sergeant G	British	32	
Turner	Flight Lieut D E	British	238	KIA*
Turner	Pilot Officer R C	British	264	KIA*
Tweed	Sergeant L J	British	111	KIA*
Twitchett	Sergeant F J	British	229-43	
Tyrer	Sergeant E	British	46	
Tyson	Squad Ldr F H	British	213-3	
Unett	Sergeant J W	British	235	KIA
Unwin	Flight Sergeant G C	British	19	
Upton	Pilot Officer H C	British	43-607	
Urbanowicz	Flying Officer W	Polish	145-303-601	
Urwin-Mann	Pilot Officer J R	British	238	
Usmar	Sergeant F	British	41	
Van-Den Hove	Pilot Officer	Belgian	501-43	KIA
Van-Lierde	Pilot Officer W E	Belgian	87	
Van-Mentz	Pilot Officer B	Belgian	222	KIA
Van-Wayen Berghe	Pilot Officer A	Belgian	236	KIA*
Varley	Pilot Officer G W	British	247-79	
Vasatko	Pilot Officer A	Czech	312	KIA
Velebrnovski	Pilot Officer A	Czech	1	KIA
Venesden	Sergeant F A	Belgian	235	KIA
Venn	Pilot Officer J A	British	236	
Verity	Pilot Officer V B S	N.Zealander	229	
Vesely	Pilot Officer V	Czech	312	
Vick	Squad Ldr J A	British	607	
Vigors	Pilot Officer T A	British	222	
Viles	Sergeant L W	British	236	
Villa	Flight Lieut	British	72-92	
Vincent	Group Captain S F	British	229	
Vindis	Sergeant F	Czech	310	
Vinyard	Sergeant F F	British	64	KIA*
Vlad	Pilot Officer	Czech	501	
Vokes	Pilot Officer A F	British	19	KIA
Von den Hove d'Ertsenrijck	Pilot Officer A E A	Polish	501	KIA*
Vopalecky	Warrant Officer	Czech	310	
Vrana	Flying Officer	Czech	312	
Vybiral	Pilot Officer T	Czech	312	
Vykdural	Pilot Officer K J	Czech	111-73	KIA
Waddingham	Pilot Officer J	British	141	DOI
Wade	Pilot Officer T S	British	92	KIA
Wadham	Sergeant J V	British	145	KIA*
Waghorn	Sergeant	British	249-111	

Name	Nationality	Sqn	Status
Wagner Sergeant A D	British	151	KIA
Wainwright Pilot Officer A G	British	151	KIA
Wainwright Pilot Officer M T	British	64	
Wake Sergeant	British	264	
Wakefield Pilot Officer H K	British	235	
Wakeham Pilot Officer E C J	British	145	KIA*
Wakeling Sergeant S R E	British	87	KIA*
Walch Flight Lieut S C	Australian	238	KIA*
Walker Sergeant S	British	236	KIA
Walker Sergeant A	N.Zealander	600	
Walker Flying Officer J H G	British	25	KIA
Walker Sergeant N McD	British	615	KIA
Walker Pilot Officer W L B	British	616	
Walker Pilot Officer J A	Canadian	111	
Walker Pilot Officer J R	Canadian	611-41	KIA
Walker Pilot Officer	British	616	
Walker Sergeant G A	British	232	
Walker Pilot Officer R J	British	72	
Walker-Smith Sergeant F R	British	85	KIA
Wallace Pilot Officer C A B	Canadian	3	KIA
Wallace Sergeant T Y	British	111	KIA
Wallen Flight Lieut D S	British	604	
Wallens Pilot Officer R W	British	41	
Waller Sergeant G A	British	29	
Walley Sergeant P K	British	615	KIA*
Wallis Sergeant D S	British	235	KIA
Walsh Sergeant E	British	141	
Walsh Pilot Officer J J	Canadian	615	DOI
Walsh(FAA) Sub Lieut. R W M	British	111	
Walton Sergeant	British	152	
Walton Sergeant h	British	87	
Want Sergeant W H	British	248	KIA*
Wapniarek Pilot Officer S	Polish	302	KIA*
Ward Sergeant R A	British	66	KIA*
Ward Sergeant W B	British	604	
Ward Flying Officer D H	N.Zealander	87	KIA
Ward Pilot Officer J L	British	32	KIA
Ward Squad Ldr E F	British	601	
Warden Sergeant N P	British	610	KIA
Ward-Smith Sergeant P	British	610	
Ware Sergeant R T	British	3	
Wareham Pilot Officer M P	British	1	KIA*
Wareing Sergeant P T	British	616	
Waring Sergeant W	British	23	
Warmsley Sergeant H W	British	248	KIA
Warner Flight Lieut. W H C	British	610	KIA*
Warren Sergeant S	British	1	
Warren Sergeant T A	British	236	
Warren Sergeant J B W	British	600	KIA*
Warren Pilot Officer C	British	152	
Warren Pilot Officer K A P	British	248	KIA
Waterston Flying Officer R McG	British	603	KIA*
Watkins Flying Officer D H	British	611	
Watkinson Pilot Officer A B	Sth. Afr	66	
Watling Pilot Officer W C	British	92	KIA
Watson Sergeant J G	British	604	
Watson Pilot Officer A R	British	152	KIA
Watson Pilot Officer E J	British	605	KIA
Watson Pilot Officer L G	British	29	
Watson Flying Officer R F	British	87	
Watson Pilot Officer	British	64	
Watson Pilot Officer F S	Canadian	3	KIA
Watters Pilot Officer J	N.Zealander	236	
Watts Pilot Officer R F	British	253	
Watts Sergeant E L	British	248	KIA
Watts Sergeant R D H	British	235	KIA*
Way Pilot Officer L B R	British	229	
Way Flight Lieut B H	British	54	KIA*
Wczelik Flying Officer	Polish	302	KIA
Weaver Flight Lieut P S	British	56	KIA*
Webb Flying Officer P C	British	602	
Webber Pilot Officer W F P	British	141	
Webber Sergeant J	British	1	
Weber Pilot Officer F	Czech	145	
Webster Flight Lt. J T	British	41	KIA*
Webster Pilot Officer F K	British	610	KIA*
Webster Sergeant H G	British	73	KIA
Webster Sergeant E R	British	85	
Wedgwood Flight Lieut. J H	British	253	KIA
Wedlock Sergeant G V	British	235	
Wedzik Sergeant M	Polish	302	
Weir Pilot Officer A N C	British	145	KIA
Welch Sergeant E	British	604	KIA
Welford Pilot Officer G H E	British	607	
Wellam Pilot Officer G H A	British	92	
Wells	N.Zealander	41-266	
Wells Flying Officer P H V	British	249	
Wells Pilot Officer M L	British	248	
Welsh Pilot Officer T D	British	254	
Wendel Pilot Officer K V	N.Zealander	504	KIA*
West Squad Ldr H	British	151-41	
West Pilot Officer D R	British	141	
Westcott Sergeant W H J	British	235	
Westlake Pilot Officer G H	British	43-213	
Westlake Pilot Officer R D	British	235	
Westmacott Flying Officer I B	British	56	
Westmoreland Sergeant T E	British	616	KIA*
Whall Sergeant B E P	British	602	KIA*
Wheatcroft Pilot Officer N R	British	604	KIA
Wheeler Pilot Officer N J	British	615	
Whelan Sergeant J	British	64-19	
Whinney Pilot Officer M T	British	3	
Whipps Sergeant G A	British	602	KIA
Whitbread Pilot Officer H L	British	222	KIA*
Whitby Sergeant A W	British	79	
White Pilot Officer B E	British	504	KIA
White Sergeant J W	British	32-3-FIU	
White Squad Ldr F L	British	74	
White Sergeant J	British	72	KIA
White Sergeant	British	604	
White Sergeant R	British	235	
White Sergeant J	British	248	DOI
Whitehead Sergeant C	British	56	KIA
Whitehead Sergeant R O	British	253-151	
Whitehouse Pilot Officer	British	32	
Whitehouse Sergeant S A H	British	501	
Whitfield Sergeant J	British	56	KIA*
Whitley Squad Ldr E W	N.Zealander	245	
Whitley Pilot Officer D	British	264	KIA*
Whitney Pilot Officer D M	N.Zealander	245	

Name	Nationality	Squadron	Status
Whitsun Sergeant A D	British	236	KIA
Whittick Sergeant H G	British	604	
Whittingham Flying Officer C D	British	151	
Whitty Flying Officer W H R	British	607	
Whitwell Sergeant P	N.Zealander	600	KIA
Wickings-Smith Pilot Officer P C	British	235	KIA*
Wickins Sergeant A S	British	141	
Wicks Pilot Officer B J	British	56	KIA
Widdows Squad Ldr S C	British	29	
Wigg Pilot Officer R G	N.Zealander	65	
Wigglesworth Pilot Officer J S	British	238	KIA
Wight Flight Lieut R D G	British	213	KIA*
Wightman (FAA)Midshipman OM	British	151	KIA
Wilcock Sergeant C	British	248	DOI
Wilcox Pilot Officer E J	British	72	KIA*
Wildblood Pilot Officer T S	British	152	KIA*
Wilde Pilot Officer D C	British	236	
Wilkes Sergeant G N	British	213	KIA*
Wilkinson Squad Ldr R L	British	266	KIA*
Wilkinson Sergeant W A	British	501	
Wilkinson Sergeant K A	British	616	
Wilkinson Flight Lieut. R C	British	3	
Willans Pilot Officer A J	British	23	KIA
Willcocks Sergeant P H	British	610-66	KIA
Willcocks Sergeant C P L	British	610	
Williams Squad Ldr C W	British	17	KIA*
Williams Pilot Officer D G	British	92	KIA*
Williams Flight Sergeant E E	British	46	KIA*
Williams Flying Officer T D	British	611	
Williams Pilot Officer W D	British	152	
Williams Pilot Officer W S	N.Zealander	266	KIA*
Williams Sergeant G T	British	219	
Williams Pilot Officer D C	British	141	KIA
Williams Pilot Officer A	British	604	
Willis Sergeant	N.Zealander	600	
Willis Sergeant R F	British	219	KIA
Willis Sergeant W C	British	73-3	KIA
Wilsch Pilot Officer	British	141	
Wilsden Sergeant A A	British	29	KIA
Wilson Flying Officer D S	British	610	
Wilson Pilot Officer R R	Canadian	111	KIA*
Wilson Pilot Officer D F	British	141	
Wilson Sergeant W C	British	29	
Wilson Sergeant W	British	235	
Wilson-MacDonald Squad Ldr D	British	213	
Wingfield Sergeant V	British	29	KIA
Winn Pilot Officer C V	British	29	
Winskill Pilot Officer A L	British	603-54-72	
Winstanley Sergeant J	British	151	
Winter Pilot Officer D C	British	72	KIA*
Wnter Pilot Officer R A	British	247	
Wise Sergeant J F	British	141	KIA*
Wiseman Pilot Officer W D	British	600	
Wissler Pilot Officer D H	British	17	KIA
Withall Flight Lieut L C	Australian	152	KIA*
Witorzenc Flying Officer S	Polish	501	
Wlasnowolski Pilot Officer B	Polish	607-32-213	KIA
Wojcicki Sergeant A	Polish	213	KIA*
Wojciechowski Sergeant M	Polish	303	KIA
Wojtowicz Sergeant S	Polish	303	KIA*
Wolfe Squad Ldr E C	British	141-219	
Wolton Sergeant R	British	152	
Wood Sergeant S V	British	248	
Wood Sergeant K R	British	23	KIA
Woodgate Sergeant J E	British	141	KIA
Woodger Pilot Officer D N	British	235	KIA*
Woodland Sergeant N N	British	236	
Woods-Scawen Pilot Officer C A	British	43	KIA*
Woods-Scawen Flying Officer P P	British	85	KIA*
Woodward Flying Officer H J	British	64-23	KIA*
Woodward Pilot Officer R S	British	600	KIA
Woolley Sergeant A W	British	601	KIA
Wootten Pilot Officer E W	British	234	
Wordsworth Pilot Officer D K A	British	235	KIA
Worrall Squad Ldr J	British	32	
Worrall(FAA) Sub Lieut. T V	British	111	KIA
Worrall Pilot Officer P A	British	85-249	KIA
Worsdell Pilot Officer K W	British	219	KIA*
Worthington Flying Officer A S	British	219	
Wotton Sergeant H J	British	234	KIA
Wright(FAA) Lieutenant A J	British	804	
Wright Sergeant B	British	92	
Wright Flight Lieut A R	British	92	
Wright Sergeant E W	British	605	
Wright Sergeant J	British	79	KIA*
Wright Sergeant D L	British	235	KIA*
Wright Pilot Officer W	British	604	KIA
Wright Sergeant R R	British	248	
Wroblewski Pilot Officer Z T A	Polish	302	
Wunsche Flight Sergeant K	Polish	303	
Wyate Sergeant J P	British	25	KIA*
Wyatt-Smith Pilot Officer P	British	263	KIA
Wydrowski Pilot Officer	Polish	607	
Wynn Pilot Officer R E N E	British	249	KIA
Yapp D S	British	253-245	
Yates Sergeant T M	British	64	
Yates Sergeant G	British	248	
Yates Sergeant W	British	604	
York Sergeant R L	British	610	KIA
Young Pilot Officer C R	British	615-607-46	KIA
Young Pilot Officer M H	British	254	
Young Sergeant R B M	N.Zealander	264	KIA*
Young Sergeant R C	British	23	
Young Flying Officer J R C	British	249	
Young Pilot Officer J H R	British	74	KIA*
Young Pilot Officer J S	British	234	
Yuile Flying Officer A	Canadian	1(401)	
Yule Pilot Officer R D	British	145	
Zak Pilot Officer W	Polish	303	
Zaluski Sergeant J	Polish	302	KIA*
Zadral Pilot Officer V	Czech	310	KIA
Zavoral Sergeant A	Czech	1	KIA
Zenker Pilot Officer P	Polish	501	KIA*
Zima Sergeant R	Czech	310	
Zimprich Pilot Officer S	Czech	310	KIA
Zukowski Pilot Officer A	Polish	302	KIA*
Zumbach Pilot Officer J	Polish	303	
Zurakowski Pilot Officer J	Polish	234-609	

Books

Available individually or as a commemorative pack:
Flying For Freedom – A Pilot's Story
The Battle of Britain –
        A Definitive Chronology of Events
The Battle of Britain – A Timeline of Events
Aircraft of the Battle of Britain
Battlefield Britain
Opposing Genius
Pilots of the Battle of Britain
Radar and the Secret Wireless War
Spitfire Pilot

Available individually or as a twin-set:
Allied Fighter Aces of World War 2
American Pilots of the Battle of Britain

Limited Edition Artwork

Spitfires 'Line-A-Stern'
'In – Readiness' (Spitfire on Airstrip)

'Into the Battlezone'
The Legendary 109
Hurricane!
Their Finest Hour Artwork 3D
Their Finest Hour 'Aircraft of the Battle of Britain'
Postcards

DVDs

Battlefield Britain	2 x 90 minutes
Aircraft of the Battle of Britain	3 x 60 minutes
Opposing Genius	1 x 60 minutes
Pilots of the Battle of Britain	1 x 75 minutes
The Civilian War	1 x 60 minutes
Britain Stands Alone	3 x 60 minutes
Spitfire!	1 x 60 minutes

Limited Edition 'Spitfire' Smart Cars

Yes, 10 'Their Finest Hour' officially branded new smart cars. Personalised to incorporate the initials of purchaser. (Finance available, subject to status)

Music CDs

The 1940s Collection: 3 CDs brought together as a musical tribute to the era in one pack:
Dame Vera Lynn's 'White Cliffs of Dover'
Dorothy Lamour's 'Thanks for the Memory'
Glenn Miller's 'Moonlight Serenade'

A4 and A5 Aicraft Illustrations

(Available individually or as a set of 12)
Supermarine Spitfire Mark 1, Hawker Hurricane Mark 1, Boulton Paul Defiant, Gloster Gladiator, Fairey Fulmar, Bristol Blenheim, Messerschmitt Bf 109E, Messerschmitt Bf 110C, Heinkel He 111 Bomber, Junkers Ju 87 'Stuka' Dive Bomber, Junkers Ju 88 Bomber, Dornier Do 17 Bomber

Die Cast Models (1/72 Scale)

Supermarine Spitfire, Hawker Hurricane, Junkers Ju 87 'Stuka' Dive Bomber, Messerschmitt Bf 109E

Plastic Models

Messerschmitt Bf 109E	1/24, 1/48, 1/72 scale
Junkers Ju 87-B 'Stuka'	1/24, 1/48, 1/72 scale
Supermarine Spitfire Mk 1	1/24, 1/48, 1/72 scale
Hawker Hurricane	1/24, 1/72 scale

Other models (1/72 Scale)

Heinkel He 111 Bomber, Junkers Ju 88 Bomber, Messerschmitt Bf 110C, Gloster Gladiator, Boulton Paul Defiant, Fairey Fulmar (FAA), Bristol Blenheim, Dornier Do 17

Sets in 1/72 Scale

Battle of Britain Airfield Set, Luftwaffe Airfield Set, RAF Airfield Set
'Dogfight Double' - Junkers Ju 88 and Hawker Hurricane

Battle of Britain 70th Anniversary Set - Heinkel He 111 Bomber, Hawker Hurricane, Supermarine Spitfire and Messerschmitt Bf 109E
Battle of Britain Commemorative Set - Supermarine Spitfire, Hawker Hurricane, Junkers Ju 87 'Stuka' Dive Bomber and Heinkel He 111 Bomber

Memorabilia and Coasters

1940s coins, stamps and other items, plus Battle of Britain coasters and original pieces of memorabilia

All 'TFH' products available from the TFH official Website. Subject to Availability.

www.theirfinesthour.co.uk or email: products@theirfinesthour.co.uk

Aircrew Statistics:		Killed in Action*
British	2353	407
Polish	146	29
New Zealand	127	18
Czechoslovakian	87	7
Canadian	96	17
Belgian	28	6
Australian	27	14
South African	24	9
Free French	14	0
American	11	3
Irish	9	0
Other	11	0

* Depicts Killed in Action during the Battle of Britain

Acknowledgements:

Maps:
Copyright T L W P Limited

Aircraft Illustrations:
Bill Dady, Copyright T L W P Limited

Photographs Courtesy Of
Francois Prins Collection
Bundesarchiv
Air Displays International
IWM Duxford

If you believe you have a friend or relative who died while a member of aircrew serving during the Battle of Britain and would like to find out more, email your request to info@theirfinesthour.co.uk - and the TFH team will see if we can help gain more information for you.